Through the Eyes of
Scholars and Journalists

眼睛里的

你

中国与以色列

杨 光

Yang Guang

主编

社会科学文献出版社

SOCIAL SCIENCES ACADEMIC PRESS (CHINA)

编委会名单

主编简介

杨　光　现任中国社会科学院西亚非洲研究所所长、研究员，中国社会科学院研究生院西亚非洲研究系主任、教授、博士生导师，兼任中国中东学会会长。主要研究方向为经济发展和能源安全问题。

编委会成员及其简介

张倩红 郑州大学副校长，兼任河南大学犹太研究所所长，享受国务院特殊津贴专家。第十、十一届全国政协委员，第十二届全国人大代表；主要学术兼职有：国家社会科学基金学科规划评审组专家、中国中东学会副会长、中国世界近现代史学会副会长、中国中外关系史学会副会长、河南省史学会会长。长期从事犹太—以色列及中东问题研究。出版《以色列史》《犹太文化》《犹太文化的现代化》《犹太教史》《以色列经济振兴之路》等学术著作。

徐　新 南京大学哲学宗教学系教授、博士生导师，犹太文化研究所所长。1977年1月毕业于南京大学英语系，1988年获美国东北伊利诺大学语言学硕士学位。1977年起在南京大学任教，1985~1986年担任英文系副主任。1988年后主要从事犹太宗教、文化、历史，以及犹太人在华散居史方面的研究，主要成果有：首部中文版《犹太百科全书》（主编）、《反犹主义解析》《西方文化史》《中国开封犹太人：历史、文化及宗教研究》（英文专著，美国出版）等。论文50余篇。其中若干用英文撰写，在国外发表。

殷 罡 中国社会科学院西亚非洲研究所研究员、中国中东学会常务理事，曾多次到以色列、巴勒斯坦、埃及、利比亚、伊朗等中东国家访问研究，熟悉中东事务，多次获中国社会科学院优秀科研成果奖。无党派人士。研究方向：中东国际关系、中东民族与宗教、中国中东关系、大国中东政策、中国古代犹太社团和穆斯林社团。

傅有德 教育部人文社会科学重点研究基地山东大学犹太教与跨宗教研究中心主任，哲学与社会发展学院宗教学系主任、博士生导师，教育部"长江学者"特聘教授、山东省"泰山学者"特聘教授；兼任教育部哲学教学指导委员会副主任委员、中国宗教学会副会长、山东省哲学学会会长、《犹太研究》

主编。主要研究领域：犹太宗教与哲学、犹太思想与儒学比较、西方哲学史。主编《汉译犹太文化名著丛书》，出版《犹太哲学史》《犹太哲学与宗教研究》等著作、译著，发表多篇论文，多项成果获奖，两次应佩雷斯总统邀请参加"以色列总统大会"（2008年、2009年）。

潘　光　现为上海国际问题研究中心副主席，上海社会科学院研究员、博士生导师，上海犹太研究中心主任，上海合作组织研究中心主任。还担任中国中东学会副会长，上海世界史学会会长和上海联合国研究会会长；被聘为国家社会科学基金评审专家，国家反恐工作领导小组办公室软科学专家，上海市政府外办咨询专家，上海市政府侨办专家咨询委员会委员，上海市信息化专家委员会委员，上海反恐研究中心副主任。2005年被评为全国劳动模范。2005年11月，联合国秘书长安南任命其为联合国文明联盟名人小组成员。2008年，联合国任命其为文明联盟大使。长期从事国际关系和世界史研究，特别在上海合作组织研究、犹太以色列研究、中东和欧洲问题、俄罗斯和中亚问题、丝绸之路与欧亚关系、民族宗教、文明对话、反恐怖问题等方面研究中取得了丰硕成果，已出版著作10余部，发表论文上百篇。1993年，获美国詹姆斯·弗兰德基金会中国—犹太研究学术奖。1996年，获加拿大政府暨国际加拿大研究委员会加拿大研究特别奖。2004年，获俄罗斯总统普京颁令授予的圣彼得堡300周年荣誉勋章。2006年，获奥地利政府授予的奥地利大屠杀纪念奖。与犹太研究有关的主要著作有《犹太人在亚洲》（中英文）、《犹太人在中国》（中英法德文）、《犹太人在上海》（中英文）、《犹太文明》《一个半世纪以来的上海犹太人》《犹太研究在中国：三十年回顾 1978-2008》《犹太人与中国：近代以来两个古老文明的交往和友谊》等。

序

杨光[*]

　　呈现在您面前的这本书，是一部关于中国与犹太和以色列关系的文集。中国与犹太和以色列的关系是一个既古老又新鲜的话题。说它古老，是因为中国与犹太这两个古老文明的交往源远流长，至少在1000多年以前已经开始；说它新鲜，是因为我们对双方交往的历史的了解还比较粗浅，大规模的相关研究工作在中国还只有短短30年左右的历史。

　　至少在公元8世纪前后，已有大批犹太人，特别是犹太商人，沿着路上和海上的"丝绸之路"进入中国，并出现在现今称作西安、洛阳、敦煌、开封、广州、杭州、宁波、北京、泉州、扬州、宁夏、南京的一些城市。及至宋朝，中国已经出现具有一定规模的犹太社团，其中最知名的是开封的犹太社团。在明朝，该社团在发展鼎盛时期，已经有500多个家庭的规模。当时，在华犹太人从事的

---

*　杨光，中国社会科学院西亚非洲研究所所长、研究员、博士生导师。

职业相当广泛，或为商贾，或为工匠，务农、行医之人亦有之，甚至有人参加科举，走上了为官的仕途。这些在古代的来华犹太人在中国的友好环境中，逐渐地学习了汉语，改换了姓名，并且与中国人通婚，到19世纪初已完全融化在中华民族的大家庭之中。

在中国近现代历史上，也出现过多次犹太人迁入中国的浪潮，并且在中国的多个城市形成了犹太人社团。从19世纪中期开始，一批犹太人为躲避奥斯曼帝国的反犹政策以及寻找商业机会，从奥斯曼帝国和印度迁移到中国。他们以经商为主并逐渐在香港和上海形成了犹太社团。19世纪80年代到20世纪初，俄国和东欧的反犹浪潮以及俄国爆发的革命和内战，导致大量犹太人穿越西伯利亚，迁移中国的东北以及内地谋生，并逐渐形成哈尔滨、天津等地的犹太社团。20世纪法西斯主义的兴起，是中华民族和犹太民族共同遭受的灾难。中国人民对纳粹迫害犹太人的行径给予了严厉的谴责，并且从20世纪30年代开始，接待了大批从希特勒屠刀下逃生的欧洲犹太人到上海避难。许多在华犹太人也以多种方式，直接参加了中国的抗日战争。尽管近现代来华的犹太人在20世纪70年代之前已经离开了中国，中国的犹太社区也成为如烟往事，但中国和犹太民族的这段友好交往和相互帮助的历史，及其为在华犹太人及其子孙后代留下的中国记忆和中国情结，为以后中国与犹太和以色列关系的发展打下了良好的基础。

1949年新中国成立以后，尽管中国和以色列的关系受到错综复杂的国际政治影响，双方直到1992年才正式建立外交关系，但建交后双方关系迅速发展，谱写了中国与犹太关系史的新篇章。到本书截稿时为止，已经有以色列的4位总统和4位总理访华，中国的国家主席和人大常委会委员长也曾赴以色列访问。两国签署了一系列经济贸易合作协议。中国以机电产品、纺织品、服装、鞋类和陶瓷制品与以色列的钾肥、机电产品、医疗仪器和电信产品等相交换，双方的货物贸易额从建交时的每年5000万美元增加到2012年的近100亿美元。同年中国公司在以色列实现的建筑工程承包营业额也达到3200万美元。中以两国在农业、生物技术、信息技术、新材料、水资源管理、纳米技术、医疗卫生、可再生能源等科技领域开展了卓有成效的交流与合作。双方在人文领域的交往也日趋活跃。近年来，每年到中国旅行的以色列人都超过 5 万人。以色列教育部已于 2011 年将中文列入中学教学内容。中国是中东和平进程的积极推动者，从 2002 年起派遣中东问题特使，为解决巴勒斯坦问题而奔走斡旋。

国内对犹太文明的研究始见于 19 世纪末和 20 世纪初。但由于受到国际政治环境和中国国内政治环境的影响，直到 20 世纪 70 年代，国内对于犹太和以色列的研究工作一直发展缓慢，研究和翻译的成果都比较少。由于研究工作的缺失，对于中国人民而言，犹太民族和以色列长期以来都是"谜一般的国家"和"谜一般的民族"。

20 世纪 70 年代末中国开始的思想解放和改革开放，推动了社会科学的发展繁荣，也使犹太和以色列研究走上了快速发展的道路。犹太民族曲折而富有传奇色彩的历史，两大文明在历史上的相互交流和影响，以及以色列在经济发展方面取得的卓越成就，深深吸引着中国学者探究的目光。从 20 世纪 80 年代开始，在上海、南京、北京、昆明、西安等地，首先出现了一些研究犹太和以色列的学者群。1988 年以后，随着上海犹太研究中心、南京大学犹太文化研究所、河南大学犹太研究所、山东大学犹太教与跨宗教研究中心、哈尔滨犹太研究中心等机构的相继创立，一批犹太以色列的专门研究机构脱颖而出，它们至今仍是国内犹太和以色列研究的重镇。除此之外，中国社会科学院的西亚非洲研究所、世界宗教研究所、外国文学研究所，现代国际关系研究院，以及云南大学、西北大学、复旦大学、深圳大学、武汉大学等研究机构，也都有专家学者加入到犹太和以色列研究的行列。1985年北京大学开办国内的第一个希伯来语班，开启了国内犹太和以色列民族语言的教学。

1992年中国与以色列建交，以及中以关系的快速发展，为犹太和以色列研究注入了巨大的新动力，加快了犹太和以色列研究的发展步伐，使国内出现了犹太和以色列研究的热潮。犹太和以色列研究的视野和领域不断扩大，研究空白被逐一填补。如果说20世纪80年代国内的犹太研究还主要集中在对古代来华犹太人，特别是中国开封犹太社团的研究，以及翻译介绍外国的研究成果，那么如今的研究范围已经覆盖了古代和近现代中国开封、上海、哈尔滨、天津、香港等地犹太社团研究，美国犹太人研究、犹太历史、哲学和宗教研究，以色列的政治、外交、经济、社会、文化、教育、军事及人物研究等众多领域。

其中又以犹太历史研究、犹太宗教哲学研究、犹太文学研究和以色列研究最为全面和深入。中国的犹太和以色列研究学者不仅在相互之间保持着密切的学术交流与合作，而且与国际研究学界的学术交流与合作也日益频繁。越来越多的专家学者成长为犹太和以色列研究领域的国际知名学者。中国的犹太和以色列研究进入了百花齐放的繁荣时代。

该文集的作者既有中国学者，也有以色列学者。其中的中国作者，都是国内犹太和以色列研究领域中我所熟知的领军人物，也是其各自研究专业领域在国内的开创者或权威专家。尽管由于篇幅所限，这本书无法全面展现中国学者对中国与犹太和以色列关系研究的成果，但我深信，通过阅读本书的文章，读者仍然可以对中国与犹太和以色列的关系的概貌和精要，获得基本的了解和认识。

2014 年 3 月 27 日

目 录

文化

中国的犹太研究

犹太文化的特征

希伯来先知与儒家圣人比较研究

以色列笔记

再访中国

中国的犹太研究

徐 新[*]

一 研究阶段

（一）1949~1978 年

严格地说，这期间，中国的犹太研究并没有得到真正开展，学术研究受到政治和意识形态的干扰与影响，发表的有关犹太问题的书籍和文章颇为有限，且大多是对中东形势发展和冲突事件的报道。尽管其中或许包含一些论析，但多属于政治性和政策性的，或以冷战思维画线，结论往往很少带学术成分。涉及以色列社会的文章更是寥寥无几，客观性和准确性有所欠缺。这当然与中国当时的国情有关。正如潘光所总结的："由于极'左'

---

* 徐新，南京大学哲学宗教教学系教授，博士生导师，犹太文化研究所所长。
* 徐新，南京大学哲学宗教教学系教授，博士生导师，犹太文化研究所所长。

思潮和十年'文革'的冲击,中国一度进入了一个相对封闭隔绝时期,犹太研究的发展也受到了严重制约。"①这显然是中国犹太研究的沉寂期。鉴此,我们无法对该时期的研究进行任何有意义的分析。

(二)1979~2009 年

改革开放促进了犹太研究在中国的重新开展。不过,最初的十年(1979~1988 年)为犹太研究复苏时期,属于思想准备、人才培养和学术积累的阶段。犹太研究的学术氛围随着中国改革开放的不断深入开始形成,学术界开始认识到此研究领域的存在和开展这一研究的意义。

从研究成果来看,首先映入人们视野的是对在华犹太人的研究。自唐代以来就有史料证明犹太人在中国的存在,著名的开封犹太社团自宋代起就生活在中国,并作为一个犹太人社团而存在。而 19 世纪中叶以来,随着中国大门被西方列强用炮舰打开,有近 4 万犹太人在不同时期来到中国一些城市生活。他们的经历与这些城市的变迁息息相关,中国人对此是有所察觉和了解的。尽管到 20 世纪 70 年代末开封的犹太人已经基本上完全融入中国社会,19 世纪中叶后来华的犹太人也都离去。但犹太人在华的这段历史并没有为中国人民所遗忘。在中国学术界恢复生机之初,首先涉及这一研究课题是十分自然的。最初发表的研究性论文包括潘光旦著的《关于中国境内犹太人的若干历史问题》② 一文,数年后又发表了由加入中国籍的犹太专

---

① 潘光主编《犹太研究在中国三十年回顾:1978~2008》,上海社会科学院出版社,2008,第 3 页。

② 本文载于《中国社会科学》1980 年第 3 期。需要指出,此时的潘光旦已经过世。该文是他在 20 世纪 50 年代研究成果的一部分,一直没有发表。同名著作于 1983 年由北京大学出版社作为专著出版。

家沙博理（Sidney Shapiro）撰写的文章《希望中国学者研究中国的犹太人历史》^① 等。关于上海犹太人的文章、书籍也不断面世 ^②，引起了不少中国学者的关注。在某种意义上，我们可以说是对在华犹太人的研究开启了中国犹太研究的新时期。与此同时，涉及犹太研究其他方面的论文也时有发表，如杨申的《论苏联犹太人》（载《外国问题研究》1981 年第 3 期）、刘邦义的《华沙犹太人反纳粹起义》（载《外国史知识》1982 年第 7 期）、赵复三的《犹太教简介》（载《世界宗教资料》1983 年第 3 期）、潘光的《古代犹太国家兴亡记》（载《历史知识》1984 年第 1 期）、余崇健的《从犹太复国主义的兴起到以色列国的建立》（载《西亚非洲资料》1984 年第 18 期）、汪池的《〈出埃及记〉的争论》（载《世界史研究动态》1985 年第 3 期）、王庆余的《旧上海的犹太人》（载《学术季刊》1987 年第 2 期）等。1984 年王仲义撰写的、作为单行本发行的《犹太教史话》（商务印书馆，1984 年版）小册子和 1986 年出版的由西北大学阎瑞松翻译的阿巴·埃班著的《犹太史》（中国社会科学出版社）具有一定的学术性。特别是阿巴·埃班著的《犹太史》一书的出版具有时代意义，影响深远，几乎所有当代从事犹太研究的中国学者都从该书中第一次较为详细地了解到犹太民族的历史，为后续研究打下了基础。

　　当然，在此阶段中国还出版了若干关于纳粹屠犹、以色列名人传记等许多方面的书籍，表明中国学术界对涉及犹太研究领域不同议题的关注。这些书籍使越来越多的中国普通民众，特别是中国青年人，对犹太人产生

---

① 参见《中外关系史学会通讯》，1983。
② 张仲礼、陈曾年著《沙逊集团在旧中国》，人民出版社，1985。

兴趣，开始关注与犹太有关的问题。若干在随后犹太研究领域发挥骨干作用的中国犹太学研究者就是在这一氛围中成长的。

顾晓鸣 1987 年发表的《犹太学及其研究视野》（载《外国语》1987 年第 3 期）和《论犹太文化对文化研究的意义》（载《复旦学报》1987 年第 3 期）论文表明中国学者对犹太研究作为一个学术领域的认识与思考。文章呼吁建立某种犹太研究的体系，以便能够推动犹太研究在中国的开展。而且顾晓鸣身体力行，其博士论文 [①] 即围绕犹太研究而作。

至此，可以说，有意义、具学术性的中国犹太研究在兴起。具体地说，它始于 20 世纪 80 年代末，2000 年后逐步形成高潮。中国犹太研究在这 20 年中取得了哪些进展？有何特色？主要成就表现在哪些方面？对这些问题的回答是对这 20 年犹太研究的概括和分析，同时也是我们判断中国犹太研究深入开展的标准。

二　研究机构的建立

犹太研究学术团体和机构的出现是犹太研究在中国向一个高起点发展的重要标志与评判标准。它们极大地推动了我国犹太研究的开展和深入。无论是 1988 年成立的上海犹太学研究会，1989 年成立的中国犹太文化研究会 [②]，还是 20 世纪 90 年代以来成立的、分布在全国各地

---

① 顾晓鸣：《犹太：充满"悖论"的文化》，浙江人民出版社，1990。
② 该研究会在 20 世纪 90 年代就设立了自己的网站，向国际社会报道和介绍中国的犹太研究。其网址为：http://servercc.oakton.edu/—friend/chinajews.htnL。

的犹太文化研究中心（所）^①，都是这样的机构和学术团体。这使犹太研究的深入开展有了组织保障和交流的平台。

　　上海社会科学院上海犹太研究中心是在中国研究界最早成立的专事犹太研究的机构，已成为一个研究基础坚实、地方学术特色鲜明的研究团体^②。2004 年，该中心由上海社会科学院确定为"特色学科"^③，受到上海社科界的极大重视，在学术研究和对外交流方面都发挥了积极作用。由该中心研究人员编撰的《犹太人在上海》（五洲传播出版社，2001 年版）、《犹太人在中国》（五洲传播出版社，2005 年版）大型画册在世界范围受到好评。多年来，该中心研究人员承担若干国家和上海市的研究课题，发表的论文和著作影响深远。

　　南京大学犹太文化研究所，成立于中以建交的 1992 年（最初名为南京大学犹太文化研究中心）。除开展犹太研究外，该研究所的最大特色是在中国高校率先开设一系列犹太文化课程，招收、指导犹太历史文化和犹太教研究方向的硕士生与博士生。该研究所举办过 3 期犹太历史文化暑期培训班，接受培训的国内各高校和研究机构的教师、研究人员和研究生超过 100 人。此外，该研究所还建立起了可能是国内最大的犹太学图书馆，收藏有上万册涵盖犹太研究方方面面的英文图书，为犹太问题研究提供了图书和资料保障。

---

①　这类研究中心在上海、南京、北京、济南、开封、西安、昆明、哈尔滨等城市先后成立。

②　潘光主编《犹太研究在中国三十年回顾：1978~2008》，上海社会科学院出版社，2008，第 2 页。

③　潘光主编《犹太研究在中国三十年回顾：1978~2008》，上海社会科学院出版社，2008，第 19 页。

　　山东大学犹太文化研究所成立于 1994 年，2004 年成功申请成为教育部人文社科重点研究基地，并更名为"山东大学犹太教与跨宗教研究中心"。该中心在犹太教与跨宗教研究方面建立起了一个较为全面的研究梯队，招收、培养硕士生和博士生，特别是在犹太哲学研究方面在国内居领先地位。

　　作为中国最大、级别最高的研究机构——中国社会科学院——尽管一直未建立专门研究犹太文化的机构，但属下的西亚非洲研究所、外国文学研究所、世界宗教研究所等均有研究人员专事相关犹太问题的研究，他们在各自领域的研究成果总体上代表中国学术界的研究水准。专事犹太研究的学术团体和机构还有力地促进了犹太研究的国内外交流，提升中国犹太研究的国际水准。

三　大量研究成果的问世

　　据不完全统计，近 20 年来，我国出版的涉及犹太文化的书籍在 600 部之上，发表的论文超过千篇 ① 。关涉犹太议题书籍和论文的大量问世反映了犹太研究的深入发展。20 世纪 90 年代，有影响力和标志性的成果有：（1）顾晓鸣主编的《犹太文化丛书》（上海三联书店出版）。这是中国出版的第一套关涉犹太文化的丛书，已出版 16 部。（2）徐新、凌继尧主编的《犹太百科全书》（上海人民出版社出版）。该百科全书共 200 余万字，有

---

① 　具体篇目可参见潘光主编《犹太研究在中国三十年回顾：1978~2008》，上海社会科学院出版社，2008，附录部分：中国犹太研究著述及相关读物索引（1978~2007）。

词条 1600 余条，于 1993 年出版，该书为中国犹太研究界提供了一本国内最具权威性的涉及犹太文化的大型工具书。（3）傅有德主编的《汉译犹太文化名著丛书》（山东大学出版社出版）。丛书共 10 部，虽均为译作，但所选篇目都是"已在西方产生过重大影响，且能够代表某一领域的学术水平的优秀力作"[①]，学术含量高。上述成果在一定程度上显示了我国犹太研究取得的成就。如果说在 21 世纪到来之前，中国出版的绝大多数与犹太研究有关的书籍还是以译介为主，那么，21 世纪以来，由中国犹太研究学者撰写、有分量和影响力的学术著作已成为犹太研究的主流。其中殷罡主编的《阿以冲突：问题与出路》（国际文化出版公司，2002 年版）、张倩红著的《困顿与再生——犹太文化的现代化》（江苏人民出版社，2003 年版）；刘洪一著的《犹太文化要义》（商务印书馆，2004 年版）、钟志清著的《当代以色列作家研究》（人民文学出版社，2006 年版）、徐新著的《犹太文化史》（北京大学出版社，2006 年版）、肖宪著的《谜一般的犹太人》（中国工人出版社，2007 年版）、游斌著的《希伯来圣经的文本、历史与思想世界》（宗教文化出版社，2007 年版）、傅有德等著的《犹太哲学史》（上下卷）（中国人民大学出版社，2008 年版）、王健著的《上海犹太人社会生活史》（上海辞书出版社，2008 年版）、张淑清著的《中世纪西欧的犹太妇女》（人民出版社，2009 年版）等均是有较高学术水准的犹太研究方面的论著，代表了国内犹太研究的最高水平。

此外，山东大学犹太文化研究所于 2002 年创办的《犹

---

① 傅有德主编《汉译犹太文化名著丛书》，总序，第Ⅱ页。

太研究》和上海社会科学院上海犹太研究中心 2007 年创办的《犹太·以色列研究论丛》^① 成为国内主要刊登犹太研究论文的刊物。

四 犹太研究在高校的开展

在中国高校开展犹太研究和教学是衡量将犹太研究引向深入的另一个重要标志。20 多年前，几乎无任何一所中国大学开设犹太研究方面的课程和进行犹太学研究。20 多年以来，中国高校中开展的这方面研究又突出地表现在犹太文化课程的开设和犹太文化研究方向的研究生招收与培养上。这对于培养犹太研究新生力量和后继人才，特别是专业人才是至关重要的。

20 世纪 80 年代中期，北京大学希伯来语专业培养了首批中国能够掌握希伯来语的年青一代。经过若干年培养和进一步深造，其中若干毕业生已获博士学位，活跃在各地的犹太研究机构中。另外，南京大学犹太文化研究所和山东大学犹太文化研究所多年来一直致力于犹太文化研究方向的硕士生和博士生的培养。在过去的 10 年中，这两个研究所每年都选送若干名硕士生和博士生去以色列或者美国大学进修、进行博士论文撰写的资料查询与研究。其中不少人毕业后充实到各高校的师资队伍中，形成新的犹太研究教学增长点。2005~2009 年，最初由南京大学犹太文化研究所牵头和组织、后由不同高校主办、每年均在中国一个城市召开的"纳粹屠犹教

---

① 这两种刊物均以集刊形式出版，目前基本每年一辑。而《犹太研究》已经数年被评为国家级核心学术刊物。

育培训研讨会"①，使中国大学生对于在第二次世界大战期间发生的屠犹事件有了深刻了解，从而有力地驳斥了国际上不断出现的否认纳粹屠犹的思潮，并对中国反击日本出现的否认南京大屠杀思潮是一个很好的借鉴。中国的其他一些高校也在开展犹太历史、文化方面的教学和研究，如河南大学犹太研究所自 2002 年一直开设犹太历史课程，培养硕士研究生，在犹太近现代史和以色列通史研究方面形成特色。云南大学、齐鲁大学、河南师范大学、西北大学、复旦大学、南开大学、黑龙江大学、同济大学、长春大学、深圳大学、武汉大学等均在开设犹太学科课程。其研究成果也不断面世，推动着中国犹太研究向前发展。

五　犹太研究的国际交流

积极参加国际学术活动和开展国际学术交流是这一时期中国犹太研究取得可喜成就与向纵深发展的另一标志。在过去的 20 年中，中国各犹太研究学术团体的研究人员经常访问北美、欧洲、以色列等，特别是各犹太研究学术团体的负责人多次应邀在国外进行学术研究，参加国际会议，举办展览，发表数以百场次计的英语学术演讲。如上海犹太研究中心主任潘光研究员访问过数十个国家和地区，南京大学犹太文化研究所所长徐新教授在国外作过 300 余场次的英文学术演讲，山东大学犹太文化研究所负责人傅有德教授几乎每年都出访，进行学

---

①　该研讨会一直获得欧盟以及国外犹太研究机构的资助，主要由国际专门研究纳粹屠犹的专家授课。

术讲演和交流。与此同时，中国的犹太研究机构每年还邀请若干国际犹太学者来华进行学术访问。通过这类国际交往，中国的犹太学者与世界范围内的犹太学术界、犹太人机构，及犹太社区建立了广泛而密切的联系，推动了犹太研究机构各项工作的开展。

举办国际学术研讨会是中国犹太研究开展国际交流的一个重要方面。已举办的大型学术研讨会包括在南京召开的"第一届犹太文化国际研讨会"（1996 年）、"犹太人在华散居国际会议"（2002 年）、"犹太教国际研讨会"（2004 年）；在山东大学召开的"犹太教与跨宗教研究国际会议"（2006 年）等。在上海召开的"犹太人在上海"（1994 年）和"犹太人在亚洲：比较研究"（2005 年）国际会议，及"哈尔滨犹太历史文化国际学术研讨会"（2004 年）、"哈尔滨犹太历史文化国际论坛"（2006 年）和"哈尔滨与世界犹太人经贸合作国际论坛"（2007 年）均吸引了大批中外学者参加。这类活动有力地推动了我国犹太学研究的开展，促进了中外学者的交流与合作及与国际学术界的接轨。

上述这一切都说明我国的犹太研究受到了国际学术界的关注和重视，我国在犹太研究方面有了自己的话语权，体现出中国犹太研究的进步和成就。

六　学术贡献与社会影响

（一）对中东研究的贡献

犹太研究的开展使国人对中东问题有了进一步了解，且有了自己的评判和观点，能够较为客观地认识和理解中东存在的一系列复杂的冲突、战争、政治、经济、文化等方面的问题，也能够更好地理解中东文化和社会，为我国能够参与中东问题的国际活动奠定了坚实基础。若干从事阿拉伯研究的学者也加入犹太研究，许多从事犹太研究的学者在中国中东学会担任领导职务，成为中国中东问题专家，为国家的中东政策建言献策就是这一贡献的最好体现。犹太研究的开展还促进了我国对以色列的专题研究。目前已经出版的关于以色列的书籍可以说涵盖以色列社会的许多方面，如阎瑞松主编的《以色列政治》（西北大学出版社，1995年版），覃志豪著的《以色列农业发展》（中国农业科技出版社，1996年版），杨光主编的《中东的小龙——以色列经济发展研究》（社会科学文献出版社，1997年版），孙正达等著的《以色列国》（当代世界出版社，1998年版），赵伟明著的《以色列经济》（上海外语教育出版社，1998年版），邱兴著的《以色列教育》（中国文史出版社，2004年版），等等。

（二）对犹太人在华散居史研究的推动

犹太研究在中国的深入开展促进了对犹太人在华散居史的研究。20年来，上海社会科学院上海犹太研究中心对上海犹太人开展了卓有成效的研究，承担并完成国家和省部级研究项目的成果丰富。除了前已提及的，该中心举办的"犹太人在上海"大型展览作为访问上海的多国领导人的参观点，成为上海外事活动的有机组成部分。而黑龙江社会科学院哈尔滨犹太研究中心自2000年成立以来，积极开展对哈尔滨犹太人的研究，承担了多项国家和省部级研究项目，该中心编撰的《哈尔滨犹太人》大型画册、举办的"哈尔滨犹太人历史展"，都堪称一流，成为黑龙江省对外宣传的一个独特窗口。此外，多年来，中国从事犹太研究学者频繁出席涉及中国犹太人的国际研讨会，成为主要发言嘉宾。而发表的关涉在华犹太人的研究量大、面广，既有用中文在国内发表的，也有用外文在国际上发表的。特别是徐新用英文撰写、在美国出版的《中国开封犹太人：历史、文化及宗教》[1]，刘爽著的《哈尔滨犹太侨民史》(方志出版社,2007 年版)等，体现出中国学者在对犹太人在华散居史这一领域的学术研究成果。

（原文刊载于《西亚非洲》
2010 年第 4 期，内容略有改动）

---

① Xu Xin, *The Jews of Kaifeng, China : History, Culture, and Religion*, Jersey City, KTAV Publishing House, Inc, 2003.

犹太文化的特征

犹太文化是一种颇有特色的民族文化，纵观其发展历程，"不难看出，从古到今，犹太人总是能够找到使其文明适应时代的挑战而又不毁灭犹太价值观的核心"①。也就是说，犹太文化能够在与其他文明的交往中不断调适自我、改造自我，完善自我，但不失去自我。本文从宗教性、民族性及世界性三个方面对犹太文化的基本特征进行归纳与分析。

一 宗教性

犹太文化历来就是一种宗教性极强的文化，犹太民

---

* 张倩红，郑州大学副校长，兼任河南大学犹太研究所所长，享受国务院特殊津贴专家。
① Adam Garfinkle, *Politics and Society in Modern Israel-Myths and Realities*, M.E.Sharpe, Inc., 1997, p.282.

族的"元典"文化就是一部完全意义上的宗教学说形成史。用宗教观念来解释社会文化现象，又以社会文化现象来论证宗教是犹太文化最显著的特征。犹太民族在失去了构成民族历史的关键要素——相对稳定的地理疆域——的情况下，仍能以民族共同体的形式顽强地生存下来，而且创造了流而不散的历史文化奇迹，在很大程度上应该归功于宗教。宗教成了保证犹太社会一体化和协调化的不可或缺的文化工具，犹太人社会生活的各个方面无不受到宗教的制约与影响。

关于犹太教的产生过程仍是一个悬而未决的学术问题，但这样一个事实是无可置疑的，即在多神教普遍流行的远古时代，希伯来人却创立了世界上最古老的一神教，而且是彻底的一神教，他们通过使自己的民族神唯一化而否认其他神祇的神圣性与合法性。

犹太教是一种不断发展、进化的宗教，它历经了圣经时代（The Biblical Period）、前拉比时代（The Pre-rabbinic Age）、拉比时代（The Rabbinic Period）、中世纪（The Middle Ages）、过渡时期（The Period of Transition）、解放时期（The Emancipation）及现代犹太教（Contemporary Judaism）等发展阶段 [1]。在整个前解放时代，犹太宗教主宰着犹太文化。随着解放运动的兴起与现代主义的冲击，犹太宗教的地位才明显下降，犹太世俗文化勃兴。但时至今日，犹太教在犹太文化体系中仍具有很强的影响力，这种影响力的保持得益于犹太教积极适应世界发展趋势，不断对教义、习俗进行改革。

---

[1] Jerusalem, *Encyclopaedia Judaic*, Keter Publishing House Ltd., 1971, Vol.10, pp.387-395.

　　犹太宗教与文化的密切关系也许可以从"Judaism"一词的内涵中略见一斑。"Judaism"一词最早被说希腊语的犹太人用来指犹太人的信仰及教规,在中世纪的基督教文学中用来指犹太教,近代以后被犹太人广泛使用。"Judaism"本意确实是指犹太人的神学思想体系,所以很多英汉词典中将它译为"犹太教",许多中文论著中至今仍把它理解为犹太人的宗教信仰。由于"Judaism"强调的是日常行为而不是教义本身,因此,它更多地反映了犹太人的行为准则及生活方式,所以,很多现代犹太学者认为,"Judaism"更确切地说应该是一种文化体系。达尼亚尔·杰里米·西尔弗(Daniel Jerany Silver)指出:"我们不再把"Judaism"严格地理解为一种信条、行为规则或崇拜的体系,"Judaism"涵盖了所有这些内容,但并不局限于此,它包括了犹太民族全部的思想文化以及深刻影响犹太人内在生活的现象。"[①] 从这个意义上看,"Judaism"对犹太人的影响绝不亚于儒家学说(Confucianism)对传统社会中的中国人的影响,其普遍性及深刻性远远超过了单一性质的宗教信仰。因此,正如我们不把儒家学说认可为一种宗教一样,我们也同样不应该把"Judaism"看做一种纯粹信仰。《犹太百科全书》英文版就把"Judaism"解释为"犹太人的宗教、哲学及生活方式"[②]。重建派犹太教的奠基人卡普兰一直主张"Judaism"不是一种宗教,而是一种广泛意义上的文明,它应该包括犹太神学、历史、文学、哲学、语言、科学、艺术、建筑、服饰、社会组织、伦理规范等各个方面。

[①]　Daniel Jeremy Silver, Bernard Martin, *A History of Judaism : from Abraham to Maimonides*, Basic Books, Inc., 1974, Vol.1, p.10.
[②]　*Encyclopaedia Judaic*, Vol .10, p.383.

犹太教作为一种意识形态成为民族文化的基本要素及传承载体，这在很大程度上及在相当长的时期里表现了犹太文化的主流与特色。不了解犹太教，就无法解读犹太文化。即便在现代化社会中，犹太教依然是犹太精神文化体系的重要内涵。一方面，它作为犹太传统的主要内容，在与现代主义的接触中通过自身所扮演的文化角色来制约犹太社会的发展；另一方面，它又通过对其他文化现象的影响而实现其文化功能。在当今的以色列，犹太教不仅是犹太人的精神支柱，而且是民族身份的鉴别标准，是以色列国民文化的本质与特征。正统派犹太教严重地制约着国家的政治、经济、文化、教育、艺术等，宗教节日是国家的法定节日，宗教禁忌渗透于社会生活的各个方面。

二 民族性

民族性是犹太文化的另一特征。远古时代，希伯来人以游牧为生，逐水草而居，靠群体力量与大自然抗衡。从定居迦南到被罗马征服为止，犹太人虽然建立过自己的王国，在大卫、所罗门时代也曾一度辉煌，但大部分时间是在四邻强国的压制下度过的。这期间犹太人始终都在与异族抗争：出埃及时与残暴的法老较量；士师时代与迦南人、腓力斯人反复交锋；王国时期先后亡于亚述和新巴比伦；后来又遭受波斯、希腊及罗马的奴役。正是在这一曲折艰辛的历史过程中，犹太人形成了以宗教为核心的极强的民族意识，在后来的大流散过程中，周而复始的反犹太主义浪潮更加强了犹太人的民族认同感。在这一宏观背景下成形、发展的犹太文化自然以弘扬民族性为主旋律。

契约观是犹太教的基本教义之一，《圣经》中多次记载上帝与希伯来人的立约。继《创世纪》中上帝与挪亚的"彩虹之约"后，上帝又与亚伯拉罕、摩西两度立约。这样，就以选民的方式建立了上帝与希伯来人之间的特殊关系。在这种关系中，上帝是群体意志的最高体现，它主宰着希伯来人（即个体）的命运。但是，除了人应当虔诚地敬畏与服从上帝之外，上帝对人也同样承担着不可忽略的承诺与责任。犹太人的契约观在人类思想史上首次给神人关系赋予了新的色彩，打破了长期以来把人置于绝对被动地位的宿命观。只是到了王国时期，国王们为了加强统治，才全面地强调契约对人的单方面约束作用，而逐渐忽略了上帝的职责。在契约观中，上帝与亚伯拉罕、摩西等人的立约，并非与个人立约，而是与整个犹太群体、犹太民族立约。因为当时那种恶劣的自然环境使个人的生存不得不依赖于群体，这在客观上迫切需要建立一种个体与群体之间的良性关系，既能发展集体利益，又能保障个人的生存，正是这种需求促成了契约观念的产生。王国分裂后，忧国忧民的先贤们在评判北朝以色列和南朝犹大的功过是非时，也始终以整个民族为立足点，以对本民族"约"的履行状况为标准，从而体现出一种以集体利益为重的原则。

犹太教作为一种"伦理一神教"，在漫长的历史过程中形成了独特的礼仪与习俗，它们是希伯来民族生活经历的结晶，也是犹太人区别于异族人的主要标志。犹太民族的宗教节日极其繁多，尽管这些节日的来源与寓意各不相同，但都不是单纯为了纪念某个人的业绩与生平，而是来源于整个民族的某种经历，把民族历史巧妙地融人节日庆典和宗教礼仪中，提醒犹太人不要忘记本民族的苦难史，增强民族凝聚力，防止被异族同化。也就是说，作为一种文化标记的宗教节日，无论喜庆还是哀伤，都是整个犹太民族所走过的历史轨迹的缩影。如逾越节是为了纪念古希伯来人胜利地摆脱了埃及法老的迫害；住棚节是为了告诫人们永远记住以色列人在西奈沙漠漂泊的艰难岁月；幸运节是为了合家欢庆犹太人团结一心，顺利地抵制了外界歧视的经历；修殿节是为了表示犹太人对光明的渴求和对马卡比起义者英勇气概的怀念；赎罪日更成了促使犹太人反省自身、励精图治的一年一度的礼仪。这些功效明确的全民节日在保持犹太民族固有文化方面起到了重要的作用，在世界各文明体系中，如此突出的民族性实属罕见。

19世纪以来，一些深受现代思潮影响的改革派思想家曾极力否认犹太宗教及文化中的民族性成分，主张犹太人应该放弃民族特性而融入主流社会。在他们看来，民族性使犹太教变成一种背离时代的狂热崇拜，使犹太文化成为一种缺乏活力的"禁锢性文化"。只有毫不犹豫地冲破"民族壁垒"，犹太文化才会像基督教文化一样成为一种普世性文化。一些推崇现代主义的学者更进一步指出："现代性倾向于和普遍主义相伴随，现代犹太人倾向于把犹太人的特殊神宠论（Jewish particularism）视为褊狭的意识。"[1] 德国改革派思想家甚至从祈祷书中删除了弥赛亚观念，把"以色列人的使命"普遍化，使之具有世界意义，其动机与目标是为了

---

[1]　Moshe Sharon, *Judaism in the Context of Diverse Civilization*, Maksim Publishers, Johannesburg, 1993, pp.21-24.

提高犹太宗教与文化的地位，吸引一些改宗者实现"信仰的回归"。然而，事实证明，宗教与文化的普世化，不是靠某些人的灵感与热情就能实现的，而是依赖于深刻的社会原因。

改革派犹太教在美国兴起后，曾在较长的时间里否定、排斥犹太文化中的民族性因素。但现代反犹太主义的兴起，已使许多人的"解放梦"破灭，并已使他们心灵深处的民族意识得以复苏。犹太复国主义运动的兴起及其所取得的成就，更促使改革派对自身反民族主义、反传统主义的一贯主张进行反思，1937 年的《哥伦布纲领》标志着犹太教改革派对犹太文化中的民族性的认可与接受。

以色列建国后，大批移民开始流入，文化差异成了"比安排衣食住行及社会就业更为棘手的问题"，融会这些差异被称作"把犹太移民造就为真正的以色列国民的最关键要素"，"以色列完成其民族融合使命的基本条件"①。在建构新的国民文化的过程中，只能以传统的犹太文化为基本的契合点，只有这样才能实现以色列社会的整合，才能使更多的犹太人来到这块"流亡者的聚集地"。但 20 世纪下半叶的犹太社会已不同于前解放时代，经过了启蒙运动及现代民族、民主思想洗礼的犹太人已发生很大的变化，宗教热情整体下降，世俗犹太人越来越多，他们虽然疏远宗教，但不怀疑自己的民族身份，这就产生了大批"世俗犹太人"。为了适应这一现象，以色列政府特别强调犹太文化中的民族性成分，使"民

---

① Eleazar Laserson, *Turning Immigrants into Israelis*, Jewish Affairs, Johannesburg, 1951, p.12.

族家园"具有号召力，从而提高了以色列在世界犹太人心目中的地位，也为以色列社会的发展赢得了不可或缺的外援。

三　世界性

犹太文化是一种典型的民族文化，但这一文化的民族性并不意味着否定自身所具有的"世界性内涵"，也就是说，犹太文化与其他民族文化的不同之处在于它同时也是一种"世界性特质的文化"。当然，"世界性特质"与"世界性文化"是两个不同的概念，前者只是具有了后者的某些品质与表象而已。犹太文化的"世界性特质"主要体现在以下几方面：

第一，文化交往的世界性。从历史的角度看，犹太民族恐怕是交往最频繁的民族。远古时代，犹太人与西亚地区的迦南人、亚述人、腓力斯人、巴比伦人等广泛交往。交往的结果使犹太教从其他地域宗教中脱颖而出，成为世界上最古老的一神教。此后，犹太人作为被征服者又与希腊、罗马文化有了交往。经过长期的接触、融合与扬弃，最终希伯来文化与希腊文化一起孕育了基督教文化。公元1世纪，犹太人被驱逐出巴勒斯坦，"大流散"把他们卷入了一种强制性的交往之中，从此，"地球成了他们的祖国"。这种特殊的历史遭际，使犹太人的交往活动远远超越了其他民族。18世纪中叶到19世纪的犹太启蒙运动堪称为意义深远的一次历史大交往。犹太人第一次勇敢地去打破民族文化的樊篱，以满腔的热情投身于学习、吸取近代科学文化的洪流之中，并以"重筑犹太教""培养科学精神"为口号，力图使犹太文化成为一种"可塑的、始终适应环境的有机的民族文化"。这次具有现代化特色的思想启蒙运动的出发点与落脚点都离不开历史交往。启蒙运动的诱发力,正是在历史交往过程中使犹太人通过对比自身的民族文化与日益发达的西方文化而产生了一种空前的危机感;而这一运动开展的结果又促成了犹太文化与西方文化的更广泛、更深入的历史交往。

频繁的历史交往对犹太文化产生了极为深刻的影响。

首先,历史交往保证了犹太文化的传承,也丰富了犹太文化的内涵。历史交往是人类存在与发展的基本形式之一,任何一种文明都必须保持一种开放性特质,在广泛的交往中保证生产力的发展与文明成果的聚合与延续。犹太历史充分证明了历史交往是社会进步、发展的推动力。试想,如果犹太人仅仅囿于巴勒斯坦的弹丸之地而不与其他民族交往,那么犹太文化就绝不会成为一种具有世界性特色的影响深远的文化。犹太历史的显著特征就是不断迁徙,不断流散,在持续位移的过程中广泛地汲取了其他文化因素。进入大流散时代后,犹太人与其他文化的交往更为广泛。犹太文化与阿拉伯伊斯兰文化在地中海区域,特别是在伊比利亚半岛的交融与结合,孕育了犹太文明中的一大瑰宝——活跃于8~13世纪的塞法尔迪文化。犹太文化与日耳曼及斯拉夫文明的交融又产生了犹太文化的又一分支——意第绪文化。近现代以来,犹太文化适应了人类现代化进程,在美洲大陆又形成了颇具特色的美国犹太文化。20世纪中叶以来,随着以色列国家的建立,犹太文化的主体又回归以色列,成为以色列新国民文化的精神支柱。可见,从犹太文化的最初发源到后来的历史演变,始终是在与非犹太文化的冲突与融会中使自身不断丰富、不断发展，从而成为一种具有世界性的博大精深的思想文化体系，并以其特有的风貌立于世界文化之林。总之，犹太文化在与异质文化的接触过程中，始终保持着一种既冲突又吸纳、既分裂又融合的交往关系，犹太文化成果在这种关系中得以保持与延续。由此看来，世界性既是犹太文化的特征与表象，也是犹太文化不断超越自我并以其顽强的生命力长期影响世界文化的必要保证。

其次，历史交往促进了民族特征及犹太精神的形成。犹太精神是犹太民族在长期的生活实践与社会实践中逐渐形成、为本民族大多数成员所认同、具有相对稳定性的价值观念与思想体系。而这种精神的产生与发展同犹太民族广泛的历史交往密不可分：一方面，交往为民族精神的产生与凝炼提供了广阔的视野与异域文化的滋养；另一方面，交往本身就是促发民族精神的重要驱动力。犹太民族商业特性的形成则印证了这一观点。

古希伯来人在进入迦南以前，一直过着逐水草而居的生活，正是迦南地区独特的环境孕育了他们的从商意识。位于地中海东岸的迦南地区东邻两河流域，北接欧亚腹地，东南为阿拉伯沙漠，西南是非洲大陆，为历史上最早的商路交汇之地。当亚伯拉罕率领希伯来人进入迦南之际，该地的文化远远先进于希伯来文化。形形色色的迦南人已建立许多小型的城邦国，掌握了农业技术和冶炼技术，手工业也很发达。各城邦国兴建的城市和城堡则是一个个贸易中心。迦南人频繁的贸易活动深刻地影响了尚未定居的希伯来人，他们中有些人逐渐放弃了畜牧业与农业，介入当地的贸易活动中。此后，随着迦南社会的发展，犹太人的贸易也日益扩大，到所罗门时代，犹太人的贸易伙伴已遍及阿拉伯半岛、两河流域、印度和非洲等地。由此可见，与迦南人的历史交往，对犹太民族商业特征的形成起到了十分重要的作用。希伯来人定居迦南的过程，不单纯是一个游牧部落向定居农业的转化过程，这个过程"正是希伯来人的商人基因同迦南地方商业特性相吻合的过程"。如果说远古时期的犹太人还是以某一块固定的地域为中心从事贸易活动的话，那么，大流散把他们赶入了真正意义上的世界市场。总体而论，他们不再同任何地方的固定市场有过于密切的关系，四处流散的生活决定了他们成为国际贸易的承担者。在流入欧洲以前，绝大多数犹太人生活在阿拉伯帝国境内，可以说，伊斯兰教的兴起使犹太商人获取了千载难逢的发展机遇。由于基督教与伊斯兰教的长期对峙，特别是由于在东西方贸易的核心地区地中海沿岸出现了两大帝国——信仰基督教的法兰克王国和信仰伊斯兰教的阿拉伯帝国，双方常因商业利益而大动干戈，不同宗教背景的商人彼此都不敢进入对方领地，欧亚之间的贸易几乎中断，而犹太人则顺理成章地扮演了东西方贸易的中介者。当时的犹太人活跃于西班牙、法国、意大利、拜占廷、巴勒斯坦、埃及、突尼斯等地，"他们在地中海和洲际贸易中起着极为活跃的作用，并作为国际商人而首次出现于西方的基督教国家"[1]。他们在各大港口都设有自己的"代表"，组成了一个排除异己、自成体系的庞大商业网，保证了长途贸易的顺利进行。

---

[1] H.H.Ben-Sasson, *A History of the Jewish People*, Harvard University Press, 1976, p.394.

可见，正是在长期的历史交往中，犹太人获得了一个又一个孕育和发展其商业特长的机遇，也正是在交往的过程中，他们对钱产生了特殊的感知与认识，钱成了他们的"防卫机制"与"生存保险"，成为他们进入外部世界的"入场券"。

第二，文化内容的开放性。犹太人在长期历史交往中积累的宝贵历史经验，就是作为民族主体，既能抵御外部社会的强大压力，又能摆脱来自方方面面的迷人诱惑，而保持其民族认同感。就文化层面而言，就是作为一个缺乏"地域疆界"的民族较为成功地把守了自己的"文化疆界"，并不断丰富其内涵，从而实现了民族文化的"闭合性"与"开放性"的统一。"闭合"与"开放"本为一对相互排斥的范畴，也是任何民族在其发展中都难以回避的一种矛盾现象，犹太民族作为一种缺乏"根基"而又不甘沉沦的民族，其文化极需要闭合，只有保持民族传统的闭合性，犹太文化的主流才能弘扬，民族特性才能延续，才能使四处漂泊的犹太人面对同化压力，仍然拥有一方属于自我的阵地。一旦失去了这种闭合性，犹太民族必将同其他许许多多消失在文化歧途上的民族一样，走上一条由同化到消亡的衰败之路。正因为如此，犹太文化曾长期被视做一种保守的"闭合性"文化。其实，这种观点是片面的，它只看到了犹太文化"闭合"性的一面，而忽略了其开放性的一面。

在公元 2 世纪以前，希伯来文化的主要成就集中体现在《圣经》中。由于《圣经》是在特定的历史条件下形成的，再加上为了树立民族独尊地位的需要，希伯来人力图使《圣经》神圣化、经典化，从而使《圣经》成为闭合性的、名副其实的《圣书》。而《圣经》越是"成圣"，它与实际生活之间的鸿沟就越拉越大。因此，时刻都在寻求发展的犹太人急需一种"准圣经"在神与人之间架起一座桥梁，为子孙后代制定一套行为准则。于是，在公元 2~6 世纪，流落在巴比伦的犹太社团就集中本民族的宗教贤哲与思想精英，编纂了洋洋 250 万字的犹太口传律法集，即《巴比伦塔木德》（简称《塔木德》）。《塔木德》不仅对传统的犹太律法加以阐释，而且内容极为广泛，包括神话故事、祖先传说、历史沿革、民俗风情、天文地理、医学、算术、植物学、历史学等诸多方面。通俗、简洁、适用的《塔木德》和《圣经》一起构成了犹太教育的蓝本。《塔木德》的问世，正体现了犹太民族的开放性心态。

犹太文化的开放性还明显地体现在对异质文化的态度上。早期的希伯来文化就是在广泛吸取四邻文化的基础上形成的。《巴比伦之囚》时期，希伯来人接触了较为先进的巴比伦文化，他们在很多方面学习了巴比伦人的生活方式及教育体制。与希腊文化接触后，犹太知识分子又掀起了学习希腊文化的热潮，在很大程度上推进了古希腊哲学与古希伯来哲学的融合，从而形成了一种新的思想——"犹太希腊化哲学"（Jewish Hellenistic Philosophy）[1]，这一思想深刻地影响了后来的西方文化。在散居欧洲的过程中，犹太文化与基督教文化虽然有不可调和的矛盾，但相融的现象还是随处可见。近代以来，随着科技革命的兴起与教育的发展，犹太人突然发现他们正面临一种不可忽视的新知识的挑战。如果犹太文化

---

[1]　Julius Guttmann, *Philosophies of Judaism-the History of Jewish Philosophy from Biblical Times to Franz Rosenzweig*, Rinehart & Winston, Inc., pp.18-29.

想在精神方面继续得到尊重，那么，就必须把现代哲学纳入他们的有关上帝、世界、理性及人的本质等问题的思考之中，就必须使犹太人广泛吸取传统之外的新知识，投身于现代化的洪流之中。于是，一些犹太知识分子便大力鼓吹世俗思想，企图通过大范围、多层次的现代化、世俗化教育，使犹太人了解西方文化，掌握现代科学技术。与此同时，还要深刻反思民族文化，提炼犹太教信仰，清除自中世纪以来弥漫于犹太宗教学说中的谬误与虚妄，消除文化孤立主义，弥合在精神与文化方面与西方文明社会的差距，"最终塑造出在思想与文化方面能适应整个欧洲社会的新型的犹太人"。在这种背景下，犹太启蒙运动及犹太教改革应运而生，犹太世俗文化也迅速兴起。

第三，文化影响的普遍性。在保留开放性特点的同时，犹太民族文化对异质文化保持着相当大的影响力，三大一神教在教义、礼仪和信众行为规范方面的继承关系便是最突出的一点。希伯来文化不仅较为合理地对待神圣与世俗、信仰与功利、传统与变革等思想范畴，实现了本体文化的丰富与完善，而且为如何处理本体文化与异质文化的交往关系树立了典范。

希伯来文化对欧洲知识界和思想界产生过极大的影响。文艺复兴及宗教改革时期，英、法、意、德等国曾一度掀起了学习希伯来文化的热潮，几乎所有的宗教改革家如伊斯拉谟、加尔文、马丁·路德等都曾潜心研究希伯来语。这一时代是不同思想交会影响的时代，是人类文化交往史上的一次奇迹，而广大犹太学者承担了文化交往的中介者及推动者的角色。

近现代以来，不同国家、不同行业犹太精英层出不穷的现象也是犹太文化世界化品质的一个反映。由于散居于世界各地，犹太文化常常表现为一种无国籍的文化。它一方面具备了民族文化的重要标识与特定内涵，另一方面在表现形式、内容及影响上又明显地超越了民族文化。以犹太文学为例，犹太作家不仅有大批希伯来语及意第绪语作品，还广泛使用英语、法语、德语、俄语等非本族语言写作，所以，如果按照国别与语种的不同，犹太作家又可隶属于不同的民族文学之列，他们的作品一方面归属于犹太文学，另一方面又归属于各居住地文学。

犹太文化之所以能在人类文化史上有如此突出的地位，其生命力与影响力的来源在很大程度上应归结于自身的世界化品质。波兰犹太思想家伊萨克·多伊彻（Isaac Deutscher，1907~1967）曾用马克思主义的观点分析了斯宾诺萨、海涅、马克思、罗莎、卢森堡、托洛斯基和弗罗伊德等犹太伟人的思想形成脉络，他认为这些人虽然被称为异端，但犹太传统已在他们身上打下了无法抹去的印记，他们的思维模式及处事方法是"非常犹太的"。但是他们绝不仅仅局限于闭塞、陈腐的古老传统，而是急于寻找超越犹太人的理想与事业，接受现代世界哲学、社会学及政治学的最新观点。他写道："作为犹太人，他们的'超前'优势恰恰在于生活在不同文明、宗教和民族文化的交界线上，他们诞生和成长在不同时代的交替点上。他们的思想成长在最为扑朔迷离的相互沟通、相互滋养的文化影响之中，他们生活在他们所居住的国家的隐蔽处和偏僻角落。他们中的每一位都既在其社会之中又超然其外，既属于它而又超乎于它。正因为如此，才使得他们创造了超越其社会、超越其国家也超越其时

代和同代人之上的思想，才使得他们的精神能遨游在宽
阔的地平线上，遨游向遥远的未来。"[①]

（原文刊载于《西亚非洲》2000 年第 3 期）

---

① Paul R., Mendes-Floh & Jehuda Reinharz, *The Jew in the Modern World*, Oxford University, 1980, p.231.

希伯来先知与儒家圣人比较研究

傅有德[*]

众所周知，犹太教是先知性宗教，而中国的儒家则是推崇圣人的。先知作为上帝的代言人在古代以色列社会的宗教、政治、道德生活中发挥过极其重要的作用。儒家圣人知天道并代天宣化，其言行和精神对个人、家庭、社会、国家影响至深至远。显而易见，作为文明的开创者或先驱，犹太先知和儒家圣人之间是有可比性的。本文的研究，希望有助于促进两个民族的相互了解，有助于推动两个历史悠久的文化传统在全球化时代的交会与融合。

---

* 傅有德，山东大学犹太教与跨宗教研究中心主任、哲学与社会发展学院宗教学系主任，教授，博士生导师。

一

从词源学上看，先知的希伯来语是"navi"（复数是
navíim），意思是"嘴唇的果实"。嘴唇的果实是什么？
在古代以色列人看来，嘴唇与说话相联系，其主要的"果
实"就是"说话"。所以，先知的字面意思是指善于言谈
的人。关于先知与嘴、嘴唇的关联，《圣经》中亦不乏例
证。如《以赛亚书》所说，以赛亚在成为先知之前是个"嘴
唇不洁的人"。他在异象中看到了雅威，又见一六翼天使
飞到他面前，把烧红的火炭沾到他的嘴上，说"这炭沾
了你的嘴唇，你的罪孽就除掉，你的罪恶就赦免了"（《以
赛亚书》6：5~7）。这里的"嘴唇不洁"，可理解为不善
于讲话，或言辞不当，在天使的火炭沾其嘴唇后就变得
洁净，言谈无碍了。

上述词源学意义尚不能表达先知概念的宗教意蕴，
所以，要完整地了解其内涵，还需进一步界说。新版
的《犹太教百科全书》这样说："先知是克里斯玛式的人
物，据信拥有接受和传达上帝启示给他们的信息的神性
禀赋（divine gift）。预言是这种信息的传达，而非预见
未来的能力。先知是上帝的意志和人之间的中介。"① 从
这个定义，我们可以明确以下四点：首先，先知具有超
乎常人的神性禀赋，能够接受和传达神的启示，因而是
具有非凡魅力（克里斯玛）的人物。其次，先知的使命
是传达上帝的启示，即把接受到的神的信息传达给普通

① Geoffrey Wigoder, *The Encyclopedia of Judaism*, Jerusalem：The Jerusalem Publishing House, 1989, p.571.

大众。因此，从功能上讲，先知是上帝在尘世的代言人（spokesman）。再次，先知就其地位而言，是神人之间的中介（intermediary）。先知是人而不是神，但因其具有神性的禀赋而担当了接受并传达上帝意志的角色，所以，他的地位超乎常人而处在神人之间。最后，就先知所做预言的性质而言，它可能预见未来事件，也可能不关乎将来之事，其使命是说出神启的真理。

无独有偶。古代儒家经典中的先知先觉，恰好与希伯来圣经里的先知遥相呼应。关于先知先觉，《孟子·万章上》告诉我们：商王成汤派人带着礼物去聘请伊尹出山。起初，伊尹不肯，宁愿身居田野以研习尧舜之道为乐。汤王三请，伊尹最终改变了主意，认识到如果把尧舜之道付诸实施，使汤王成为和尧舜一样的君主，使百姓们成为和尧舜时代一样的百姓，那将会更有意义。他说："天之生此民也，使先知觉后知，使先觉觉后觉也。予，天民之先觉者也。予将以斯道觉斯民也。非予觉之而谁也？"意思是：上天降生这些百姓，使先知的人帮助后知的人觉醒，使先觉的人帮助后觉的人觉醒。我，是百姓中天生先觉的人。我将拿尧舜之道去帮助这些百姓觉醒。我若不去帮助他们觉醒，还有谁能去呢？[1] 后来，伊尹辅佐汤建立了商朝，还辅佐了汤之后的几个君主，成为历史上有名的贤相。后辈儒家多有谈及先知先觉者，如南宋大儒朱熹就说过"人性皆善，而觉有先后。后觉者，必效先觉之所为，乃可以明善而复其初也"之类的话[2]。

---

[1] 原文见杨伯峻《孟子译注》，中华书局，1960，第225页。现代汉语翻译参考了刘方元《孟子今译》，江西人民出版社，1985，第192、193页。

[2] 朱熹：《四书集注》，岳麓书社，1986，第70页。

孟子不仅说有先知先觉，而且认为先知先觉也就是中国古代常说的圣人。关于这一点，孟子说："伯夷，圣之清者也；伊尹，圣之任者也；柳下惠，圣之和者也；孔子，圣之时者也。"[①] 意思是说，伯夷是圣人中高洁至清的典范，伊尹是圣人中特别富于才干而能担当大任的典范，柳下惠是圣人中喜怒哀乐皆能中节的典范，孔子则是应时而生的圣人。在孟子心目中，他们都是先知先觉，也是各具特点的圣人。

《辞源》在解释"圣"字时说："无事不通曰圣"。反映子思、孟子思想的《郭店楚简·五行》有这样的话："闻而知之，圣也。圣人知天道也。……圣，知礼乐之所由生也，五（行之所和）也。"[②] 在子思、孟子看来，圣人是知天道者，而圣人所知的天道就是"礼乐所由生"的根据，也即五行（仁、义、礼、智、圣）统合而成的"天德"。由此可知，儒家圣人之为先知先觉，指的是他们先于常人而认识了"天道""天德"，因而拥有最高的智慧。结合前面有关"先知觉后知，先觉觉后觉"的引文，我们可以推知，圣人的所作所为就是用自己先知先觉的"天道""天德"教化后知后觉者，使普通百姓也"知道"并成为有智慧、有德行的人。可见，儒家的圣人不仅是知天道者，而且肩负着"代天宣化"的使命。

在希伯来《圣经》中，上帝是至高无上的实在，他不仅是天地万物的创造者，还是真理和律法的最终源泉，先知向人传达的话语就是从上帝那里来的。至于儒家所信奉的天的内涵，历来的学者众说纷纭，如"主宰之天""义

① 刘方元：《孟子今译》，江西人民出版社，1985，第 197 页。
② 李零：《郭店楚简校读记》（增订本），中国人民大学出版社，2007，第 102 页。

理之天""自然之天"等。从现有的历史资料，我们尚不
能找出一个众人皆可接受的对儒家之"天"的理解。但是，
有一点应该是公认的，即在周代以降的文献中，天被看
做至高无上的实在。这就是说，儒家的天与犹太教里的
上帝是同一个层面的存在。既然如此，儒家所知、所言
之"天道"自然也和先知所传达的神的话语是同一个层
面的东西。既然儒家的天与犹太教的上帝是同一个层面
的存在，而且儒家圣人所得的"天道"和犹太教先知所
传达的"神言"也是同一个层面的东西，那么，作为知
天道且代天宣化的主体——儒家圣人，也逻辑地与希伯
来先知是同一个层面的人物。或可说，从性质和功能上看，
圣人与先知是同类的。正是在这种意义上，英国学者罗
利（H.H.Rowley）非常明确地称中国的孔子、孟子（还
有墨子）是先知式的人物。他说，希伯来先知和中国的
圣贤"属于不同的社会，各有不同的传统。但中国人及
希伯来人都同样自觉有受令于天去对他们的社会说一种
重要的话的责任"。在这一点上，中国的圣贤"并不较
弱于以色列先知"。古代中国的圣贤，如孔子、孟子（和
墨子），"姑勿论他们与以色列先知们有许多不同之处，
他们可公正地被视为先知性的人物，且可与以色列先知
放在同等的地位，而两者的训言的某些部分，可以相互
参对"① 。

不仅如此，和希伯来先知具有神性的禀赋相似，儒
家的圣人也具有卓越的天资或与天的授命有关联。在中
国的典籍里，至少孔子和孟子都说过才德、使命源于天

---

① H.H.Rowley, *Prophecy and Religion in Ancient China and Israel*,
New York : Harper, 1956, pp.20-21, 26.

授之类的话。如孔子说："天生德于予。"(《论语·述而》)表明他意识到自己先天有配天之德。《论语》还说："天下无道久矣，天将以夫子为木铎。"(《论语·八佾》)意指上天让孔子扮演警世摇铃的角色，好让"无道久矣"的天下复归于有道。孟子说："天将降大任于斯人也，必先苦其心志，劳其筋骨……"(《孟子·告子下》)按孟子的意思，以往的历代圣人都是"天降大任"，历经磨炼而后成圣的。可以这样看，圣人意识到的配天之德和源于上天的使命，是圣人之所以成为圣人的先天主观条件，如果没有这样的条件，他们是无从"知道"而成圣的。

在犹太教中，先知的地位处于上帝与普通人之间。先知虽然具有神性的禀赋，但他们仍然是人不是神，而且永远也不能变成神。他们能够能常人所不能，即接受神的启示并代神传言，因此得以高于常人而成为神人之间的中介。在儒家传统中，圣人具有配天之德，能够先知先觉而得天道，但他们也是人，而不是神。可以说，圣人之于普通人，是"出乎其类，拔乎其萃"的人杰，其地位也与希伯来先知类似，属于沟通天人的中介人物。

先知是圣经犹太教时期的重要现象。按照传统的犹太教，摩西作为以色列人的民族领袖和犹太教的创始人一直被看做最伟大的先知。摩西之后，以色列还出现过为数众多的先知。这些先知的相继出现及其活动构成了以色列历史上的"先知运动"。王国前夕出现的是一个先知群体，撒母耳（Samuel）是其代表；后来进入王国但无成文《圣经》时出现了个别先知，有名的先知包括以利亚（Elijah）、以利沙（Elishah）、拿单（Nathan）、米该亚（Micaiah）、亚希亚（Ahijiah）等 ① 。在公元前 8 世纪至前 5 世纪中叶，在北部的以色列国，南部的犹大国以及第二圣殿的以色列，涌现出了一批著名先知，他们是阿摩斯（Amos）、何西阿（Hosea）、以赛亚（Isaiah）、弥迦（Michah）、西番雅（Zephaniah）、那鸿（Nahum）、哈巴谷（Habakkuk）、耶利米（Jeremiah）、以西结（Ezekiel）、俄巴底亚（Obadiah）、哈该（Haggai）、撒加利亚（Zechariah）、约珥（Joel）、约拿（Jonah）、玛拉基（Malachi）等。这些先知尤其受到西方思想界的关注。20世纪德国著名哲学家雅斯贝尔斯指出，这些希伯来先知是与希腊的苏格拉底、柏拉图，印度的释迦牟尼，中国的老子、孔子等一样的伟大思想家，他们共同开创了人类思想发展史上的一个奠基性的繁荣时代——"轴心时代"。

在古代中国，各家各派的思想家对圣人的理解不尽相同，有的用以指君王，有的指某一方面的天才或大德 ② ，但在儒家圈子里，大都认可《孟子》书最后一段话所宣示的圣人道统："由尧、舜至于汤，五百有余岁，若禹、皋陶，则见而知之；若汤，则闻而知之。由汤至于文王，五百有余岁，若伊尹、莱朱，则见而知之；若文王，则闻而知之。由文王至于孔子，五百有余岁，若太公望、散宜生，则见而知之；若孔子，则闻而知之。由孔子而来至于今，百有余岁，去圣人之世若此其未远也，近圣人之居若此其甚也，然而无有乎尔，则亦无有乎尔！"

---

① 参见休斯顿·史密斯《人的宗教》，刘安云译、刘述先校，海南出版社，2006，第 310 页。

② 例如老子讲的"圣人"，就是具备"玄德"的人。古人还把在某一方面达到最高境界的人称为圣人，如称关公为武圣，张仲景为医圣，李时珍为药圣，杜甫为诗圣，等等。

（《孟子·尽心下》）这里明确提到的圣人有尧、舜、禹、皋陶、汤、伊尹、莱朱、文王、太公望、散宜生、孔子，再加上《孟子》别处提及的伯夷、傅说、百里奚、柳下惠、武王、周公，这样算来，孟子心目中的圣人不下十几位。与《圣经》时代的希伯来先知相比照，我国古代儒家认可的圣人队伍也是不逊色的。

二

希伯来先知与儒家圣人之间不仅具有以上相同、相近之处，还有许多重要的差别。正是这些差别体现了先知与圣人各自的突出特征。

在希伯来《圣经》中，我们经常看到这样的说法："雅威对摩西说"，"雅威晓谕摩西说"，"万军之主、以色列的大能者说"，"雅威的话临到我，说"，"雅威这样说"，"这是雅威说的"，诸如此类。按照传统犹太教的解释，《摩西五经》向众人传达的是神赐予的"摩西十诫"和其他律法；阿摩斯、以赛亚、耶利米等希伯来先知是得到上帝的启示，然后传达给众人的。先知们明确知道，他们所宣示的是直接来自上帝的话语。也正是在这个意义上，犹太教把先知界定为"上帝的代言人"。

与此不同，翻开中国古代的典籍，呈现在我们面前的是"尧曰""舜曰""殷汤曰""子曰""诗云"等，未发现有"天曰"或"上天曰""昊天曰"之类的字眼。不同典籍的"主人公"不同，发言者也自然不同。但有一点是相同的，这就是，圣人们直接说的话是他们自己的话，或是转述先王圣祖的意思。就孔子而言，他"信而好古，述而不作"（《论语·述而》），"祖述尧舜，宪章文武"（《中庸》），即弘扬古已有之的尧舜文武之道。要而言之，无论孔子等圣人自己说的话，还是转述往圣的话，说出的都是"人的话"。这与希伯来先知所说的"神的话"厘然有别。这一差别极其重要，它反映了先知与圣人在获得超越知识上的不同方式，由此进一步生发出彼此人格上的重大区别。

先知获得神的意志和目的的方式是神的启示。"启示"的意思是开显、显示。神的启示指的是上帝向人显示其存在、属性、意志、计划或目的的言行。从希伯来《圣经》看出，上帝对先知的启示就是和先知说话。例如，上帝和亚伯拉罕说话，令其子孙繁茂并赐其迦南地为永久的产业（《创世记》17 : 1~8）；上帝和摩西说话，明确讲出"十诫"的具体内容（《出埃及记》20 : 1~17）；上帝预言耶路撒冷的败落与犹大国的倾倒（《以赛亚书》3 : 4~13）。此类的例证在《圣经》中俯拾即是。不仅如此，按传统犹太教的解释，希伯来《圣经》的律法书部分，即《摩西五经》，全部是摩西书写下来的上帝在西奈山启示给他的话语，《先知书》的主要内容也是上帝话语启示的宣示。不论摩西在清醒时刻所听到的，还是其他先知在梦境或异象里听到的，都是从神而来的话语。一句话，希伯来先知接受的是神的话语启示。在宗教神学中，话语启示属于特殊启示（special revelation）的主要形式。

儒家圣人得天道的方式则较为复杂，需要仔细梳理与概括。有一点是明确的，这就是：圣人所知的"天道"不是上天对他们所说的话，因为在《诗》《书》《礼》《易》《春秋》以及《论语》《孟子》这些早期的儒家经典中，没有记载有关天对人说话的事情，尧、舜、禹、汤、文、武、周、孔等圣人也未曾说他们的话是直接来自上天的。还有一点也是明确的，即圣人的话不是自己心里先天固有的。孔子就明确说他"非生而知之者"。既然圣人所言不是直接来自天的话语，也不是他们头脑里固有的，那么，其得道的方式就一定是后天的学习和求索。孔子说："我非生而知之者。好古，敏以求之者也。"（《论语·述而》）他还说过"唯上智与下愚不移"（《论语·阳货》）之类的话。综合孔子这些话的意思，我们似乎可以说，孔子乃至以往的圣人是靠"上智"之人的卓越天资加后天勤奋求索而"上达"天道智慧的。

中国传统文化里没有明确、系统的知识论，因此我们无从清晰地得知圣人是如何运用感性、知性、理性或直觉能力而认识天道的。从现有的资料看，圣人求道的方式主要表现为"闻道"和"悟道"。"圣"字的繁体是"聖"，从耳，从声，有善于听音的意思；从口，有口问、口传的意思。《郭店楚简·五行》有言："闻而知之，圣也。"[1]《马王堆汉墓帛书》也说："聪也者，圣之藏于耳者也。——聪，圣之始也。"[2] 耳聪，即善于倾听是圣人的品质。实际上，"闻"与"问"相联系，就是说，从何而闻，闻什么是与向谁发问相联系的。就孔子而言，他"信而好古"，曾"问礼于老聃，学鼓琴于师襄子，访乐于苌弘"（《孔子家语》）。他孜孜求教的对象是前辈圣贤，希望从他们那里谛听到天道的"玉音"。他说"朝闻道，夕死可矣"（《论语·里仁》），足见其求道的拳拳诚意和迫切心情。前面援引过《孟子》书最后那段有关圣人道统的话，从中也可得知，从尧、舜到孔子的历代儒家圣人，或者耳濡目染，"见而知之"；或者间隔数代，"闻而知之"。总之，无不经过一个向先

---

① 李零：《郭店楚简校读记》（增订本），中国人民大学出版社，2007，第 102 页。

② 《马王堆汉墓帛书》（壹），文物出版社，1980，第 20 页。

贤求学问道、闻道的过程。

圣人得天道的另一个途径是悟道，即通过亲身的体察与参悟而得道。如果说"闻道"主要指向同代人与前贤学习，那么，悟道则主要指从自然界与社会现象中觉察到上天之真实的意图。《孟子》中有这样的意思："天不言"，但是，像改朝换代这样的大事，如舜从尧那里接受天子位，仍然是由天决定的。但是，天的决定并非"谆谆然"下达明确的命令，而是"以行与事示之而已矣"。孟子还举例说，派舜主持祭祀，众神都来享用，这就意味着上天接受了。让他主持政事，政事有条不紊，百姓非常安乐，这就意味着百姓也接受了（参见《孟子·万章上》）。天虽然不说话，但以自然界和社会中发生的"行与事"显示其意志。普通人不知其意，但天资卓越的圣人，如尧、舜等，则能够通过体察、思虑而觉悟到上天之道。从广义上说，天向人显示的"行与事"也是一种启示，但不同于以色列的上帝所说的话语那样的直接而显白的启示，而是一种不明确的一般性启示。因其不明确，所以常人不得真谛；因其是启示，所以作为人杰的圣人能够受到启发而悟得超越的天道智慧。当然，圣人悟道的过程，也是他们修身立德的过程。他们是在修身立德的实践中去体会、理解、亲证上天之道的。

从西方的知识论哲学和认知心理学的角度看，也许"闻道"和"悟道"很难完全对应于那些认知范畴，或可说，其中掺杂了感性、理性、内省、体验、直觉等各种认知方式，但无论如何，它们在本质上都属于人的认知功能，而绝不是天启。圣人虽然天资卓越，但他们没有希伯来先知那样幸运，不可以从上天那里直接得到话语性启示，而必须付出认识上的努力，在实践中反复体会、印证、修正已有的知识，最终得闻天道。在这个意义上，儒家圣人是一批虔诚的求道者，是靠自己的认知获得天道的睿智大哲，因此可以说是先知型的哲学家（prophet philosopher）。希伯来先知无需自己去认识神的启示，只需传达上帝在人清醒时，或在梦境、异象中告知的话，因此，他们只是先知，而不是哲学家。

进一步分析还可以看出，圣经犹太教的先知仅为先知而不是哲学家，儒家圣人则既类似于先知，又是哲学家，最终的根源在于犹太教与儒家信奉的对象不同。

凡是读过《圣经》的人都知道，犹太先祖信奉上帝，而上帝是一个有情感、有意志、会说话，能够直接命令、教诲、奖励或惩罚的人格神。《创世记》开篇就昭示人们：上帝是会说话的。上帝说有光，就有了光；说有穹苍，就有了穹苍；说有海洋和旱地，就有了海洋和旱地——总之，上帝说出什么，什么就被创造出来。《出埃及记》中摩西接受"十诫"和其他律法，《先知书》中诸先知得神的"默示"而传达给众人。由此推想，先知之所以能够说出神的话语，是因为他们接受了神的话语启示。假如犹太祖先信奉的不是这样一位用话语启示人的上帝，那么，先知们就无从传达上帝的话语，因而也不成其为先知，犹太教也就全然是另一副面目了。可见，希伯来先知之能够成为"上帝的代言人"，其根源在于，犹太教信奉的乃是一位会说话的人格神。

与《圣经》中会《说话》的上帝相反，儒家信奉的是"不言"之天 ① 。最能表明这一点的经典文本莫过于《论语》

---

① 关于天是否为人格神，国内学界多年来争论不休。笔者认为，在先秦儒家经典中，天有人格神的特征是不容置疑的。但是，这些典籍关于人格天神的描述是零散而不系统的。本文关于圣人为何必须通过认知而知天道的观点只涉及天的不言特征，故不展开阐述其人格性。

中的那段话：“天何言哉？四时行焉，百物生焉，天何言哉？”（《论语·阳货》）意思是：天不说话，一年四季照样运行，大地上的百物依然生生不息。结论：天不必说话！既然天不说话，而是“以行与事”昭示天道的，那么，圣人就只有靠自己的认知禀赋去体察、参悟；因为天不言，圣人就必须善于向先贤往圣问道，听从已有传统的教诲。在这个意义上，儒家圣人之为哲学家，是由他们信奉的不言之天成全的。反观犹太教里的先知，因为他们有一个会说话的上帝，可以直接接受上帝的话语，所以不必成为靠认知得道的哲学家。

三

　　希伯来先知的一个突出特征是无畏的社会批评家。《旧约圣经》的《先知书》告诉我们，古代以色列的先知们激烈抨击国王的腐败和堕落，谴责人们背离了雅威，制造并崇拜偶像，揭露假先知，斥责谎言、淫逸、抢劫、不公、无义等不道德的行为，预言以色列、犹大、亚述、巴比伦、推罗、埃及等国的覆灭和以色列民族的复兴，宣告上帝有罪必罚，绝不偏袒；呼求人们真诚忏悔，远离罪恶，“行公义，好怜悯，存谦卑的心，与你的上帝同行”（《弥迦书》6：8）。他们所处的时代不尽相同，有的是在亚述吞并以色列之前，有的是在犹大国灭亡之前，有的是在“巴比伦流放”时期，有的是在波斯帝国时代。所处的国度、地域也不一样，有的在以色列，有的在犹太，有的在巴比伦，有的在耶路撒冷，等等，但他们无不对当时的政治腐败、社会无序、道德败坏痛心疾首，义无反顾地予以尖锐的批评并指明出路。他们传达的是上帝的话语，反映的是社会下层普通民众的利益诉求，代表的是社会的良心。先知在犹太——基督教文明中影响极其深远，以至于直到现在，人们仍然用"社会良心"来指代希伯来先知。

儒家圣人对现实也有批判，如孔子就曾表达了对于"礼崩乐坏"的忧虑，说："德之不修，学之不讲，闻义不能徙，不善不能改，是吾忧也。"（《论语·述而》）也发出过"苛政猛于虎也"的声讨（《礼记·檀弓下》）。孟子也警告说："生于忧患而死于安乐也。"（《孟子·告子下》）但是，和以色列先知的无畏批判精神相比，儒家心目中的圣人对社会现实的批判在程度上就微弱多了。圣人们或为帝王，或为辅相，或为参与朝政的重臣，或为具有政治抱负、极力争取君王见用的思想家。作为在位的统治者，他们不可能把矛头对准自己，批判自己或自己统治下的家国社会；作为那些不在官位却极力争取见用的思想家，如孔子，他们间或有些批判或建议，但不可能站到和统治者直接对立的立场上去批判君王与他们统治的国家。另外，儒家经典所描述的是传说中的"王道乐土"，圣人们作为君王、辅相、大德之人，其人之圣明，贤良、智慧，所处社会、民风之淳朴都近乎理想。据《孟子》载，舜辅佐尧 28 年，尧把帝位让与舜；禹辅佐舜 17 年，舜把帝位让与禹；益辅佐禹 7 年，禹也把帝位让与益，但臣民们不接受益而接受禹的儿子启，于是启继承帝位，从此禅让制度不再，帝位的传承改为儿子继位（参见《孟子·万章上》）。尧舜禹在自己的国家实行"仁政"和"王道"，以仁、礼、爱、敬之道治天下，致使天下归心，国泰民安。帝位的禅让制昭示着那个时代君王的贤良，社会的和谐和人心、民风的良善。在这样几近理想的"黄金时代"里，先知式的批判是没有用武之地的。

其实，在儒家的圣人较少批判精神而犹太先知皆为激进的批评家这样的差异背后，我们看到的是两个全然不同的政治制度和统治模式。

在中国的古典文献中，尧舜禹所处的时代是华夏民族及其文化初创的阶段。"大道之行也，天下为公"正是那个初始的"黄金时代"的写照。那时，天子、大臣治理国家不是靠霸道，而是靠王道或仁政；换言之，不是靠暴力，而是靠德化。而舜则是行此德化的典范。据《孟子》书，舜之父瞽瞍极不喜欢舜，曾多次企图置之于死地，如让舜爬到粮仓上面去做修缮，而后抽去梯子并放火烧毁粮仓；让舜去淘井，然后把井口封死。但舜成为天子后不仅不记父仇，反而认为可使之"窃父负而逃，遵海滨而处，终身然"（《孟子·尽心上》）。舜的弟弟象"以杀舜为事"，可谓"至不仁"，但舜成为天子后非但不杀他，反而把他封为有庳国的王（《孟子·万章上》）。舜对于屡次企图杀害自己的父亲和弟弟，没有"以其人之道还治其人之身"，而是极力地"尊之""亲之"，以孝敬之心和仁人之爱去对待他们。因此，在孟子和儒家后人看来，舜是孝子的典范，也是仁人的典范，是实行"德化"的楷模。

夏商之后，周代制定了颇为完备的礼制。孔子对周礼推崇备至，说"周监于二代。郁郁乎文哉，吾从周"（《论语·八佾》）。周礼的目的是规范人际关系，其主体是"君君臣臣，父父子子"的伦理纲常。因此，周朝的礼制在本质上仍然是人治，并且是德治。所以，推崇周礼的孔子是力倡德治的。他说："为政以德。譬如北辰，居其所而众星共之。"还说："道之以政，齐之以刑，民免而无耻。道之以德，齐之以礼，有耻且格。"（《论语·为政》）

其后的儒家经典《大学》开宗明义讲"三纲领""八条目",也无不围绕着德治这个核心。

大致说来,从尧、舜、禹的帝位禅让,到先秦儒家的治国之道,都体现了人治社会和"以德治国"的特征,而儒家所推崇的圣人——尧、舜、禹、汤、文、武、周公、孔子等,恰好是这种人治与德治的政治理念和制度的体现者。

在先知起作用的古代犹太史上,我们没有发现这样一个人治与德治的时代。摩西和其后的一段时间是一个完全神治的时代。那时,以色列人信奉的神是立法者,摩西是神的代言人,即律法和制度的颁布者,在他之下的长老、祭司、千夫长、百夫长、五十夫长、十夫长都是律法的执行人和监督者。他们共同维系着一个"神治"即神法统治的社会。在两个世纪的士师时代,士师们平时管理民事,战时率兵打仗,肩负着先知、统帅等多重职能,但其背后依然是神的统治 ① 。在后来的王国时代,神权与世俗权力并驾齐驱,神权的代表是先知和祭司,世俗权力的代表是国王。但在理论上,上帝是真正的国王,神权高于世俗的王权,因为国王是由先知膏油、加冕的,而且国王要和他的臣民一样遵行神的旨意。然而在事实上,王权有时盖过神权,以致国王目无上帝的存在,大搞偶像崇拜,导致道德败坏,世风日下。不少先知就是在这种情势下挺身而出,针砭时弊,匡正世风,发挥社会良心和精神领袖作用的。可见,先知的产生和存在与其置身其中的政治制度——神权政治有关。在那样的制

---

① 参见 J.Maxwell Miller and John H. Hayes, *A History of Ancient Israel and Judah*, Philadelphia : TheWestminster Press, 1986, pp.111-112;张倩红:《以色列史》,人民出版社,2008, 第 11 页。

度里，从本质上看，作为上帝代言人的先知是实际的立法者；先知作为神权的代表和社会批评家，起到了限制、监督王权的作用。

四

儒家素有效法圣人的传统。这是因为，儒家心目中的圣人不仅是先知型的哲学家，还是具有完美人格的道德表率。如《辞源》所释，圣人是"人格品德最高的人"。而在犹太教中，先知则不具备这样的理想人格，也不是道德教育的追求目标。

孔子按道德标准把人分为若干等级，其中，君子和圣人都是人应当追求的道德榜样。在日常生活中，"君子敏于事而慎于言"（《论语·学而》），任劳任怨地做事却不张扬，说话谨慎有度。具体到义与利的抉择，"君子喻于义"（《论语·里仁》），是重义轻利的人；而且君子是"乐天知命"的人，"不知命无以为君子"（《论语·尧曰》）。到了孟子那里，圣人不仅是人们追求的道德理想，而且还是可以在现实中实现的，所谓"人皆可以为尧舜"。孟子还告诉人们，成圣的法门则是修身养性、"尽心知性"，即努力扩充、发展与生俱来的"善端"，使之臻于完美。由于孔孟的提倡以及汉代以后"独尊儒术"，做君子，成圣人就成为儒家知识分子终生追求的目标，圣人崇拜也成为儒家传统的重要组成部分。在国人心目中，尧舜是最早的也是最高的圣人，孔子是"无冕之王""至圣先师""万世师表"，他们都是中国人心目中最具人格魅力的道德典范。

自孔子始，儒家就认同榜样的无穷力量。孔子说："其身正，不令而行；其身不正，虽令不行。"（《论语·子路》）"上好礼，则民莫敢不敬；上好义，则民莫敢不服；上好信，则民莫敢不用情。夫如是，则四方之民，襁负其子而至矣。"（《论语·子路》）孟子说："君仁，莫不仁；君义，莫不义；君正，莫不正。一正君而国定矣。"（《孟子·离娄下》）后世儒家信徒无不循此而强调道德楷模的作用。

先知则不同。在圣经时代，先知是因为站在神的立场上抨击君主和社会上一切背主的行为，体现了社会的良心才得到群众爱戴和尊敬的。《圣经》没有号召以色列人效法先知，他们也不是人们学习的楷模。先知之所以不是人们学习的楷模，首先在于犹太教是以神为效法对象的宗教。在这样的宗教里，人被说成是"按照上帝的形象，照着上帝的样子"造成的，因此，人活着就是要仿效上帝来生活。上帝是超越的，但他和人立约，把律法赐给了人，为人提供了追求模仿他的方式——履行上帝的律法。先知是上帝在尘世的代言人，但他不是神，而且也不能变成神，所以不能成为人们效法的榜样。其次在于先知是不可学习的。按照《圣经》，先知之成为先知是靠神选，不是因为他有模范事迹而被群众根据道德标准认可或推荐的，因此不是可供学习的道德典范和理想人格。

在犹太教中，带有理想人格和道德典范意味的是义人（righteous man）。和代神传言的先知不同，义人的最大特点是虔诚地信仰神，认真听从神的教导，无条件地服从神的安排，模范地遵守神的律法。在《圣经》中，这样的义人有诺亚、亚伯拉罕、罗得、约伯等。尽管义人在《圣经》中被描述为众人该学且可学的榜样，但义人在圣经犹太教中的意义远没有圣人在儒家传统中那样重要。这是因为，在神法统治的古代以色列社会，义人作为道德的楷模所起的作用比之信仰和律法的作用是微乎其微的。与此不同，在人治—德治的古代中国，因为个人成圣，社会秩序的维系，民族的兴旺均需依靠理想人格的指引，所以圣人作为道德的典范和理想的人格，其榜样的作用是巨大的。

五

举凡一种宗教或文化传统，大都同时倡导仁爱与公正。但是，比较犹太教里的先知和儒家宣扬的圣人，我们可以清楚地看到，在仁爱与公正之间，他们的选择不是"半斤八两"，而是各有侧重的。如果说先知是公正的化身，那么，圣人则是仁爱的人格化。

《圣经》所宣扬的爱包括两个方面：爱神与爱人。《申命记》（6：4~5）说："以色列啊，你要听，雅威我们的神是独一的主；你要全心、全性、全力爱雅威你的神。"这是犹太教徒每天必颂的"经训"，后被基督教确定为"大诫命"，即一切诫命中最重要的诫命。《利未记》（19：34）这样说："与你们一起寄居的外人，要看他象你们中间的本地人一样；你要爱他好像爱自己。"这里说的是人与人之间的爱，即仁爱。爱神也爱人，而且"爱邻人如爱自己"。这是犹太教奉献给人类的"爱经"。

与仁爱相对的是公正。仁爱表达的是怜悯、同情、关心、仁慈等道德情感，而公正则主要指社会学和法学意义上的公平、正义、不偏袒、不徇私、一视同仁、赏罚分明。在犹太教中，公正经常表现为先知为下层人民追求权利和利益所作的呼求和斗争。如果说以色列先知在仁爱与公正之间有所偏重的话，他们所偏重的是公正。《摩西五经》作为"律法书"，充斥着有关公平处罚的条文。其中最引人注目的大概是下面这段众所周知的经文："以命偿命，以眼还眼，以牙还牙，以手还手，以脚还脚，以烙还烙，以伤还伤，以打还打。"（《出埃及记》21：23~25）① 不仅立法要公正，而且司法也要公正："不可做假见证去陷害你的邻人。"（《出埃及记》20：16）"不可在诉讼的事上随众说歪曲正义的话"（《出埃及记》23：2）；"不可杀无辜和正义的人，……不可受贿赂，因为贿赂能使明眼人变瞎，又能歪曲义人的话。"（《出埃及记》23：7~8）先知敢于坚持正义，为处于弱势的人打抱不平的例证有很多。例如，先知以利亚听说以色列王亚哈设计打死了平民拿伯并霸占了他的葡萄园的时候，立即跑到还在葡萄园里的国王面前，当面斥责他，致使他心里害怕并真心悔改（详见《列王记上》：21）。还有一个更有名的故事：大卫王看上了手下将领乌利亚的老婆拔示巴，就与她私通并使之怀孕。为了得到她，大卫王就把乌利亚派往前线，让敌人在战场上杀死了他。随后，大卫王就娶了拔示巴为妻。先知拿单得知后，马上奉神的旨意来到大卫的王宫，严厉质问并指责大卫王。结果，大卫王低头认罪，他与拔示巴的私生子也病死了（详见《撒母耳记下》11：1~23）。如果说《先知书》之前的经文提到的先知事迹，如撒母耳或拿单的事迹，表达的是某个先知通过神谕对某一个别的不公正事件的谴责和警

---

① 按照拉比们的解释，此段经文并非指一个人受了伤害以后一定要肇事者受同样的伤害，而是说要得到相应的补偿。但无论如何，我们在这里看到的是，不论是什么伤害，相应的处罚应该是公平对等的。

告,那么《先知书》则更多地指责一个民族,如以色列人、以法莲人、亚兰人、亚述人;一个阶层,如祭司阶层;一个国家或地区,如以色列、犹太、耶路撒冷,他们更多的是"挑战社会秩序中的腐败和压迫人的制度"①。先知们关于社会公平和正义的心声在下面这句话里得到了最明确有力的表达:"惟愿公平如大水滚滚,使公义如江河滔滔。"(《阿摩斯书》5:24)

20世纪最伟大的科学家爱因斯坦是犹太人,他的话也表达了公正是犹太教之核心价值的意思:"几千年来使犹太人联结在一起,而且今天还在联结着他们的纽带,首先是社会正义的民主理想,以及一切人中间的互助和宽容的理想。甚至在犹太人最古老的宗教经文里,就已浸透了这些社会理想,这些理想强烈地影响了基督教和伊斯兰教,并且对大部分人类的社会结构有良好的影响……像摩西、斯宾诺莎和卡尔·马克思这样一些人物,尽管他们并不一样,但他们都为社会正义的理想而生活,而自我牺牲;而引导他们走上这条荆棘丛生的道路的,正是他们祖先的传统。"②

儒家也有公正的思想。但是,在儒家圣人那里,仁爱才是其核心价值。"仁"是《论语》中谈论最多的概念。《论语·颜渊》说:"樊迟问仁。子曰:'爱人'。"按照孔子的说法,"仁"是人天生就有的道德禀赋,其首要的表现是"爱人"。所谓"仁者爱人",就是超越自我而承认、尊重他人存在的价值,并把爱心传达于人,把爱的行为

---

① 休斯顿·史密斯:《人的宗教》,刘安云译,海南出版社,2006,第312页。
② 爱因斯坦:《爱因斯坦文集》(第3卷),许良英、赵中立、张宣三编译,商务印书馆,1979,第164页。

施之于人。在孔子那里，仁和爱关系最近，所以后来的儒者常常"仁爱"并称。

"仁"在孔子那里是核心，其他的道德原则和规范都是由它衍生出来的。孔子的"忠恕之道"，即"己欲立而立人，己欲达而达人"，"己所不欲，勿施于人"，不是与仁爱不同的原则，而是具体实现"仁"的方法，即孔子所说的"仁之方"。"礼"也是为了践仁的："克己复礼为仁。一日克己复礼，天下归仁焉。"和"仁"相关的范畴如"温""良""恭""俭""让""孝""弟"（悌）"忠""信"等，无不是"仁爱"的具体化。孔子认为一个品行高尚的君子必须具备"智""仁""勇"三种美德。他说："智者不惑，仁者不忧，勇者不惧。"（《论语·子罕》）而在这三种美德之间，"仁"是居于核心地位的。"仁者安仁"，"智者利仁"，即说，一个有仁德的人会以仁为本，而他又有才智，能理解、达到"知人"的境界，进而实行仁德。所以他说："仁者必有勇，勇者不必有仁。"（《论语·宪问》）至于孟子谈论很多的尧舜，以及文王、周公、柳下惠诸位圣人，也无不是仁爱、孝悌的典范；他极力主张的"王道"政治也是一种"仁政"或德治，是仁爱在政治领域的具体运用。总之，孔孟及其心目中的圣人不是把"公正"，而是把"仁爱"放在核心地位的。

如前所述，先知的主要功能之一是社会批判。我们发现，社会批判需要一个评判的尺度，也需要一个应该且可以实现的目标，这个尺度和目标就是"公正"。凡不符合"公正"这一尺度的，就是背离神的意志的、邪恶的、有罪的，因而都是应该受到抨击和谴责的。可以说，以色列先知是利用公正这面镜子鉴别和批判负面的、丑恶的社会现象，从而发挥其批判功能的。与此不同的是，圣人的主要功能是道德楷模，而且是在一个人治和德治的社会里发挥道德楷模作用的，这就需要把他们塑造成仁爱的典型，他们的言论和行为都应该体现一个仁者所具备的品质，其核心的品质当然是"仁"或"仁爱"。可见，先知之强调"公正"与圣人之突出"仁爱"，都是有其社会历史和政治根源的。

六

我们研究的是距今 2500 年前后的希伯来先知与或许更遥远的儒家圣人。在时间上，他们无疑都属于"过去时"了。然而，他们的言行却超越了时空而化为不朽的思想和精神，影响着犹太的、欧洲的、亚洲的乃至整个人类的历史发展和文明进程，至今仍然表现出顽强的生命力。因此，比较希伯来先知与儒家圣人，应该发掘活的价值和精神。通过上述比较，我们发现，先知接受神启并代神传言的功能，是我们今天所不可思议，因而也是无法效法的。但是，先知的许多品质，例如先知的无畏批判精神和正义优先原则，却是当今时代依然需要的。在社会转型中致力于民主与法治建设的当代中国，尤其需要这样的精神和原则。另外，儒家圣人倡导的"君臣父子"之类的价值，也许已经不再适用，然而他们提出的另外一些价值如"仁""义""礼""智""信""温""良""恭""俭""让"等，则仍有发扬光大的必要。更为重要的是，孔子确立的仁爱原理，作为儒家的核心精神，无疑是当今国人应该继承和大力弘扬的。

在这里，我们也看到了希伯来先知与儒家圣人的互补性。古代犹太先知那种正义优先原则、大无畏的批判精神、法治的理念等，显然可以补充儒学之不足。同样，我们也认为，儒家圣人作为"仁爱"的化身与道德楷模，其仁爱精神、个人修养、人格魅力、君子风范、德化作用，对于犹太文化乃至与之密切相关的西方文化，也许是一个有益的补充。实际上，没有一个健全的社会不需要道德教化，以及理想人格的示范；没有一个健全的社会，尤其是现代社会，不需要民主与法治，其中包括对当权者的限制、批评和监督。既如此，本文所阐述的希伯来先知和儒家圣人的不同社会功能、特征、价值和精神，对于中国社会和中国人民，以及犹太民族和犹太文化，其现实价值和意义，就是不言而喻的了。

（原文载于《中国社会科学》2009 年第 6 期）

以色列笔记

黄 恒*

2008 年，北京奥运会前，我来到了以色列工作，2012 年春天，我离开。在中国，其实不仅是中国，在意大利、法国、英国、西班牙、日本、韩国……每个知道我曾在以色列长时间生活的人，都会问："那是一个怎样的国家？"

其实，作为一名职业记者，我不得不说，这是一种非常正常也非常差劲的提问方法。一个负责任的人，很难想象他会使用简单的几个词汇来描述一个国家，如果不是带有傲慢与偏见的话。因此，每次面对这个问题的时候，我想了又想，最终只能蹦出一个单词：神奇。

以色列是个神奇的地方。

它的神奇不在于创造了什么，或者毁灭了什么，它的神奇在于当下的存在。全球化时代中，虚无越来越成为一个社会学课题，但在以色列，实在的存在，冲突和妥协，喧嚣与

* 黄恒，新华社前驻耶路撒冷记者。

寂静，清真寺的宣礼塔，背负十字架行进在耶稣受难"苦路"上的游客，构成每一日生活，而非学院派书本中的词句。

一 大马士革门

开车经过耶路撒冷大马士革门，就像在两个世界间穿越。

一边是有秩序的，阳光下看着不论什么季节都一身黑衣黑帽面色苍白的犹太学者，看着他们走在老城墙的白色石块下，不时有种回到千年之前的错觉。

另一边是混乱的，却也是充满生活气息的。白天，一卡车一卡车的蔬菜和日用品拉过来，皮肤黑糙的阿拉伯壮汉和孩子们忙着卸货，店主飞快敲打着计算器，捧着英文书本的女学生安静穿行。夜晚，湿漉漉的地上，到处是菜叶和包装纸，年轻人开着车，车窗摇下来，舞曲震天动地。

有一天，黄昏时分，正在老城阿拉伯人聚居区闲逛，刚进大马士革门不远，突然看见一位犹太教士从狭窄的街道中穿过，向马克·吐温以前住过的地中海客栈走去。如今的地中海客栈是一所犹太宗教学校，房屋产权属于不同的犹太人，以色列前总理沙龙也买了一间，这被认为是一种姿态，就像上面飘着的大卫星旗帜。所有声音似乎在那一刻都消失了，教士和其他阿拉伯路人的眼睛里写着同样的东西。教士走过去，后背僵硬，人们很快收回凝视的目光，棋盘上有人挪动了下一步。

这就是再普通不过的以色列生活，游客找不到的生活，就像很多背包客坐着轻轨在耶路撒冷几进几出，却不知道这条线路。通过大马士革门前向北延伸的一段，就是1967年中东战争前的"绿线"——在各种语言的时政新闻中，反复出现，大多数观众却又不知的东西。

耶路撒冷不仅有老城和大马士革门，即便按照 1948
年联合国划分的界限，以色列还有国境之内的其他生活，
夹杂着问题和幸福。

二　以色列的时尚

在以色列，极端正统宗教人士，自不必说，从早到晚，
黑西装黑裤子白衬衣黑皮鞋，似乎没什么不同，离近点看，
大多数人外衣质地不错，鞋子厚底、圆头、粗鞋带，在
雨季沾上些草屑和泥巴，让人觉得很有生活气息。

正统宗教家庭的女人们不穿花衣服，黑白两色居多，
偶见蓝灰，收拾得都很干净。初来乍到，看惯其他城市
霓虹夜色中放荡的色彩，颇有一种清新美感。特别是
十四五岁的犹太少女，娇小居多，骨架单薄，色彩单薄，
再加上羞涩的眼睛和苍白的脸，颇为别致。

以色列最近这几年夏天流行 Croc，好多小洞的那种塑料
凉鞋，从老太太到婴儿，差不多人脚一双。冬天流行穿 UGG
那种爱斯基摩式的鹿皮靴子，小女生和中年妇女都不甘落后。

安息日去犹太会堂的时候——那是重要的社交场合，
时尚全部体现在体面上，可以看到诸多大牌的基本款衬
衣、领带、马甲和外套，没有花哨的装饰和裁剪，只有
熨烫得笔直的线条和一丝不苟的袖口、帽子和胸针。

三　"老大哥"真人秀

"老大哥"是起源于荷兰的真人秀节目，2009 年以版
"老大哥"创下了收视率新纪录，高达 30%。报纸说，这
是有史以来，以色列最成功的电视节目，赚了大概 2500

万美元的广告费，共收到 600 万条手机投票短信，光电信公司就从这些短信里赚了差不多 50 万美元。

街边买菜的一领退休金的老太太告诉我，她特别喜欢看这节目，白天一醒过来就上网打开直播画面，晚上还看电视台播的当日精选剪辑版。

我很佩服的一个老牌专栏作家解释说，该节目之所以收欢迎，是因为它展现了以色列犹太人之间的冲突。参赛者实际上按生活背景自然而然地变成了两个阵营，一个代表着以前住在中东和北非的东方犹太人后裔，另一个代表了来自欧洲的阿什肯纳兹犹太人移民。

四　考古和诗人

在以色列，媒体宣传渗透在每个地点和每个时间，不仅是总理办公室或者国防军总部的 Facebook 和 Twitter，还有考古学家的每一次发现和报告。他们试图说明：这块土地上，自古以来居住的便是犹太人，而不是巴勒斯坦人，即便罗马帝国和 19 世纪的英国委任统治者都将此地称为巴勒斯坦，但那只是一个地名概念，而不是民族概念。

2009 年达尔维什安葬的时候，阿拉伯世界最著名的一群知识分子发出请愿信，呼吁让他安然回到家乡，现在以色列北部的加利利地区，他在那里出生。

要理解以色列，需要有时间感，也只有有了足够的时间，才能够去理解以色列的现实。当然，这也不是以色列人或者犹太人的特色，全世界都差不多，并不因是否信仰摩西五经而有质的差别。正如房龙所写："3000 年前、2000 年前和现在的犹太人，都是普通人，和你我一样。既不像他们有时声称的那样，比别人好到哪里去，也不像他们敌人经常指责的那样，比别人坏到哪里去。"

这是一个停滞在理论体系中的所谓国际问题专家想不到的变化，时间像一架钟摆，不慌不忙地晃悠到顶点，终于随着 2009 年以色列选举中左翼的崩溃而落下。

（原文刊载于《同舟共济》
2013 年第 4 期，部分内容有删减）

再访中国 [*]

桑德拉 · M. 鲁宾斯坦 **

一 首访中国

你是否曾经有过突然发现自己的观念已经落伍于当今现实的经历？通常，这种经历会让你出现认知失调的不适感。除非，你像我一样，是因为中国。对于我来说，证明自己关于中国的旧有观念是错误的是一种非常美妙的感觉。

---

    *   引自 *Women of china*，2005（03）。陈亮译校。

   **   桑德拉 · M. 鲁宾斯坦，在美国出生并接受教育的媒体专家。她长期担任纽约霍夫斯特拉大学（Hofstra University）新闻与大众媒体系的系主任，直到 2001 年退休并随丈夫移居以色列。她曾两次来中国，第一次是 1986 年，受霍夫斯特拉大学一个交流项目资助来到中国；第二次是在 2004 年，受一个中国—以色列合作项目的资助。短短十余年间中国发生的巨大变化给她留下了深刻的印象。

　　我对中国的首次访问要追溯到 1986 年秋天。当时我在霍夫斯特拉大学一个交流项目的资助下，被分配到位于上海的华东师范大学外语系当老师。我之所以申请学校这个项目源于我对中国及其历史和文化的热爱，还有对当时中国的领导人、后来广受爱戴的邓小平先生发起的经济改革的强烈兴趣。

　　因此，当 1986 年 8 月飞抵中国时，我满以为会看到一个比当时实际情况"开放"得多的中国。我们的中国同事们对大多数"外国专家"——这是我们当时获得的称呼——都敬而远之，显然是害怕对我们显得"太过友好"。

　　入住华东师范大学校园的第二周，我买了一辆自行车，然后经常骑着它去逛上海的大街小巷。那个年代，路上行驶的汽车不多，一到晚上整个城市的街道几乎是一片漆黑，只偶尔几处有黯淡的路灯。我和另外一位教授经常在白天骑车到处逛，途中经常跑进当地的餐馆里吃一碗面条或饺子，特别是在寒冷的冬日。我至今还记得那些劳动人民的友善，他们总是给我们让出位子来，让我们和他们坐在一起。

　　除了骑车逛遍上海，我还在学校外事官员的安排下去一些外地旅游观光。我去过南京、北京、西安、广州和其他一些地方的景点。我喜欢自己的工作，热爱学生，有一两个中国同事对我也很好，但是我总感觉和外国人打交道的氛围是比较紧张的。

　　因此，当 1987 年 1 月中旬我准备离开上海时，心情是很糟糕的。在我即将飞离中国的头一晚上，学生们一个一个地来跟我道别。所有人都带来了礼物并且送给我衷心的祝福。其中一个学生——他是一位敏感的诗人——感觉到了我的情绪，问我为何如此难过。我回答说："我很后悔，我也许曾经把你们国家的未来描绘得过于乐观了。"他很理解我的心情，握着我的手说："你和其他外国教授已经帮助我们播种下美好未来的种子。但要开花结果还需要时间。"

二　故地重游

首次访问中国之后的很多年里，我都会认真地急切地阅读关于中国发展的报道。但是，我显然还没有放下我的"陈旧思想"，对这些报道抱着怀疑态度，并固执地认为1986年之后的中国不会有什么太大的改变。2001年8月，我从霍夫斯特拉大学退休并与丈夫移居以色列，在那里执教于海法大学的新闻传播系。同时，我也开始偶尔去海法的卡梅尔山国际培训中心做讲座。

我很高兴地接受了卡梅尔中心和以色列外交部委派的前往尼泊尔和埃塞俄比亚与当地新闻记者一起工作的任务。同样的，当他们给我提供了去北京做两周讲座的机会时，我也欣然答应。在卡梅尔中心的研讨班上，我已经认识了一些来自中国的记者。他们的开放态度和宽广知识面给我留下了深刻的印象。当我着手为2004年8月为期两周的研讨班做准备时，我又想起了我那位中国诗人在我离开中国前夜跟我说的话。"开花结果需要时间"，我告诉自己不要抱太大的期望。

"社会变革中的媒体战略"中以研讨班由中国妇女外文期刊社、哥达梅尔卡梅尔山国际培训中心和以色列外交部主办。我的同事拉斐·曼恩（以色列《星报》高级编辑、希伯伦大学新闻传播系讲师）和我为自己能代表以色列参加这一活动而骄傲，我们希望竭尽全力提供专业知识，促进中以两国的友谊。

我们到达崭新而漂亮的北京国际机场时,受到了会议组织方的热情欢迎。从那时起,我开始意识到中国已经发生了巨变。在组织方驱车送我们去气派的好苑建国酒店的路上,我被车窗外面的景色迷住了:穿着得体、打扮时尚的骑自行车者、川流不息的汽车车流、宏伟的建筑物和畅怀大笑、满脸幸福的人们。北京,已经成为一座"国际化"都市。

抵达的第一天下午,我们被介绍给为我们做翻译的四位年轻人。他们都很自信、开心、外向,非常阳光。对我而言,他们是中国正在发生的变革中最美好的部分。

我们课程的第一周过得飞快。我们很享受与研讨班学员的互动。她们的提问和评论都很有水平也很有挑战性,她们的幽默让我们轻松愉悦,暖人肺腑。我不由得再次想起我在上海时那些消沉而沉默的学生。这两次在中国教书的经历简直就是云壤之别。

三 上海变了

听说上海外滩附近已经发生了天翻地覆的变化,我觉得必须去亲眼看一下,"眼见为实"嘛!记得在1986年的时候,我一周总要骑车从华东师范大学到这个面对海湾的街区去好几次。古老的"和平宾馆"还在,附近的建筑也保持着传统的风格。但外滩那条崭新的、挤满了早起的上海本地人和来自全世界的旅游者的海滨步行街对面的风景却与十八年前迥然不同。

"它很像曼哈顿南区,只不过比曼哈顿南区要美丽、优雅十几倍,建筑风格也更具有想象力。"后来我这样在信中向以色列和美国的朋友们描述道。外滩对面的风景令我目瞪口呆，惊讶得合不拢嘴。我曾经骑车通过的那座联通浦东和老城区的旧桥已经被一座更加坚固的桥代替。上海海员酒店的老楼还在，但已经粉刷一新，矗立在它的新邻居之间。这座楼保留着旧貌，是中国历史上贸易被外商垄断的遗迹，令人浮想联翩。而它周边宏伟的摩天大楼则更像是中国新时代和不断增长的经济实力的宣言书。

那天深夜，我们到灯火通明的街道上走了走，看见不同年龄的中国人在许多餐馆里吃饭，还有的在购物，或者什么都不做，就或坐或站在那里聊天。每一个人都比我记忆中更加自由、开放和幸福。

四　北京印象

接下来，我回到北京去上最后一周的课程。我开始尽量去北京的各个地方走走，显而易见，这座城市无论是新建筑还是旧遗迹都给我留下了难以磨灭的印象。我知道中国已经取得了巨大的经济进步，并且还在继续向前发展。尽管漂亮的新建筑群、汽车数量激增、灯火辉煌的街道、移动电话和其他现代技术装备普及到个人……这些都令人难以忘怀，但最打动我的心的是人们脸上再没有了恐惧，而代之以灿烂的笑容。于我而言，这才是所有变化中最深刻的。

我不记得1986年时年轻的情侣会在大街上挽手而行，我也不记得那时候在大街上听到开心的笑容，看到人们拥抱，年轻人当众开玩笑，老人们微笑。我不是说，1986年这些都不存在，我是说我从来没有在公众场合看到过。

一天晚上，我绕到天安门广场去散步。我看见许多夫妻带着孩子们在放风筝。看着孩子们欢笑着注视各式各样、色彩鲜艳的风筝飞翔在高高的天空中，那一刻我觉得我心中关于中国的旧印象远去了，一股幸福的浪潮在我心中荡漾开来。

在我离开北京前的那个星期六，我再次参观了天坛，然后在巨大的北海公园里游玩了好几个小时。公园里满是不同年龄段的人们。有的人在参加一个大型团体活动，还有的躲在僻静的地方图清静或者跟爱人在一起。人们在跟随着音乐锻炼身体，聚在一起练习合唱，或者，在挺拔的松树树荫里纳凉，玩牌，听业余京剧爱好者表演，野餐或者仅仅坐在那里安享这个美丽的公园里的美好一天。

是的，我再次访问的这两个大都市在物理空间和经济上的变化都是深刻的。但最让我感到温馨、让我永远抹去不好的老印象和内心恐惧的变化是人们的笑意。这些笑意呈现在中国人——从参加我们研讨班的优秀记者和编辑们，到我会见过的人，或者我观察过的、沉浸在其日常工作生活或安享公园里的休闲一天的普通中国人——的脸上。

（原文刊载于《中国妇女》英文版 2005 年第 3 期）

经济

中国西部的农业挑战：中以合作

中国和以色列水资源战略比较分析

以色列的经济发展与环境保护

中国西部的农业挑战：
中以合作*

沙雷夫 **

中国西部大开发首先意味着该地区的农业开发。

作为外交官向在座的各位专家详述中国农业即将面临的困难与挑战，我也许不是行家里手；但作为了解以色列农业技术的国家代表，我希望能够向这一值得敬慕的论坛提供一些有用的意见与信息。我集中简述四个要点：

（1）缺水问题与向中国农业引进节水技术的必要性；

（2）先进的农业技术在农业持续发展中的作用，特别是中国西部农业；

（3）技术推广进程的重要性与技术的成功应用；

（4）以色列在中国加大西部省份开发力度期间的作用。

---

* 本文系作者在"2001·中国西部论坛"上的讲话。

** 沙雷夫，以色列前驻华大使。

一 缺水问题与节水技术

干旱不仅仅困扰中国，而且是全球性问题。

缺水是制约包括中国在内的任何国家经济发展的一个主要因素。合理分配水资源与节水灌溉技术的应用已经成为农业发展的基础。这一点适合干旱地区占陆地总面积 1/4 的中国。

为了使我提出的问题有充分依据，现提供一些事实。

中国每年人均可用水量为 2440 立方米；这不足世界平均可用水量的 1/4。20 年前农业用水占中国总用水量的 88%；但现在已经降到 72%。

人口爆炸与持续都市化，到 21 世纪中叶会将此比率降至 52%。

受干旱影响的农田面积从 20 世纪 50 年代的 1100 万公顷逐年递增到了 90 年代的 2060 万公顷。

中国是世界上 13 个面临严重水资源缺乏的国家之一。

中国有 1.3 亿公顷可耕地，其中的 5300 万公顷可以灌溉；但仅有 5% 的可浇地在采用节水灌溉技术。

中国水利用效率较低，下面的例子可以说明这一点：平均而言，生产 1 公斤粮食在中国要用 1 立方米水，而在一些发达国家仅用 0.2~0.3 立方米。

从上述事实可以得出结论：在中国特别需要推广水的有效利用。

我有意不用节水技术这一通用术语，因为节水仅是有效用水这一综合体系中的一个组成部分。节水是有效用水的表现之一。

先进农业的终极目标是在节水前提下的优质高产。

基本标准应该是从每一滴水中获取最高产量。

二　先进的农业技术

中国加入世界贸易组织会迫使中国农业迎接国外低值收成的挑战。

例如，中国农民种的玉米在质量和价格上不能和将从北美大批进口的玉米相比。

应付这一新情况的办法是引进新的、先进的农业技术。创新中国的农业技术并提升其水平会是应付这一新处境的最佳途径。这一提升过程是对不同要素的综合；灌溉、施肥、合格种子等要素在其中起着重要作用。

三　技术推广

认为技术从发达国家向发展中国家的转让会解决多数问题是人们常犯的一个错误。在某些场合也许是对的，但在农业方面并非如此。

农业持续发展的关键是加强源于研究的技术与该技术欲被采用的对象之间的转化进程。

在许多情况下，一个国家专门技术的开发源与该国的技术采用对象之间有脱节。形成这种脱节是由于在沟通研究与农民的体系中少了技术流通推广这一中介代理渠道体系。

中介代理是专门技术发送者，人们称其为"技术推广经纪人"或简称"培训系统"。技术可源于国外或国内，但如果少了中介代理，任何现有技术就会尽失价值。

四 以色列在中国促进西部省份开发中的作用

严重的缺水问题、引进高效用水技术的必要以及西部省份在新技术方面需要对专家和农民进行培训这一切致使以色列愿和中国共享其多年积累的专门技术。

以色列政府基于以上考虑提出的项目是在干旱地带建立一个农业中心。该中心特别重视在干旱地区发展有效灌溉农业。中国政府决定该中心将设在新疆维吾尔自治区。

该中心将开展三项工作：培训、研究与开发、生产。

（1）培训。中心的目标是培训来自西部省份所有地区的技术员和农民，引进有效用水方法以便实现优质高产。

（2）研究与开发。研究与开发将与当地的研究机构合作进行，包括在先进的灌溉、施肥与管理情况下种植高值蔬菜、水果、经济作物与花卉，也会注意种植"绿色"有机蔬菜。

（3）生产。该项目将示范在干旱地带采用先进的有效用水技术会达到的潜在目标。示范旨在鼓励其他团体与公司在强化农业附加项目的实施中进行创新实践。以色列将为该中心提供所需的设备主体并以派遣专家与当地专家和农民交流经验的形式提供技术支持。

中国—以色列干旱地带农业中心的预期目标如下：

（1）生产和使用适宜高热高寒地域、含盐与干旱条件下采用的优质栽培品种与合格种子。

（2）示范提高灌溉作物水肥使用效率的技术，包括咸水与已处理废水的使用。

（3）驯化新的沙漠作物，引导大规模种植。

（4）革新丰收后的存储方法。

（5）示范农作物保护技术的应用（包括塑料和网膜覆盖）。

（6）示范土壤曝晒、作物轮作和表土覆盖的益处。

（7）示范选择性植物保护措施和生物农药的应用方法。

（8）示范在干旱地带经济体系中以农业起步的经营如何维持发展环境。

中国和以色列希望这一联合项目能加强中国西部的农业并提高其水平。

（原文刊载于《西部大开发》2001 年第 10 期）

中国和以色列水资源战略比较分析

郇　际 *

　　水资源是基础性的自然资源和战略性的经济资源，是经济社会发展的重要支撑，是生态与环境的重要控制性要素，是一个国家综合国力的重要组成部分。水是地球万物生存之本，全世界淡水年用水量达 3 万亿吨，远远超过其他任何资源。水对一个国家发展的影响程度远远超过石油，所以将水作为一种战略资源是十分恰当的。以色列把水资源放在国家安全战略高度来认识，通过立法强化水资源的管理与利用，在水资源的管理与利用上远远领先于世界各国，有很多值得认真学习、借鉴的地方。

---

　　*　郇际，郑州大学教授，研究方向为国际战略环境。

一 中、以两国地理、气候特征比较

中国位于亚洲东部，太平洋西岸，海陆兼备，大部分地区位于北温带，四季分明，适宜人类居住与生存。以色列位于亚洲西部，地中海东岸，海陆兼备，中北部为丘陵裂谷，南部为沙漠，生存环境恶劣，属地中海亚热带气候区。

（一）相同点

中国和以色列同是北半球背陆面海的国家。若分别以北京、耶路撒冷为中心，北京位于北纬39°9′、东经116°3′，耶路撒冷位于北纬31°47′、东经35°13′，两地的纬度接近。

中国西北干东南湿，北冷南热，降水东南多西北少，水资源分布不均。以色列东南湿西北干，北冷南热，降水量南北差异大，多年平均降水量北部约为800毫米，中部约为600毫米，南部内格夫沙漠地区不足50毫米，南北水资源分布不均。

（二）不同点

中国经纬度跨度大，地势西北高东南低，气候复杂多样，季风气候显著。南方河流水量大、汛期长、无结冰期、含沙量小；北方河流水量小、汛期短、有结冰期、含沙量大。东部以森林草原为主，西部以荒漠草原为主。

以色列经纬度跨度小，地势东北高西南低，地处亚热带，每年11月~翌年3月为多雨的冬季，4~10月为干燥的夏季。由于以色列坐落在海洋与沙漠之间，且各个地方受到海拔、与海洋距离等因素影响，各地气候多变。以色列全境主要河流为约旦河，水源单一。沙漠气候与地中海气候之间是过渡性的半干旱地区。

二　中（黄河流域）、以两国水资源比较

黄河流域降水分布不均，总的趋势是由东南向西北递减，多年平均降水量为 466 毫米。根据 1956~2000 年系列资料，黄河河川年均天然径流量为 535 亿立方米，地表水资源量为 594 亿立方米，流域水资源总量为 707 亿立方米，流域内人均水资源量为 647 立方米 [①] 。

以色列境内降水分布不均，由北向南骤减，多年平均降水量约为 360 毫米，地表淡水资源主要集中于北部地区，以约旦河和加利利湖为主要水系，约旦河年均天然径流量为 6 亿平方米，全部淡水资源约 20 亿平方米，人均水资源量不足 370 平方米。

（一）相同点

黄河流域与以色列水资源的相同点：降雨分布不均，区域内水资源差异大，人均水资源量少。

黄河河川径流量仅占全国的 2%，却承担了占全国 15% 耕地面积和 12% 人口的供水任务，流域单位面积河川径流量仅为全国平均水平的 15%。随着城市化进程的加快，流域用水量激增，水资源供需矛盾日益突出，还出现了水质恶化、水体功能降低或丧失等水环境问题。

以色列 2/3 需要灌溉的土地在南方，却只有全国 20% 的水资源。以色列的水环境也曾面临过用水量增加、水量减少、水质污染、地下水位下降等问题。

[①] 　魏昌林：《以色列的北水南调工程》，《世界农业》2001 年第 10 期，第 29~30 页。

（二）不同点

黄河流域是中国流域管理中调度管理体制相对完善的流域，于 1987 年开始在流域内实施取水许可总量控制，但此方案是多年平均情况的宏观分配指标，没有制订出不同来水情况下水量分配方案和控制意见，因此未能很好地执行 [①]。流域内水资源仍存在分配不均的问题，城市、工业、农业用水缺乏科学规范的制约机制，农业用水基本上还是粗放型的。

约旦河在以色列境内全长约为 300 公里，流域总面积约为 15000 平方公里。以色列水资源 1/3 为地表水、2/3 为地下水。加利利湖是境内最大的淡水湖，水面面积为 160 平方公里，是约旦河的源头。自 20 世纪 60 年代以来，以色列农业用水总量一直稳定在 13 亿立方米，而农业产量却翻了 5 番，农业产值增加则更多。以色列的农产品不仅能够自给自足，而且每年还出口价值 13 亿美元的农业产品 [②]。以色列较好地解决了水资源和可持续发展的关系。

三　中、以两国水资源战略比较分析

与以色列约旦河相比较，黄河属于内流河，整个河段均在我国境内，水资源战略环境安全。约旦河对以色列来说属过境河流，水资源战略环境不安全。以色列地处中东，水资源问题造成的和周边国家的矛盾日益突出。

---

① 马建琴：《黄河流域与澳大利亚墨累—达令流域水管理对比分析》，《河南农业科学》2009 年第 7 期，第 69~73 页。

② 魏昌林：《以色列的北水南调工程》，《世界农业》2001 年第 10 期，第 29~30 页。

（一）相同点

中、以两国均将水资源列为国家宏观调控的范畴，通过法律手段强化水资源的管理与利用，如规定水资源是公共财产，由国家控制，私人不得拥有水资源，但可以拥有使用权；通过法律确定了水资源配置的优先程序，居民使用最优先，之后依次是工业、农业、其他用途。

（二）不同点

1. 法律法规

以色列水资源战略目的明确，在建国初期就充分考虑所处的地理环境和自然条件的特殊性，视水资源为国家存在和经济社会发展的命脉。以色列自1959年起，先后制定了《水法》《水计量法》《打井取水控制法》《河溪法》等法律法规，且执法机关分工明确。中国于1988年正式颁布实施了《水法》，并作过多次修改，但可操作性却较差，其问题在于配套法律跟不上，并且常出现有法不依、执法不严的情况，在跨区域、跨行业执法的过程中尤为明显。

2. 水价机制

以色列水委员会作为执法机构，为政府提供了供水管理以及供水收费方面的法律依据，用法律手段约束各部门和全体国民科学合理利用水资源。以色列实行有偿用水制，实施用水许可证和配额制，政府对城镇居民用水以及农民用水实行阶梯价格，超定额用水大幅度加价，同时，政府向城镇居民收取污水处理费，实行使用回用水价格优惠政策。

中国近些年才逐步将水资源纳入商品价格管理，但水价机制还不完善，水价普遍偏低，大都低于供水成本，使城市、工业、农业用水缺少制约。回用水技术在中国处于起步阶段，由于缺乏回用水技术开发和利用的明确政策导向和价格机制，因此浪费了大部分可回用水。

3. 节水意识

以色列通过执法和舆论宣传，使全民形成了良好的节约用水社会风气，节约有奖、浪费受罚的奖惩制度已经成为全社会的共识[①]。国家和地方政府积极倡导居民节水，"不要浪费每一滴水"的口号在以色列家喻户晓，让全民知道以色列的生存一直依赖于极有限的水资源。

中国节水意识比较淡薄，主要体现在用水缺乏市场制约机制、水价偏低、节水观念淡薄。在严重缺水的情况下，城市景观、绿地仍使用城市生活用水，这在以色列是严格禁止的。同时，国内水资源浪费现象严重，农业用水利用率仅 40%~50%，工业用水重复利用率为 20%~40%，单位产品用水定额往往比发达国家高 10 倍以上。

4. 科技手段

以色列利用科技手段使水资源利用率达到世界先进水平，如再生水利用、雨水利用、海水淡化、农业节水灌溉等。以色列的雨水资源利用率高达 98%，再生水利用率达到 72%，80% 以上的农田应用滴灌技术。以色列的自动化管水程度高，蓄水、输水、供水全部由电脑控制。达到一定规模的城市园林绿化供水都采取系统控制，针对不同绿化品种、不同时间段的需水要求，全部智能控制供水。城市生活用水供应系统也全部实现了智能控制。

中国在采用现代化科技手段提高水资源利用率方面远远落后于以色列，在许多方面甚至没有可比性。仅就

---

① 朱建民:《以色列的水务管理及其对北京的启示》,《北京水务》2008 年第 2 期, 第1~5 页。

雨水利用上来讲，黄河上游部分严重缺水的农村广建储水窖，较好地解决了缺水问题，但也仅是试点，还并未广泛推广；流域中下游城市、农村的雨水利用几乎空白。黄河流域的汛期段，雨量较大，若能充分利用，则将大大改善缺水状况。

四　结语

通过对中、以两国水资源战略的对比分析，不难看出，中、以两国在水资源开发利用方面存在着巨大差异，其核心问题是水资源管理，而管理的核心是立法。为了保障我国的水资源满足国民经济可持续发展的需求，必须采用严格的法律体系管理好水资源；通过对《水法》的宣传，提升全民水资源安全意识，把水资源放在国家安全战略高度来认识；完善水价机制，提倡节约用水，反对浪费；引进、借鉴和吸收国外先进的科技手段和经验，提高水资源利用率。

（原文刊载于《人民黄河》第 32 卷第 7 期，2010 年 7 月）

以色列的经济发展
与环境保护[*]

Amram Pruginin^{**}

  以色列现有人口 470 万, 面积 1.49 万平方公里, 是世界上人口最密集的国家之一。以色列水资源匮乏, 国土面积约一半是半沙漠和沙漠地区。建国后 40 多年里, 不仅在农业上自给有余, 而且在工业上向国际市场提供许多高精尖产品, 经济长期保持 9% 左右的增长率, 人均国民收入将近 8000 美元水平, 是中东地区非产油国中发展最快的国家。

  在经济持续发展和人口增长的过程中, 必然遇到许多环境问题。以色列很早就开始了保护环境的工作, 并在 1988 年 12 月将原有的几个有关机构合并, 正式成立

---

  * 该文节译自 "The Proceedings of the Third International Symposium of Biopolitics", *Biopolitics*, 1991（3）, 张毅、王小群译校。

  ** Dr.Amram Pruginin, 任职于以色列环境部。

了以色列环境部。现在，环境部已颁布实施了十三个有关的环境保护法，在环境监督管理工作中发挥了积极有效的职能作用。

为了解决以色列自身的环境污染问题，改善不利的自然条件，环保部门主要从以下十二方面积极采取措施，综合性地治理污染，保护环境，并取得了显著成效。

1. 严格控制燃料中的污染物含量和排放量

随着经济发展，各行业大量使用燃料造成严重污染已成为以色列的一个突出问题。对电力的需求从 1950 年的 5.43 千瓦时上升到 1970 年的 66.10 千瓦时，到 1988 年已达到 187.61 千瓦时，1988 年的装机容量为 4062 兆瓦，以目前趋势预计到 2017 年将达 11200 兆瓦。对此，以色列环保部门已制定了若干规章，要求发电、炼油等行业多使用低硫的燃料和原料，对越来越多的厂家实行更为严格的监测和规章管理，分别降低各种燃料中污染物的最高允许量，今后将逐步停止使用重性燃油发电，并在条件成熟的时候关闭污染严重的特拉维夫电厂，同时，在内陆地区大力开发太阳能、风能、抽水蓄能及利用油页岩，可以生产出 3200 兆瓦电力，以期减少燃料污染的一部分负荷。

以色列现有汽车约 80 万辆，随着人口增加和生活水平提高，汽车将会继续增加，到 2000 年时汽车年平均增长率为 5.9%，到 2000~2025 年为 2.5%，预计到 2025 年将达 374 万辆，是目前汽车数量的 4.5 倍，汽车尾气污染日趋严重。以色列已颁布并正在执行汽油含铅标准，已全面推广使用无铅汽油，在汽车污染管理工作中借鉴并采用了发达国家实施的法规和标准，并引进外国汽车厂家防治汽车尾气及噪声污染的技术改进措施，通过改造汽车发动机的办法实现了汽车改用无铅汽油的一次性转变。

近几年，环保部门通过法律、技术和行政等手段，对交通、工业、能源等生产所用燃料中污染物含量及排入大气的污染物总量进行了严格的控制，取得了较好的效果，在一些地方直接改善了大气环境质量。

2. 强化大气质量标准

能源、交通和工业这三大行业向大气排放出越来越多硫、碳、氮的氧化物等污染物。为此，除了进行技术改造和调整燃料结构外，以色列环境部正在修订有关标准，准备制定更为严格的二氧化硫、一氧化碳、铅颗粒物等的几个环境排放标准，不久将批准颁布，对各污染源实行严格控制。例如，通过管理和改造，1400 兆瓦的 Hadera 电厂，第一批四台机组的最大污染排放量在以色列国家标准的一半以下，1989 年批准该电厂扩充到 2500 兆瓦规模，仍要求其排放量保持在原有水平。有关部门正在设法降低海法市的电厂和炼油燃料中硫含量，以改善海法市的空气质量，并将阿什杜德地区电厂的烟囱升高，同时计划在某些特殊的时期、季节里使用含硫量更低的燃料。

3. 处理污水的数量和比例大有提高

前几年，以色列曾多次发生饮水受污染的事故，如 1990 年夏季，由于水质污染，特拉维夫 Dan 区的居民在一段时间里不得不将饮水煮开后再喝，公众反映十分强烈，越来越多的人使用各种家用水质净化器，同时很多人改为喝开水。有关单位的多份调研报告均对以色列水源环保工作提出了批评意见。公众的反映、批评同时推动了污水处理、水源保护工作。

现在，先后建立起了一些污水处理厂，接纳和处理大部分工业及生活污水。在农村，大量污水（占全国污水总量的 1%~2%）主要排入化粪池作为农用。20 世纪 70 年代初，处理污水量占全国污水总量的比例为 26%，1987 年达到 81%，预计 2000~2025 年将达到 100% 处理。

由于经济发展、人口增加、生活水平提高，城市、家庭、工业的需水量不断增加，预计城市用水将从 1985 年的 4.6 亿吨上升到 2000 年的 6.1~7.1（亿吨），2025 年可达 9.1~11.0（亿吨），工业用水也将从 1985 年的 1.04 亿吨增长到 2000 年的 1.2~1.6(亿吨)和 2025 年的 1.5~2.0（亿吨），换言之，生活及工业用量占去了以色列全国总耗水量的一半。因此，扩大污水处理能力已是当务之急。计划将扩建特拉维夫城市污水处理厂及其与新建的市政设施之间的联网管线，同时在耶路撒冷、Nahariya 和 Kiryat Gat 等地（市）新建和改建一批污水处理设施，争取在近几年达到以色列大部分污水都能够经过现代化污水厂工程处理的水平。

由于缺水日益严重而需水量不断增加，提高污水处理量是当前缓解农业水源危机的一个有效措施，预计将已处理过的污水用于农灌的总量可从 1985 年的 6000 吨增加到 2000 年的 2.6~3.0(亿吨)和 2025 年的 4.3~5.0(亿吨)，能够代替并节省下原来用于农灌的相应数量的淡水，效益十分显著。

4. 加强生活垃圾的收集填埋处理

过去 15 年中，引进了大小不同的各类垃圾桶、垃圾车等现代化收容装备，并采用了城市垃圾的现代的集装技术，防止原来那种环境脏、乱、臭问题，使垃圾收集工作走上更为程序化的轨道。由于建立了垃圾运输站，从垃圾装车到运抵填埋场全过程一次完成，无须多次装卸，同时加强对垃圾车的覆盖封闭，杜绝了运输途中垃圾飞场的污染。政府建立了一些大型的区域性垃圾处理场，代替了原先那些零乱分散的小垃圾堆，并且每天都在新到的垃圾表面覆盖一层土，同时辅助以隔离、紧压等其他措施防止污染扩散，从而使城市环境状况大为改观。为了尽量减少垃圾场对地下水的潜在污染，在全国垃圾处理的总体规划中，经反复研究选定出 30 个垃圾场址。环保部门准备进一步强化特拉维夫和海法等大城市地区垃圾运输管理，提高垃圾场运转效率和处理质量。

5. 加强公共场所的环境卫生工作

设置许多垃圾桶，大量采用特种车辆清扫道路，经常在公共场所开展"清洁卫生运动"，这些工作在过去十年中改善了公共卫生状况，转变了人们对公共卫生的看法。随着生活水平提高，人们希望在生活、教育、工作中拥有更好的环境和条件，因此，环保部门正在加强实施《环境清洁卫生保护法》，促进各种公共卫生条件和设施的改善。对丢弃的废汽车也将进行回收和集中处理。

6. 美化城市市容和旅游环境

旅游业是以色列经济中最赢利的部门之一，在国民经济中发挥着重要作用，1985 年旅游收入为 12 亿美元，入境的外国游客达 120 万人次。以色列拥有众多世界著名的历史名胜和考古遗迹，以及世界三大宗教的胜地，同时还具有许多独特的自然景观、娱乐设施和优美的城市景观，吸引了国内外的大批游客。据统计，到 2025 年入境游客可达 700 万人次。旅游业兴旺必然会给环境造成较大的压力。因此，地方政府一直致力于整治、改善和美化市容环境，譬如建造极富特色的街边人行道路，在特拉维夫海滨、Abu Tor 周围地区及耶路撒冷东Talpiot 邻近地区大量建造海滨胜地的临水大道，特别设计和装饰入城的路口，等等。重视房屋临街面的清洁美化，不断补充技术力量，在旅游区广泛安装一些标准的标识牌，建造各具特色的街道设施（长椅、垃圾桶、路标、广告牌、海报板、汽车站、街灯、街道花坛、地面瓷砖），加强公共场所的园林化、绿化工作。在公寓楼区和私人住宅区，特别是新建的地区，把居民区结构与公共绿地统一规划，使房屋从建筑格式到建筑材料上都形成多种多样、变化有致的视觉美感，改善建筑质量和室内居住环境的条件，加强居民区内的各种社会服务职能配套，这些工作对从总体上美化市容起到了很好作用。

商业建筑物的临街楼面，包括各种标志和陈列橱窗，从建筑设计质量、清洁美观程度及其保洁情况都有了较大改进，这点在大城市最为明显。居民也做了改善市区环境的工作，居民广泛积极地参与住房临街面的装修整治工作，私人绿地、花园大大增多，屋顶立体绿化已经普及起来。现在人们已渐渐注意到，在屋顶放置各种物品（如太阳能热水器水槽），确实有碍观瞻，因此，大多数人已清除了屋顶的杂物。由于普遍采用公用天线，逐渐消灭了"电视天线丛立如林"的杂乱景象。

在市中心、新建居民区、主要旅游干线等区域，市容、街景有了很大的改观。

在一些具有很高景观价值的区域（主要在北部区），在建造通信发射塔、风力电站等工程设施及其道路管网时，进行严格的环境评价和规划，重视保护重点景观及其周围环境协调。

随着生活水平的提高和每周工作时间的缩短，加上人们互相之间的竞争，城市景观不断改善的趋势将进一步发展。

7. 改善海滩卫生状况和保护沿海水质

过去，由于大量污水直接排海造成的细菌滋生污染，加上大量化学污染物和工业废物（如柏油、重油等），地中海海滨环境一度极其恶劣。大量生活垃圾、建筑垃圾堆弃在海滨，海水冲来各种海上垃圾，使游人望而生畏，一些海滨浴场由于达不到卫生标准而不得不关闭，而另一些浴场则人满为患。通过强化管理和狠抓治理，这种恶劣状况在过去十年中逐渐改善。现在，海滩上柏油的数量已减到 1/150，污水排海已大部分停止，杜绝了向海滩倾倒垃圾的现象，海滩经过清除、恢复和综合治理后，环境质量和卫生条件明显提高，达到了国际水质标准，均重新对游人开放。新近颁布实施的《陆源污水排放环境保护法》可以解决海滨的工业废物问题。随着区域性垃圾处理场和建筑垃圾处理场的扩大和使用，将彻底解决海滨垃圾污染。

8. 扩建和加强有毒废物处理场

20 世纪 80 年代初，建成了 Ramat Hovav "全国有毒废物处理场"并投入使用。起初只做一些废物的收集和存放工作，从 80 年代中期起，逐步开展有毒废物的中和、处理，该处理场每年接纳的废物量逐年增加。为了确保今后有更多的废物入场处理而不乱倒，专门由国营的"环境质量服务公司"负责废物的运输工作。不久将新建一些处理设施，包括建造一座废物焚烧炉，并准备在 Negev 地区建立一个新的有毒废物处理场。即将颁布的《有毒废物法》有助于强化对有毒废物的处理、管理工作。

9. 建立并加强专门处理化学污染事故的机构

过去几年中，国家领导人越来越认识到必须建立处理化学事故的专门机构，现在组建工作正在进行，该机构的职责和机能均已明确划定。同时，已建立起了与之配套的有害废物数据库和事故应急报警系统，该机构不久将开始工作。

过去十年中，以色列妥善处理了一些小规模的海上污染事故，但尚无力应付大规模海上石油泄漏等大型事故，因此，采取了与有关国际组织密切合作的办法以处理随时发生的大型海上污染事故。环境部准备在此方面投入更多的人力物力予以加强。

10. 扩大自然保护区

1963 年以色列颁布实施了《国家公园、国家保护区和国家保护场地法》，这方面的工作开展至今。每年以色列的保护区和公园的面积都在不断增加。如果把"犹太人国家基金会"资助建立的植树区和国有林区包括在内，保护区面积约占全国土地的 25%~30%。新近将在 Negev 建立一个大保护区，保护区在今后十年将有很大发展。

Kinneret 湖长期以来一直保持较好的水质，除了修建排水渠、采取环保措施、减少污染物入湖量以外，实施"国家 Kinneret 沿海地区总体计划"，通过"Kinneret 湖区管理局"划设出湖面保护区，加强保护区监测和管理等工作，都起到了有效的保护作用。

以色列现已建立了两个野生动物保护区，Yotvata 划为沙漠野生动物保护区，Carmel 划为地中海地区特种野生动物保护区。据统计，以色列地中海区至少有 54 种脊椎动物，沙漠地区有 29 种动物均被列为濒临灭绝危险的种群。建立这些保护区的目的在于恢复当地野生动物的自然栖息生态环境，尽可能促进野生动物的繁殖和种群恢复，目前已取得了较好的效果。

11. 恢复地中海沿海山丘地区的自然植被

以前，在地中海沿海山丘地区，由于滥伐、滥砍、烧荒，严重破坏了当地自然生态系统，20世纪40~50年代开始了植被恢复工作。譬如，在该地区禁止砍树和限制牧羊，在某些被破坏较严重的区域则明令禁止牧羊，实行全封闭恢复。过去的秃山现已长满了灌丛，过去的灌木山地现已形成了规模树林。北部加利利高原和Carmel的许多地方，山坡自然植被已得到较好恢复。同时，还在全国几个地方建立起了一整套负责沿海丘陵植被恢复工作的专职管理系统，很有成效。

12. 大力植树造林

以色列每年造林面积平均增加1.5万~2.0万dunams（以色列本国通用的面积单位）。造林主要集中在城市近郊区和沿海平原河流两岸区域的植树带，这些林木起到了缓冲带作用，阻止了沿海平原上城市向外杂乱延伸，并且成为城市居民的娱乐休闲场所，大大改善了城市外围环境。为了保护土地，将着重在Negev的北部及西部地区植树造林，并在一些主要污染源（如采石场、交通干线、工业区等）周围大力种树，形成林木隔离带，通过造林来恢复自然景观，复垦采石场，固定移动性沙丘和蚀退的河岸、沟岸。

现在，人们在逐渐改变单一树种、密植松树的传统造林方法，采用多层次、多树种的综合立体造林结构，近些年的造林已取得显著成果。以色列耕地面积约440万dunams，使用不当、水土流失、盐碱化、沙漠化等问题都会破坏和减少现有耕地。

尽管到目前为止，以色列环保部门已做出了不少成绩，但仍有许多工作亟待开展，除了加强环境部自身管理和国内的环保投入之外，将进一步扩大国际合作和交流，为保护"我们共同的地球"而不懈努力。

（原文刊载于《污染防治技术》1992年第5卷第4期）

科教

软实力支撑以色列 60 年

以色列教育的特点

中国与以色列的职业教育比较研究

软实力支撑以色列 60 年

殷 罡[*]

以色列得以生存和强盛的原因很多，强大的军事力量和美国的鼎力支持至关重要，但关键还是这个国家的软实力。以色列的软实力突出体现在延续千年的民族认同感、毫不松懈的危机感、高度的国民凝聚力，以及严格运作的法制体系。

一 信仰维系民族存在

以色列是世界上绝无仅有的"死而复生"的特殊国家，是犹太人在亡国1900年之后从世界各地返回故土重新建立起来的国家。仅此一点，就说明了这个民族和这个国家极为强大的凝聚力。罗马帝国灭亡了古代犹太

---

* 殷罡，中国社会科学院西亚非洲研究所研究员。

人的国家之后，幸免于难的犹太人就开始流散到世界各地，在延续千年的种族歧视和宗教迫害之下顽强地恪守自己的信仰，在非常苛刻的生存条件下顽强地繁衍生息。之所以能做到这一点，关键在于犹太教的维系作用。

犹太教是世界上最早产生的一神教，其特点不仅在于信奉创造万物的唯一的神（上帝），也在于坚信自己是神的"特选子民"，而迦南地（巴勒斯坦）则是神授予犹太人万世享用的土地。显而易见，犹太教是一种民族宗教。但世界上的民族宗教很多，犹太教的特殊之处在于它不仅仅是犹太人自己的宗教，同时也是基督教和伊斯兰教得以产生和发展的根基。正是由于犹太教、基督教和伊斯兰教有共同的属性，信奉同一个神，"正统之争"便贯穿着以往 2000 年的历史。

在正统之争中，犹太人的"特选子民"资格不被他人所接受，犹太人也不承认居于主导地位的异族异教的权威，群体实力弱小的犹太人被歧视被迫害的命运便不可避免。与此同时，歧视和压迫又不断强化着犹太人的身份认同和民族凝聚力。19 世纪末期，渴望彻底摆脱压迫和杀戮的犹太人终于整体性觉醒，犹太复国主义运动最终导致了以色列国的诞生。

为了恢复故国，犹太人坚持了半个世纪有目的、有组织、有谋略的筹备。到 1947 年联合国大会辩论分治决议的时候，犹太自耕农和犹太复国组织已经有选择地分散购买了巴勒斯坦 6.8% 的土地，建立了 300 个定居点，形成了"连点必成片"的战略态势，而购买土地的资金除了来自犹太富商的捐助，还有世界各地的犹太平民每周一次的开支结余汇集，甚至包括犹太儿童节省下来的零花钱。这些资金在犹太土地基金会的极为严格的管理之下，购买的土地则成为犹太民族的共有财产。正是以这不足 7% 的土地和 50 多万定居者的存在为资本，以及数百万犹太人在"二战"期间被屠杀而得到的同情，犹太人奇迹般地得到了恢复故国的法律依据。

二　凝聚力是不可战胜的力量

复国之前的巴勒斯坦犹太控制区被称为"犹太家园"。在这个家园里，犹太人主要以集体方式生存。复国决心、集体主义精神、有组织的家园建设、未雨绸缪的武装训练和精明执着的外交努力，使得犹太民族集中了所有能够集中的实力，经受了周边国家的集体围攻，取得了求生存战争的胜利。

恪守集体主义信念的"基布兹"是犹太家园最主要的基层组织。在建国前的近 300 个定居点中，基布兹就占去了一半，来自世界各地的早期犹太移民几乎都在这样的集体农庄里生活过。基布兹是社会主义和犹太复国主义结合的产物，其宗旨是建立"共同劳动、共同占有、共同生活、没有剥削压迫、人人平等、和睦民主"的理想社会。在这样的集体农庄里，犹太移民没有私有财产的概念，有的只是集体利益和个体责任。借助于这样的组织形态，犹太移民不仅形成了超强的凝聚力，还为犹太复国主义组织的有效运作和犹太地下武装的建立提供了极好的条件，以色列军队就是在基布兹里诞生的，早期以色列军队的大多数士兵和将军也是在基布兹里接受训练的，赫赫有名的独眼将军达杨则是第一位出生在基布兹里的以色列军队统帅。诞生于各派基布兹的犹太武装成功地保卫了犹太定居点，并在独立战争中发挥了至关重要的作用。

犹太人内部的宗教派别和政治派别的争斗令人眼花缭乱。但是在民族命运和国家利益面前，没有规避者，没有叛徒，只有明智和极端之分。大敌当前战争临近之时，从来都是举国一致，同仇敌忾。战争爆发后争先恐后，绝无见死不救、互相拆台之事。1848 年独立战争初期，世界各地的犹太壮丁和犹太资金源源不断地涌入巴勒斯坦，接济处于危难境地的同胞和家园，保证了以色列国的生存。1973 年战争突然爆发，美国的犹太青年和远在印度和尼泊尔的以色列旅游者纷纷在一天之内就赶回祖国参战。

高度的民族凝聚力和共同的危机感，是以色列得以存在和发展壮大的最关键、最宝贵的力量。

三　无条件锻造统一的国家军队

早期的犹太武装分属不同的派别，既有奉行社会主义的巴勒斯坦工人党（工党前身）领导的"哈加纳"，也有受犹太复国主义修正派影响、奉行激进民族主义的"伊尔贡"。"哈加纳"是犹太武装的主体，理性而务实，处于半合法、半地下状态；"伊尔贡"立场激进，为达目的不惜采取极端和恐怖手段。在同委任统治当局和阿拉伯武装对抗时，"伊尔贡"尽管战斗力极强，但其极端手段不仅损害了犹太复国主义武装的名声，也加剧了阿犹之间的仇恨。"哈加纳"竭力反对"伊尔贡"的极端行径。为了遏制"伊尔贡"势力，"哈加纳"甚至还将一些无关紧要的"伊尔贡"成员抓起来交由英国委任统治当局的司法机关管教。

独立战争中，尽管"哈吉纳"同"伊尔贡"是并肩战斗的。但以色列开国总理本 - 古里安决心不让以色列存在两支武装，在颁布相关法令之后，对"伊尔贡"的特立独行的举动采取了铁腕手段。

1948 年 6 月 10 日，正当以色列利用第二次停火积极备战的时候，"伊尔贡"的军火走私船载着 5000 支步枪、250 挺机枪、3000 枚炸弹、几百吨炸药、300 万发子弹、大量火箭筒和迫击炮，连同 800 多名回国参战的新移民抵达特拉维夫港口。政府下令没收全部军火，而"伊尔贡"领导人贝京坚持要求将 20% 的军火拨给自己的武装使用，在紧张的对峙之后，本 - 古里安在重申"一个国家不能有两支武装"和"这 5000 支步枪足以葬送整个国家"之后，亲自下令击毁"反叛"的军火船。炮击造成数十人伤亡和大量以色列急需的军火被毁，同阿拉伯人的停火期变成了以色列的内战期。尽管本 - 古里安从此背上骂名，但"伊尔贡"武装最终服从了政府权威，并入了国家军队。

当然，只要服从规则，机会就是均等的。那位一度被称为"恐怖分子头目"的"伊尔贡"领导人贝京，在战后组建了合法政党，最终于 1977 年领导利库德集团赢得了大选，名正言顺地当上了以色列军队最高统帅，并以总理身份签署了同埃及的永久和平条约。

以色列政府不惜代价无条件统一全国武装力量之举，为独立战争的胜利和日后国内的长治久安奠定了基础。

四　财富在头脑中积累

"财富在头脑里"是犹太人的口头禅，也是犹太人容易发家致富的根本。

犹太人重教育是出了名的。在千年流散期间，大多数犹太人不被允许拥有土地、矿山和工厂等不动产，生存手段受到极大限制。依靠智慧和知识生存便成了犹太人的一个主要特点。知识来源于教育，犹太教育首先是犹太教知识的教育，然后才是生存手段的教育。由于不被允许拥有"硬资产"，依靠知识形成的"软资产"就成为犹太人的最大财富。犹太人的"软资产"表现在对商业、金融、法律、医疗、艺术、思想理论等领域占有优势。而在这些领域的占有份额又使得犹太人得以在很大程度上控制一个国家或地区的经济，并影响该地区的政治发展。"软资产"是不易被剥夺的资产，也是拥有高度教育水准的犹太人有能力转移和重新聚集的资产。正是由于犹太人的这种特性，使得犹太人在欧洲地区一次又一次对其财产剥夺和驱赶之后，能够在较短的时间内重振家业，恢复社团兴旺。

注重教育是以色列人得以成功的一个主要因素。无论是建国之前还是建国之后，犹太复国主义组织和以色列政府都在教育上倾注了超过一般水准的精力和资金。以色列的教育经费长期占据 GDP 的 8%~9%，为世界平均额的 2 倍，全民实施 12 年免费义务教育，从幼儿园直至高中。60 年过去了，以色列的人均 GDP 已经从建国初期的不足 300 美元增长到目前的约 2 万美元，与海湾石油出口国不相上下。高水准、高普及的教育使得以色列人在狭小的土地上积累了巨大的财富，使得以色列的多项科技水平保持世界领先地位，并为国家的硬实力建设和强大的军事力量的建设提供了基础。

五 法制建设重中之重

以色列的政治制度和法律体系也有强烈的犹太色彩。这个国家没有宪法，但有一系列保证国家机器和社会生活运行的单项内容的"基本法"，如《议会法》《土地法》《总统法》《司法制度法》《经济法》《国防军法》《人的尊严与自由法》等。建国初期，考虑到犹太教宗教力量对维系犹太民族的巨大作用，以色列政府和立法机关尊重了宗教人士的意见，在国家政治和社会生活中保留了宗教势力的影响。以色列的立法机构和选举制度不是"最好"的，运作起来弊端很明显。但毕竟是"复国"，在建国初期制定这样的法律不可避免。

以色列的议会体制、议会名称和议员人数均遵从古制。单一选区比例代表制的选举制度使得以色列小党林立，政坛争斗频繁而复杂。在这样的制度下，每4万名选民就可以选出一名议员，成就一个政党。一般情况下，每次议会选举都有30多个参选集团相互角逐，最终取得议会席位的总在20个左右，从来没有单一政党得到过议会多数席位，从来都是联合政府执政。

这样的体制，保证了以色列所有特定群体的参政机会，也保证了这个"犹太国"中20%阿拉伯公民的基本利益，而复杂激烈的权力斗争则极大地加强了对政府和政府成员的监督，使得以色列的廉政建设有突出成效，甚至被人认为是过于苛刻的成效。这方面有代表性的例子有很多。

由于以色列国是建立在实行犹太共有制的犹太家园基础之上，以色列公民的主人意识和监督意识非常强烈。

占有公共财产、贪污受贿和营私舞弊被认为是绝对不可接受的。即便在股份制企业，监督意识和监督手段也非常严格。例如在以色列乘过公共汽车的人时常可以看到突然上车检查乘客车票的稽查员，司乘人员对亲友的任何关照都是不被允许的。

以色列强大的军事实力和源源不断的外部支持无疑是以色列在动荡中生存发展的重要因素。

（原文刊载于《当代世界》2008 年第 6 期）

以色列教育的特点

　　犹太民族具有尊师重教的优良传统，长期以来，教育在维系民族凝聚力、保持民族传统、构造民族特性、繁荣民族文化等方面发挥了不可低估的作用。以色列建国后，"把教育继续视为以色列社会的一种基本财富以及开创未来的关键"[1]，在百业待举、战火连绵的情况下，花费了大量的人力、物力和财力，在短期内建立了一整套较为完备的教育体制，使教育在提高国民素质、促进社会文化整合、推动资源经济向知识经济[2]的转化等方面起到了不可替代的作用。本文仅就以色列教育的特点作一探讨，总结其教育立国的成功经验，以期对我国的现代化建设有所启迪。

---

* 　张倩红，郑州大学副校长，兼任河南大学犹太研究所所长，享受国务院特殊津贴专家。
[1]　以色列新闻中心：《以色列概况》，耶路撒冷：哈摩科出版公司，1997。
[2]　吴季松：《知识经济》，北京科学技术出版社，1998。

一 教育方针的灵活性

　　早在建国之前，犹太复国主义者就曾把教育作为复兴犹太国的手段之一，学校成了最早在巴勒斯坦地区建立起来的犹太人组织。早期的犹太移民们在生活条件极为恶劣的情况下，始终保持着兴办教育的热情，建国前犹太儿童的入学率已高达85%。建国初期至20世纪50年代，以色列政府把教育工作的重点放在了推行义务教育、建立统一的国民教育体系上。1949年4月，以色列教育文化部成立，其职责是：保持和发展教育体系；确定稳定的教育标准；培训和指导教师；推广教育计划和教学课程；改善教学条件，并组织和鼓励成人的教育文化活动[①]。教育文化部成立不久，就颁布了《义务教育法》，对6~14岁的儿童以及14~17岁未完成初等教育的少年实行免费义务教育。1953年，以色列政府颁布了第二个重要的教育立法——《国家教育法》，全面推行义务教育，对伊休夫时期及建国初期存在的多元性教育体制进行改革，把全国教育分成普通教育和宗教教育两种，并对一些政党、团体及社会组织主办的学校实行国家统一管理。新法律还规定了以色列教育的基本原则，即"基于对犹太文化和科学知识的重视；基于对故土、对国家、对民族的挚爱；基于对农业及其他技能的训练；基于对开创性原则的实现；基于对一个建立在自由、平等、宽容、互助及人类友爱基础上的社会的向往"[②]。为了实现教育一体化，教育文化部还就教学内容、课程设置以及考试等问题提出了一些指导性方案。随着政治稳定与经

① Dr. Moshe Avidor, *Education and Science*, Jerusalem, 1974.
② Dr. Moshe Avidor, *Education and Science*, Jerusalem, 1974.

济发展，20 世纪 50 年代以来，大批移民移居以色列，1948~1960 年，移民人数近百万。新移民来自世界上 103 个国家和地区，操 70 多种语言，有着不同的文化和知识结构。以色列政府便从教育入手，来消除文化差别，促进社会融合，以期创造一种融东方传统的农业文化与西方工业文化于一体的新型的"以色列文化"。为了尽快加强集体认同和社会整合，以色列政府从 60 年代开始对教育方针进行了调整，在教育机会均等的前提下，推行教育多样化原则，其主要措施如下：

第一，改革教育结构。以色列最初的教育体制是仿效西方模式建立起来的，可大批东方犹太人的子女并不能很快适应之。为此，1963 年，以色列政府改革教育机构，把幼儿园（3~5 岁）＋小学（6~13 岁）＋中学（14~17 岁），改为幼儿园（3~5 岁）＋小学（6~11 岁）＋中学过渡部（12~14 岁）＋中学高级部（15~17 岁）。设立中学过渡部的目的就是把来自不同环境的小学生吸收在一起，使他们适应新的教学体制，然后再升入同一中学的高中部。这一改革取得的明显成效是，在最初的 10 年中升入中学高级部的学生人数增加了 20%。

第二，兴办文化补习班，为移民提供第二次受教育机会。随着移民的增加，以色列把移民教育提上了正式的议事日程。中央政府与地方行政部门、工会、社区及企业联合起来，在全国设立不同层次的文化补习班和培训点，为不同文化程度的人提供学习语言、增长知识及职业培训的机会。据统计，以色列国内为新移民设立的教授希伯来语的教学点就有 150 个，还有上百个扫盲中心与文化补习班，传授各种文化知识。中央与地方政府联合建立的移民安置系统，为许多接受完再教育的移民优先安排就业。

第三，为亚非裔学生创造受教育条件。由于亚非裔学生的受教育水平普遍低于欧美犹太人，因此，以色列政府对亚非裔学生进入公立学校实行多种优惠政策，如在入学分数线上给予照顾，在以色列，小学毕业生都要经过名为"Seker"的统考，80分以上者为合格，而亚裔、非裔学生的合格线仅为68分；在收费标准上，亚非裔学生可根据其家庭收入状况而减免学费，所减免部分基本上都由政府承担。1978年，以色列开始依据其收入高低征收教育税，以解决高中的免费教育问题，低收入的亚非裔家庭尽管纳税较少，但仍能享受同等的教育机会。此外，政府和学校还向亚非裔学生提供多种形式的奖学金与寄宿条件。由于采取了上述措施，亚非裔学生接受教育的平均年限提高很快，从1961年的5.9年延长到1981年的9.7年。

第四，推广特殊儿童教育。为了挖掘高质量的人才，以色列建立了一套"天才儿童培训计划"。在班上名列前茅的3%的天才儿童通过资格考试之后可送入专业学校和校外特殊班，对其进行专门的知识和技能训练。对那些学习能力特别低下和身有残疾的儿童则提供特殊教育课程，采取延长学时、个别辅导等办法进行补救教育，这项任务由学校、家长、医疗保健人员、特殊教育专业人员以及社区资助团体共同承担。对某些逃学者或厌学者，还由儿童心理学家提供专门心理咨询，并推行社会引导服务。采取这些措施的宗旨是社会和公民要对每个儿童负责，把儿童视作整个社会的宝贵财富。

1948~1973年，以色列经济经历了一个黄金时期，不仅建立起了结构较为合理的工业、农业及国防工业体系，而且实现了年增长率为10%的高速度。由粗放型经济向集约型经济转换，走知识密集型的发展道路已成为以色列经济的主导方向。经济的发展对教育提出了新的要求. 一般意义上的普及性教育已很难适应发展的需要。为此，从20世纪70年代中期起，以色列再度调整教育方针，除了延长免费教育年限、发展贫困地区的教育之外，政府在政策方面有两个倾斜：一是发展职业教育；二是扶持高等教育。

为了大批培养技术人才，政府设立各类技术职业学校，鼓励学生及成人选修经济发展所急需的相关课程，如电脑培训、企业管理、市场策略等。1974年，政府通过了关于提高公民(不论其年龄和受教育程度)工业水平的决议，为此，教育文化部创办了公开大学。在全国各地设立了25个教学中心，分别接纳中学水准以下、中学水准及大学水准的学员，每个学员都有接受导师指导的机会。教学中心设有齐全的图书馆、实验室及其他教学设备，提供80多种学位培训和职业培训。公开大学的设立，为发展经济培养了大批人才。

20世纪70年代以色列开始酝酿高科技产业，到80年代，高科技产业已普遍兴起。在发展高科技产业的过程中，政府对高等教育寄予了很大的希望。以色列的大学在供应合格的工业工程师及技术人才方面起着重要的作用，1972年，大学所培养的此类人才为11500人，而到1984年则增至30800人。每千名工业劳动力中工程师所占的人数由1965年的8人提高到1982年的33人 ①。到1984年，以色列全国劳动力总人口中大学毕业并获得学位者的比例已高达13%，而1973年这一比例仅为7.6%。1992年，以色列每353人中就有1人获得博士学位。总之，教育方针的灵活性，使教育更符合于国情、民情，更好地推行社会进步与经济的发展。

---

① Paul Rivlin, *The Israeli Economy*, Westview press, 1992.

二 教育体系的独特性

在几十年的教育实践中，以色列政府从实际出发，建立了一整套完备的教育体制。该体制由以下层次组成：学前教育—小学教育—中学教育—中学后期教育—高等教育。从 1978 年起，开始实行 12 年即全部中小学（含一年学前班）的免费教育。以色列的教育体制具有自身的独特性，其特点主要表现在：

第一，中央集中领导与地方自主管理相统一。以色列的教育属中央统一领导，教育文化部负责制定教育政策、分配教育基金、规划教育标准及设立教学大纲，而地方政府则拥有具体的管理权，如接受政府拨款、雇佣初中和高中教师、建筑校舍、购置教学设备等。在服从政府领导的前提下，各个学校也拥有一定的自主权，如教学大纲虽然由教育文化部统一颁发，但所涉及的科目极其广泛，学校有权根据本校的情况，设置课程，选择教学方法；从理论上讲，所有教师都是教育文化部的雇员，但各校校长拥有聘任权，从而保证了教师队伍的淘汰制与流动制。为了调动全民兴办教育的积极性，以色列政府还鼓励一些地方团体与民间组织建立私立学校，如妇女国际犹太复国主义组织在1962~1963年，拥有80个幼儿园、30个日托中心、70个俱乐部。目前，各种形式的私立学校遍布各地，成为以色列普及教育的主要形式之一。

第二，建立了行之有效的学前教育系统。在早期的希伯来教育中，就极为重视对儿童的早期教育。当时，学校并未兴起，家庭教育则是主要的教育方式。犹太法律要求家长尤其是父亲要对孩儿进行启蒙教育，为其日后成为道德之民、律法之民和智慧之民创造条件。有些犹太社团还要求幼儿至少从3岁开始，就必须接触犹太圣典《塔木德》。以色列建国后，为了保证"先起步"的优势，大力普及学前教育。一般情况下，幼儿从2岁开始接受教育，主要培养幼儿的语言表达能力、身体运动能力及对周围环境的认知。3~4岁儿童要进入由地方当局、妇女组织及某些私人团体兴办的学前班，接受较为系统的知识训练。一些贫困地区的学前教育要由教育文化部拨专款资助。按国家教育法规定，这一年是免费义务教育的开端。据1996年由英国出版的《中东经济手册》统计，以色列3岁儿童中接受学前教育的达97%，这一比例在世界上名列前茅。1993~1994年，在以色列学前教育系统学习的儿童达32万名，年龄为2~6岁，占适龄儿童的90%以上。以色列的学前教育成就很早就引起了联合国及一些国际教育机构的关注。国际教育计划学院在20世纪70年代末80年代初所作的比较研究中就指出，以色列的幼儿教育系统最为完善，其数量与质量均令人满意。发达的学前教育，不仅使孩子们从小就开始了基本知识教育，而且培养了他们的创造能力、判断能力、分析能力、学习能力、社交能力及审美能力，使儿童从小养成了热爱知识、热爱集体、热爱劳动、遵纪守法、讲究公德的良好习惯。

第三，现代文化教育与传统文化教育相结合。以色列虽然是一个现代化的民主国家，但仍保留了浓厚的宗教文化传统。在这样一个融传统与现代、东方与西方、宗教与世俗为一体的环境中，教育必须适合多元文化的趋势。为此，以色列政府在大量吸取现代文化精华的同时，特别注意加强本民族的传统教育。1959年，教育文化部还在全国推行了"强化犹太意识规划"，教育国民不要忘记以色列是当今世界上唯一的犹太国家，而每一个人都是犹太社会中负有责任与使命的一员。在教育文化部规定的教学计划中，希伯来语、犹太历史、犹太律法、犹太教义及教规等是每个犹太学生从小到大的必修课程。为了保持国家的属性，也迫于宗教势力的强大压力，以色列办起了许多公立与私立学校，这些学校把传统教育放在了首要位置上。建国之后的以色列曾长期致力于建设一种能融东西方文化于一体的新型的国民文化——以色列文化，这一主导思想已贯穿于教育方针的确立、教育体制的建设及教育活动的开展等各个环节之中。

第四，犹太教育与少数民族教育并举。根据义务教育法，以色列的少数民族（以阿拉伯人为主）与犹太人享有同样的权利与义务。以色列政府在全国推广阿拉伯语教育，明确规定阿拉伯语为初等学校的必修课程。在阿语学校中，开设的基本课程与希伯来语学校相同，只是阿拉伯语为第一语言，小学四年级开始学习希伯来语，六年级学习英语，学校的节假日也遵循阿拉伯人的民族习惯。由于政策的重视，阿拉伯人的受教育程度大为提高，如 1948 年，阿拉伯女孩的入学率为 25%，而 1964 年增加到 80%。1949 年在校的阿拉伯学生为 140000 人，而 1973 年增加 920000 人 [1]。当然，从目前的受教育程度与文化水准上看，阿拉伯人和犹太人还存在着很大差距，要实现真正意义的平等（尤其是观念上），还有很长的路程。此外，以色列教育体制还具有正规教育与成人教育相结合、知识教育与技能教育同兼顾等特点。

三　教育经费的稳步增长

以色列领导人一直视教育为立国之本，为维系民族

---

[1]　Dr. Moshe Avidor, *Education and Science*, Jerusalem, 1974.

发展的纽带，历任领导人在教育投资问题上达成了高度的共识。本－古里安强调："没有教育，就没有未来。"梅厄指出："对教育的投资是有远见的投资。"前任总统纳冯教授卸任之后，又兢兢业业地当上了教育部长，这在其他国家是罕见的，正是因为他认识到"教育上的投资就是经济上的投资"。自20世纪70年代中期以来，以色列的教育投资在国民生产总值中的比重一直没有低于8%，超过了美国等发达国家（见表1）。

表1　以色列全国教育经费占国民生产总值的百分比

年度	百分比（%）	年度	百分比（%）
1962/1963	6.0	1982/1983	8.6
1965/1966	7.6	1983/1984	8.4
1972/1973	7.5	1984/1985	8.5
1975/1976	8.0	1985/1986	8.5
1979/1980	8.8		

资料来源：达洲、徐向群：《中国人看以色列》，新华出版社，1990。

1995年，以色列的教育投资高达9.5%，同年，佩雷斯政府还宣布把国防开支占国民生产总值的比重由33%降至9%，其节约资金用于教育和科技事业。以色列的教育经费大部分由政府提供。1978年以前，政府的教育投资主要来自一般性的政府收入，1978年之后国家开始征收教育税，教育税由全国保险协会根据家庭收入的高低统一征收，其税额相当于应纳税收的0.4%。与此同时，政府很注意吸收国外援助款项用于教育事业，如经过犹太代办处提供的国外犹太人的捐款在以色列教育投资中曾占很大的比例，特别是1968年高达27.7%。以色列的地方政府虽然也负担了一部分教育开支，但比重不大，如在

1990 年，中央政府提供了国民教育开支总额的 60% 以上，而地方政府仅承担了 8%。1992 年，在国民教育支出中，中央和地方政府共占 77%，其中绝大部分来自中央。在整个 20 世纪 90 年代，以色列的国民教育支出一直呈上升趋势，高额的投资为教育的发展奠定了物质基础。

四　教育与社会生产相结合

犹太民族自古以来就是一个务实的民族。犹太人认为，接受教育是每一个人的责任与义务，但学习知识、钻研律法都不能代替劳动的技能。《塔木德》上说："凡不教子女学习职业的人，便是教育子女从事盗窃。"犹太智慧书《阿伯特》上引用了拉比迦玛列的话，精辟地论述了学习"托拉"与劳作之间的密切关系："最好的是学习'托拉'能与一项脚踏实地的劳作一起进行。同时致力于这两项将使人摒除恶念。而任何不伴以劳作的'托拉'学业都终将被荒废并引发犯罪。"在这一传统观念的影响之下，从古代开始，希伯来人就极为强调掌握一门技艺，要求"儿童无论贫富贵贱等级高低，到成年时都必须掌握一门手艺。部落所有的头领也都有技术，甚至可以和街上的匠人媲美"[1]。建国之前，在巴勒斯坦犹太人建立的基布兹组织中，就很重视对幼儿进行劳动教育。老师不仅给孩子们讲授劳动的价值与意义，还把孩子们组成"儿童社团"，每天都要参与劳动，让孩子们从小便了解各种农活，掌握最基本的饲养知识。在老师的指导下，孩子们还经营自己的小农场、小饲养场、小植物园等。

---

[1]　戴本博：《外国教育史》，人民出版社，1990。

建国之后的以色列，继承了犹太人这一传统，小学生从一年级开始接受系统的劳动教育，使他们熟悉劳动的基本知识，了解主要的生产原料和加工过程，学会使用基本的劳动工具。小学高年级和初中学生要掌握各种劳动技术，如材料加工、制图、制表、电力、电子、裁剪缝纫、家务操持、家政管理等。普通学校8年级（相当于我国初中二年级）要学习"以色列工业和国民经济"课程，要求学生了解工业生产的基本原理、国民经济的主要运行机制、产品的生产及市场营销、财政金融的基本法则等。中学高年级的劳动教育有了明显的职业化倾向，学校把劳动教育分成农业技术教育和工业技术教育两种，学生根据自己的兴趣与爱好，培养一门专门技艺。这种教育方法使学生学完中学课程时，已基本上完成了基础的劳动教育训练，相当一部分学生还学有专长，这对其选择专门化的大学教育方向以及未来的就业都有帮助。

以色列有极为发达的高等教育。1948~1949年，全国仅有0.164万大学生，而1984~1985年大学生人数达9.9万，即每千名劳动力中有77名大学生（美国为111名，日本为42名，英国为30名，法国为50名）。1993年，以色列在校大学生已增至20万，占全国职工总数的18%。在受教育人口不断增长的同时，高等教育的产业化趋势日益明显。以色列的大学在开展科研活动的同时，把大量精力投入产品开发，大多数高校成立了自己的企业，如希伯来大学的伊瑟姆研究开发公司、魏茨曼科学研究院的耶达研究开发公司、特拉维夫大学的拉默特公司、以色列工学院的研究开发公司等，这些企业对促进科研成果的商业化起到了重要作用。在政府的支持下，以色列大学校园附近还建立了许多以高科技产业为方向的工业园，这些工业园在信贷、税收方面享有优惠条件，凡申请进入工业园的企业必须经过大学的审查与评估，主要进行技术水平与生产能力的可行性论证。在工业园区内，大学与企业互相配合、密切合作，对研究出来的新成果进行快速的投产和开发，当生产规模达到一定程度时，便迁出工业园区，进行扩大化生产。如今，以色列魏茨曼科学研究院所属的魏茨曼科学工业园、特拉维夫大学与特拉维夫市合办的阿蒂迪姆科学园、希伯来大学所属的哈尔霍茨维姆科学工业园等都已成为国家高科技产业的摇篮。此外，"以色列的大学获得的专利数量是衡量大学与产业部门之间关系所带来的效益的一个尺度。最近一项研究已经表明，大学是国家内外专利权的主要所有人，以色列大学专利活动的规模远远超过了其他国家高等教育部门。而且，在研究与开发经费方向，以色列大学所获得的专利经费是美国大学的 2 倍多，是加拿大大学的 9 倍多。"①

总之，正是由于与社会生产的密切结合，使以色列教育在挖掘智力资源、提高劳动力质量、促使产业结构更新等方面起着无法替代的作用，因而成为推动经济现代化的持久动力。尽管目前的以色列教育仍面临着许多难题与挑战，如怎样摆正宗教与世俗的关系、如何使福利式的教育模式更适合市场化的经济发展趋势等，但从整体看，以色列的教育体制是较为科学的、卓有成效的体制，以色列人在教育兴国方面的成功经验值得进行认真的总结、研究与借鉴。

[原文刊载于《西北大学学报》(哲学社会科学版)
第 30 卷第 1 期，2000 年 2 月]

---

① 以色列新闻中心 :《以色列概况》，耶路撒冷 : 哈摩科出版公司，1997。

中国与以色列的职业教育比较研究

知识经济让从业者向着终生学习方向发展。在这种背景下，我国职业教育受到重视。但是不能忽视的是，我国职业教育还存在问题。本文通过审视以色列经济腾飞和科技文化奇迹般的成就，拟对以色列从职业教育的视角进行研究。

一 显著差异

将中国和以色列的职业教育在定位、课程设置和教学水平三方面进行对比。

（一）定位不同

长期以来，我国职业教育界对职业教育的认识是：培养职业能力。他们所持的是注重认知能力的能力观，

认为"能力就是个体的心理特征，是在个性化过程中表现与发展的对主客观世界的认识、实践的本领及其态度"。以色列在考虑职业教育的目标和内容时就形成了重应用性知识、重实际工作能力的职业教育知识观和能力观。正是这种不同的定位，他们才偏重实践和应用的内容。

（二）课程设置不同

我国职业教育课程设置是把学科整体作为课程设置的基础。长期以来，我国的课程设置工作主要集中在教学计划和教学大纲的编写方面，而且这一工作一直是在国家教育部门的领导下，委托专门机构完成的。就总体而言，我国职业教育的课程设置是注重理论。以色列虽然国家有统一的教学大纲，却高度肯定各地的多样性，学校有权根据本校的情况，设置课程。这使得职业学校可以根据社会实际需要灵活设置课程，进行教学。以色列职业教育的课程设置非常注重实际。

（三）教师水平不同

我国的职业教育学校的老师多来源于高专院校、短期职业大学以及高职院校等。这几类学校的原有师资水平与教育部的要求存在差距。一方面，高职院校中，教师学历层次整体水平偏低；另一方面，具备较高学历的教师绝大部分来自高校，缺乏相应的工作经历与工程技术实践经验。而以色列职业教育师资的发展趋势与我国的截然不同。以色列认为，兼职教师通常具有丰富的理论与实践知识，职业教育团队应专兼结合，以兼职教师为主。总的看来，兼职教师团队是支撑以色列职业教育发展的重要力量，作用在不断提升。教师从业标准更加严格，以色列几乎全部建立了高标准的教师资格制度。

二　差异成因

中国职业教育与以色列职业教育存在显著差别，这些差别的形成是多种因素综合作用的结果。

（一）传统因素

犹太人认为学习知识、钻研律法都不能代替劳动的技能。在以色列人们心中，职业教育是让他们安身立命的支撑物，因此职业教育在以色列不是低层次、低水平的教育，是一个人立足社会、谋求发展的必备工具，以色列的社会有尊重技术和职业教育的传统。

在中国，儒家思想统治中国千年之久，"君子不器"的思想封锁着中国职业教育。我国历来没有培养劳动者的教育观念，不论是"官学"还是"私学"，都把科举取士作为目的，视技术、技能为"奇技淫巧"，职业技能的传授仅存在于民间，以师带徒的方式承传着，这导致我国传统观念中具有鄙视职业教育的因子。

（二）制度因素

以色列把培养高素质的人才作为其科技立国成功的关键因素。专门的职业中学和农业中学是为工厂和农业生产培养大量的熟练工人、初级工程师。为了保证让青年在进入劳动力市场之前，能基本适应市场的需求，以色列制定了《职业培训法》。这就从政策、法律和法规的高度，根本上保证了职业教育的发展。

而在中国，政策文本的繁荣与职业教育发展却产生了尴尬。进入 21 世纪的短短几年，国务院、教育部先后出台了《关于大力推进职业教育改革和发展的决定》《国务院关于大力发展职业教育的决定》等重要的职业教育政策，创造了政策文本的一派繁荣。然而，国家希望通过制度设计引领职业教育快速发展的急切心情似乎并没有起到立竿见影的效果。资料显示，我国的职业教育正面临着严重的困境。我国职业教育政策文本繁荣与职业教育实践的滑坡，彰显出来的是职业教育政策执行失效的问题。这是中国职业教育发展的巨大瓶颈。

（三）经济因素

建国初年的以色列经济并不发达，人均仅 1000 美元多一点，但他们能以大量资金进行短期内看不见任何效益的职业教育投资，实在是大胆之举。政府在各种职业教育设施上不惜投入巨资。以色列全国每年通过劳动部门用于职业培训教育的经费约为 130 万美元。今天看来，对于职业教育倾力于可持续发展，颇具远见卓识。

而中国，政府对职业教育的投入不足，是职业教育出现滑坡和发展相对缓慢的重要因素。国家对职业学校教育和技工学校的财政投入增长慢于财政收入增长，甚至慢于整个教育的财政投入增长。由于教育经费投入上的不均衡，结果造成在整个教育经费的投入格局中，职业教育的投入比例呈较大幅度下降。

三　启示

通过上面的差异比较和因素分析，我们认为，要借鉴以色列职业教育的先进经验，改变我国当前职业教育的现状，启示有三。

（1）从职业教育办学的定位上来说，要从整体上综合把握。职业教育是一个系统，系统内有许多元素，如教师、学生、学校资产、负债、收益。如何对职业教进行有效管理，使其达到整体优化，创造最大的社会效益与经济效益，是职业教育考虑的中心问题。这样的定位才能促进职业教育的发展。

（2）从课程设置上来说，我们要改变课程设计中实践课一边倒的倾向，适当增加实践学习的深度和广度，提升学生自主思考、自主学习、自主总结、自主动手等方面的能力，促使学生具备从实践中学习和总结理论、甚至发展理论的能力，真正做到理论联系实际的要求。

（3）从教师的角度来看，职业教育教师要认真进行业务学习，职业教师要真正完成职业教育院校向社会输送适应社会需要的合格人才的使命，就要不断强化职业教育内容的充实，接受新观念、新文化、新知识。只有这样，教师才能完成新时代的教学任务。

以色列资源奇缺、路途坎坷，却创造出了经济、科技和文化传奇，我们仅从职业教育的角度进行比较，找出我国与以色列的不同点，并分析形成差异的原因，从而为我国职业教育的发展寻找更好的途径。

（原文刊载于《出国与就业》2011 年第 3 期）

中以关系

中国与以色列关系 60 年述评

中国—以色列关系的历史演进和现状分析

中以关系大事记（1949~2013）

中国与以色列关系 60 年述评

殷 罡[*]

中以关系是国际关系史上十分罕见的特例。中华人民共和国和以色列国同期诞生，两国没有直接的利益冲突，中华民族和犹太民族之间也无历史积怨，具备平等发展双边关系最好的自身条件。然而，尽管以色列是中东地区第一个承认中华人民共和国的国家，却是该地区最后一个同中国建立正常外交关系的国家。中、以两国终于在 1992 年实现了关系正常化。目前，中国同所有中东国家都保持着正常和友好的往来，同以色列也不例外。

一 亲善的历史交往，最佳建交机遇的丧失

中国和犹太民族的亲善关系可以追溯到一千年以前。

* 殷罡，中国社会科学院西亚非洲研究所研究员。

金大定三年（1163 年），从中亚辗转迁徙到中国腹地的犹太人在开封建立了犹太会堂①，标志着中国境内犹太社团的形成。这一社团在明、清时期还同宁夏和扬州等地犹太社团之间保持着人员、宗教文献和资金往来②，而元代杭州的犹太社团则在经济领域里表现得十分活跃，社团规模甚至超过开封③。无论是开封犹太人的自述史料，还是明、清时代外国传教士的实地调查和中国官方典籍的相关记述都表明，定居中国的犹太人在金、元、明、清四个朝代都受到中国官方和民间的平等对待，一些犹太人甚至身居要职。由于受科举制度的吸引、明代同化政策对外来民族语言文字的限制，以及犹太社团的封闭性和同境外断绝交往等综合作用，规模曾达数千人的开封犹太社团在 19 世纪中期解体。

在中国古代犹太社团解体的同期，来华经商的犹太人又开始形成近代中国社团。1887 年和 1907 年，上海和哈尔滨相继修建了犹太会堂。随着中东铁路沿线的开发、沙皇俄国对犹太人的迫害和十月革命的影响，哈尔滨犹太社团在 20 世纪初年急剧扩大，1920 年社团成员超过了 1.2 万人④，并辐射到天津、大连和青岛等城市，对当地的社会文化和经济发展影响很大。而活跃在上海的沙逊和嘉道理家族，以及地产巨头哈同，则在相当程度上控制着上海近代工业和城市建设的发展。第二次世

---

① 参见明弘治二年（1489 年）开封犹太会堂碑文《重建清真寺记》。
② 参见明弘治二年（1489 年）开封犹太会堂碑文《重建清真寺记》，并见明正德七年（1512 年）碑文《尊崇道经寺记》。
③ 参见利玛窦、金尼阁著《利玛窦中国札记》，何高济等译，中华书局，1983，第 116~117 页。
④ 徐新：《哈尔滨犹太人简况》，《以色列动态》1992 年第 19 期。

界大战期间，纳粹德国的反犹运动迫使约 3 万名犹太难民涌入上海。1939 年，经德国犹太银行家雅各布·贝尔格拉斯的游说和时任立法院院长的孙科提议，国民政府各部曾就接受 10 万犹太难民并在腾冲建立"犹太人寄居区域"的计划进行认真会商，计划得到云南省政府主席龙云的积极呼应，但受战况进展不利、中德关系和国内安全等诸多因素的牵制，该计划被放弃 ①。

由于中国不存在反犹意识、犹太社团领袖的积极游说和资助，一些国民党上层人物对犹太复国运动持同情立场。一些犹太人还积极参加了中国的抗日战争，其中包括坚持在新四军从医 4 年、后任东北民主联军一纵卫生部长的罗生特，以及在山东反扫荡战场上牺牲的德国共产党员希伯。

对于 1947 年联合国巴勒斯坦分治决议和 1948 年第一次阿以战争，国民政府持中立态度，在第 181 号决议表决时投了弃权票。而解放区各主要报纸均对以色列建国表示积极支持，指出这是一场由英国人挑动阿拉伯反动政府发动的反犹战争，而犹太人在进行坚决和正义的抵抗 ②。中国共产党对阿以冲突的早期立场同苏联是一致的。

1949 年 3 月 1 日，已败退广州的国民政府外交部宣布了对以色列国的承认 ③，但以色列方面采取了礼貌的回避态度。

---

① 参见《重庆国民政府安置逃亡犹太人计划筹议始末》，《民国档案》1993 年第 3 期；"One Hundred Thousand Jews May Find Home in China", Israel's Messenger, Shanghai, July 14, 1939, pp.114-151。
② 参见新华社陕北 1948 年 6 月 2 日电，《人民日报》1948 年 6 月 5 日。
③ 参见中央社广州 1949 年 3 月 1 日电，《中央日报》1949 年 3 月 2 日。

1949 年 10 月 1 日，中华人民共和国成立。1950 年 1 月 4 日，以色列外交部法律顾问签发了同意承认新中国政府的文件，并决定"一旦联合国出现中国席位之争，应赞成将席位让给新政府"[①]。1 月 9 日，以色列外长夏利特致电中国外长周恩来，正式宣布承认中国新政府。1 月 16 日，由刘少奇签发了以周恩来外长名义的回电，对此表示感谢。1 月 28 日，中国外交部曾致电驻苏联大使馆，询问以方是否有正式承认文件送达[②]。而以色列外交部则认为中方的回复仅仅是礼貌性的，并未决定同以色列建立正式关系，便采取了不急于同中国发展直接关系、双方在莫斯科进行接触的决定[③]。同年 6 月 13 日，中国外交部将同意和以色列互派使节的决定电告驻苏联大使馆，中方代表随即会见以色列公使，询问以色列何时向中国派出外交使团。

对于 1950 年的中以外交接触，中国方面还有这样的认识：中国同以色列"已经建立外交关系而没有交换使节"[④]。

二 中国的政策调整和中以关系

1953~1955 年，中以双方驻缅甸等国的外交官为此

[①] 国际司—亚洲司：《对中国立场问题》，1950 年 1 月 4 日，以色列国家档案馆，外交部档案 1561/9。

[②] 参见中国外交部档案馆，原档编号 107-D0035，开放编号：107-00087-01（1），第 4 页。

[③] 外交部部长致东亚司司长函，1950 年 1 月 29 日，以色列国家档案馆，130.02/2385/31。

[④] 《中华人民共和国四年来的外交胜利》，《世界知识手册》，世界知识出版社，1954，第 54 页。

进行了多次接触，而阿拉伯国家也开始调整对华政策。1954 年 6 月 29 日，周恩来总理在访问缅甸期间曾会见以色列驻缅甸公使哈科汉，并邀请他访华 [①] 。同年 9 月 23 日，周恩来总理在人大作政府工作报告时宣布：中国同以色列建立正常关系的事宜正在接触当中。但又表示，中国希望同中东和近东国家发展事务性关系，即经济和文化关系 [②] 。

1955 年 1 月，在中国同埃及谈判建交期间，哈科汉率以色列贸易代表团访华，随行的有以色列外交部亚洲司司长列文。双方签订了一项贸易协定，但没有就建交事宜进行具体磋商。中国报纸比较醒目地报道了此次访问，目的是"通过邀请以色列代表团访华从反面推动阿拉伯国家与我建交" [③] 。

此时，第一次亚非会议（万隆会议）的预备会议已经结束，阿拉伯国家拒绝让以色列参会已成定局。值得一提的是，针对阿拉伯国家的立场，《人民日报》曾发表社论指出，"亚非会议不应该成为一个排他性的区域集团"，"亚非会议的大门对未被邀请的亚非国家是开着的" [④] 。显然，中国对排斥以色列的做法持保留态度。

万隆会议期间，周恩来总理同埃及总统纳赛尔进行了两次单独会见，并认真听取了叙利亚代表团副团长关于巴勒斯坦问题的介绍，而这位副团长就是 9 年后成立

---

① David Hacohen, *Time to Tell*, Herzl Press, New York, 1985, pp.227-228.

② 《世界知识手册》，世界知识出版社，1955，第 976 页。

③ 《周恩来致刘少奇、陈毅、邓小平、习仲勋函》，外交部档案馆，开放档案编号 107-00087-01，第 19 页。

④ 《人民日报》社论，1955 年 1 月 5 日。

的巴解组织第一任主席舒凯里。以色列在万隆会议结束3天后便正式致函中方："决定同中国建立全面外交关系"[①]，中国外交部亚洲司司长3周后回复："愿意就两国建交事宜保持私人接触。"[②] 5月30日，埃及终于断绝了同台湾当局的关系，正式同中华人民共和国建交。中国外交部副部长章汉夫1956年7月对以私人身份来访的以色列驻莫斯科公使坦言相告："在目前形势下，两国之间建立外交关系的时机还不成熟"[③]。

三 支持阿拉伯解放事业，但不否认以色列的生存权

在1956年后的阿以冲突中，中国始终坚持反对以色列的政策，但不否定以色列生存权的立场，并反对巴解组织中激进派别的做法，周恩来总理曾多次对来访的巴解组织代表团表示，中国反对的是以色列政府的政策，但并不把以色列人民当作敌人，并对劫持民航班机和杀害人质等恐怖主义手段提出严厉批评，明确表示反对"把以色列扔到大海里"的口号[④]。

中断了官方交往，并不等于中断了两国之间的所有关系。在中国共产党和以色列共产党之间，一直保持着正常的交往。以共代表团列席了1956年的中共八大和

---

① 《以色列外交部亚洲司司长致中国外交部亚洲司司长函》，1955年4月29日，以色列国家档案馆，外交部档案号3334/37。
② 《以色列外交部亚洲司司长致中国外交部亚洲司司长函》，附件《陈家康致列文的函》，1955年5月21日。
③ 外交部档案馆，开放档案编号107-00039-01（1），第30~32页。
④ 参见裴坚章主编《研究周恩来——外交思想与实践》，世界知识出版社，1989，第132~134页。

1959 年中华人民共和国国庆十周年庆祝活动，以共文件集被译成中文版，周恩来总理和毛泽东主席都同以共领导人保持接触。1957 年 11 月莫斯科世界共产党和工人党会议期间，毛泽东曾单独会见以共总书记米库尼斯，认真听取了米库尼斯关于苏联的犹太文化正在消失的抱怨，并对苏联禁止出版犹太教的祈祷书表示不可理解。事后，毛泽东还亲自就此事同赫鲁晓夫交涉。一年后，莫斯科的书店里便出现了数以万计的犹太祈祷书，以及大量犹太文学著作和希伯来语词典。在同米库尼斯的谈话中，毛泽东还介绍了中国古代犹太人的情况，令以共领导人深感意外 ① 。

1963 年 8 月 2 日，针对美、英、苏一周前签署的部分停止核试验的条约，周恩来总理致函各国政府首脑，建议召开世界各国首脑会议，讨论全面禁止和彻底销毁核武器问题，以色列总理艾希科尔也收到了周恩来签署的正式函件。艾希科尔在回函中表达了同中国建交的愿望 ② 。

中以关系冻结期间，参加中国革命并留在中国的犹太人始终受到中国领导人的高度尊重。1988 年第七届政协会议的 7 位外裔委员中，有 5 位是犹太人。

中国境内犹太社团的正常活动也没有受到影响，数以万计的犹太人都是和平和自愿离境的。仍未撤离上海的犹太人得到了中国政府和人民一如既往的礼遇，上海、哈尔滨和天津的犹太社团都在登记后取得了合法地位，并同国际犹太组织和以色列保持着联系，直至"文革"开始后的 1967 年中国境内的外籍犹太人基本撤离完

---

① 参见〔以色列〕《最新消息报》1973 年 5 月 6 日。

② 以色列国家档案馆，外交部档案号 3426/16-17，《周恩来与艾希科尔信件往来》。

毕。留华犹太人的良好境遇可以从上海"犹太人联合委员会"1957~1958 年度致《国际犹太人大会》报告结束语得到证实："必须指出，中国人民和中国人民的政府对在华犹太居民及犹太社团组织均宽宏友善相待。当局一直对我们的宗教需求给与特殊的尊重和关心。本理事会诚挚地在报告中记录下对这个伟大国家的感激"[1] 。

以色列数十年一直坚持承认中华人民共和国为中国唯一合法政府，始终没有同台湾当局发生往来，并支持我国恢复在联合国的合法席位。

四 中以建交后双边关系的发展与障碍

中国实施改革开放政策以后，许多具有双重国籍的犹太商人和企业家活跃在中国各地，犹太资本再次涌入中国，其中主要来自原上海犹太社团成员控股的财团。从 1979 年起，中国开始接待以色列非官方商业代表，两国开始在经济与科技领域开展民间交往。同以色列的非正式交往，对中国提高国防能力和科技水平起到了积极的作用。

20 世纪 80 年代中期，随着阿以关系整体走向政治解决，中国及时调整了对以色列的政策，并于 1985 年正式恢复了同以色列的外交接触，中以间的学术交流、贸易往来和邮电通信也逐渐走上正轨。

1990 年春季，中国和以色列分别在各自首都建立了准官方联络机构。即中国国际旅行社驻以色列代表处和

---

[1] Report, "Council of the Jewish Community", Shanghai, July 1, 1957-June30, 1958.

以色列科学院驻中国联络处。

1991 年 11 月，继埃及和以色列在 1979 年实现关系正常化 12 年后，阿拉伯国家终于在马德里和会上同以色列坐在了一张谈判桌上。1992 年 1 月 24 日，中、以两国终于在北京签署了建交公报。

中以关系从此进入了蓬勃发展的新时期。自 1992 年 10 月起，两国签署了政府间贸易、避免双重征税、投资保护、经贸合作、工业研发合作等多项协定，以及高技术领域合作的谅解备忘录。2005 年 11 月，以色列正式承认中国完全市场经济地位 ① 。

中、以两国农业领域的合作尤为突出，以色列在北京建立了中以农业培训中心，在北京、山东、陕西、云南及新疆等地相继建立了农业培植、花卉种植、奶牛饲养等示范基地，对提高中国农业技术起到了促进作用。除数以千计的中国技术人员在本国接受以方培训外，中国每年赴以色列留学人员也保持在百人左右，以色列在华留学生亦保持在百人左右 ② 。

中以建交后，担任过总理和总统的以色列领导人都访问过中国。在 2000 年中东和平进程陷入停顿之前，中国总理和国家主席都对以色列进行了国事访问。

目前，以色列有 260 多家从事商业和技术贸易的公司在中国设有办事机构 ③ 。中国建筑公司在以色列承建了多项工程，其中包括隧道和铁路建设项目，在以色列

---

① http：//www.fn prc.gov.cn/chn /pds/gjhdq/g j/yz/1206-4/xgxw/ t3849161 htm.

② http：//www.fn prc.gov.cn/chn/pds/gjhdq/gj/yz/1206-41/sbgx/.

③ http：//www.israeltrade. org. cn/zhongw en/comp an iesphp#8.

的中国劳工一度接近 4 万人 [①]。据中国海关统计，2008年，中以贸易额已逾 60 亿美元，其中出口 42 亿美元，进口 18 亿美元 [②]。以色列方面的目标是在几年内将这项数额提高到 100 亿美元。

特别需要指出的是，前上海犹太社团成员及其后代在推进中、以两国经贸合作方面发挥了特殊的、巨大的作用，嘉道理和艾森伯格等犹太财团在对中国的能源、高科技、核电站等项目上进行了大规模投资，受到了包括邓小平等中国领导人的赞扬。

（原文刊载于《西亚非洲》2010 年第 4 期）

[①] http://www.china news.com.cn/news/2006/2006-04-11/8/7153461 shtml.

[②] http://il.mofcom. gov. cn/aarticle/zxhz/tjsj/200903/20090306140350. html.

中国—以色列关系的历史演进和现状分析

潘　光 *

中以建交 60 多年来，中国—以色列关系沿着一条十分罕见的轨迹演进，经历了风风雨雨后终于达到了全面、稳定发展的良好状态，但在具有强劲驱动力的同时仍面临一些障碍。本文拟对此作一回顾、分析和展望。

一　从建国到建交：一波三折的中以关系

20 世纪 40 年代末，在中华民族和犹太民族的历史上都发生了划时代的事件：中华人民共和国和以色列国分别于 1949 年和 1948 年在亚洲东部和西端建立。当时两国之间并无任何直接的利害冲突，建立外交关系本来

* 潘光，上海国际问题研究中心副主席，上海社会科学院研究员、博士生导师，上海犹太研究中心主任，上海合作组织研究中心主任。

是顺理成章的事，必定会给中犹两个民族进一步发展传统友谊提供一个极好的契机。然而，由于种种复杂的原因，两国关系的正常化直到 43 年后才实现。在这 43 年里，中以关系走过的曲折历程大致可分为四个阶段。

第一阶段：友好接触时期。1948 年 5 月 14 日，以色列国宣告成立。当时，包括中国共产党办的报纸在内的中国舆论界普遍表示欢迎。5 月 27 日，华北解放区的《冀中导报》指出："定名为'以色列'的新犹太国家，于 14 日宣告成立。两千年来没有祖国而到处流浪受着侮辱与屠杀的犹太人民，他们要求建立犹太国家的愿望，开始实现了。"①

1949 年 10 月 1 日中华人民共和国的成立，也受到以色列政府和人民的欢迎。1950 年 1 月 9 日，以色列政府正式承认中华人民共和国，成为中东第一个承认新中国的国家。《人民日报》1950 年 1 月 17 日在头版报道这一消息，使用的标题是："以色列、阿富汗、芬兰决与我国建外交关系，周外长分别复电表示欢迎"②。此后几个月，中以两国朝着建立正常外交关系的方向迈进。与世界上大多数国家不一样，以色列与旧的国民党政权没有官方关系，因此中以之间并无影响建立邦交的直接障碍。1950 年 6 月，中以双方代表在莫斯科首次会晤，开始讨论建交的具体事宜。但就在这时，朝鲜战争爆发了，中国与美国极有可能在朝鲜发生正面冲突。在这样的形势下，来自美国的压力使以色列政府对中以建交的态度发生了微妙的变化。6 月底，以色列外交部通知以驻苏代表："政府原则上决定与中华人民共和国建立外交关系，

---

① 《冀中导报》1948 年 5 月 27 日。
② 《人民日报》1950 年 1 月 17 日。

但在远东局势明朗之前，政府在这方面不会做出任何决定。这点只有你知道，在得到进一步指示前，你只能静观事态发展。"[①] 这样，冷战在全球愈演愈烈使两国失去了建立正常关系的第一个机会。

1953~1954年，中以双方在莫斯科、仰光、赫尔辛基、伦敦频频会晤，仰光成了中以接触的主要地点。

1954年9月23日，周恩来总理在第一次全国人民代表大会第一次会议上作报告时指出："中国与阿富汗和以色列建立正常关系的接触正在进行之中。"[②] 此后，在万隆会议筹备和召开过程中，中国与阿拉伯国家的关系迅速发展。

1956年5~9月，中国先后与埃及、叙利亚、也门建立了外交关系。此后，中以问就建交进行的接触均告中断，中以关系进入了长达20年的"冻结"时期。

第二阶段：关系"冻结"时期。虽然这一时期中以国家关系处于"冻结"状态，但中国人民与世界各国犹太人之间的友谊并没有中断。双方在反对侵略战争、维护世界和平等方面仍然互相支持，双方之间的经济交往和文化交流从未停止。在中国与美国等西方国家改善关系的进程中，一些犹太裔政治家如美国国务卿亨利·基辛格等发挥了重要作用，他们也曾试图在中以两国之间牵线搭桥。

与苏联和东欧一些社会主义国家不同，在中华人民共和国的土地上从未出现过像欧洲那种反犹主义。就这一点而言，在从古至今的中国历史上是一脉相通的，并没有因改朝换代而发生任何变化。

---

① ［美］M. 柯蒂斯、S.A. 吉特尔森（Michael Curtis & Susan Aurelia Gitelson）编《以色列在第三世界》（*Israel in the Third World*），新泽西出版社，1976，第225页。

② 新华社北京1954年9月23日电。

在中国发生"文革"前的 17 年里，仍然有许多犹太人生活在新中国的土地上，代表他们的主要组织——上海犹太社团委员会（简称"犹联"）在中国政府支持下顺利地开展工作。同时，那些离开中国的犹太人纷纷到世界各地定居，形成了一个"中国犹太人"群体，保持着强烈的中国情结。

1956 年，周恩来总理在与来访的新加坡犹太裔政治家戴维·马歇尔（曾任新加坡首席部长和驻法国大使）交谈中，了解到一些在华犹太人在移居其他国家方面仍面临若干政策性障碍，随即指示有关部门协助他们尽快办理离境手续，使这些犹太人很快就顺利离境移居其他国家 [①]。经过中国方面做工作，苏联政府也改变了政策，同意接收部分在华犹太人移居苏联 [②]。同时，由于新中国与大多数西方国家尚无外交关系，香港成了中国与西方国家进行间接贸易的主要通道，而与中国内地有着传统联系的香港犹太社团，特别是塞法迪犹商集团在其中发挥了极其重要的促进作用。

第三阶段：关系"解冻"时期。1976 年"文革"结束后，走上改革开放之路的中国与越来越多的国家建立了外交关系，与包括美国等西方大国在内的世界上大多数国家的关系得到了改善和发展。在这样的形势下，中

---

① 〔新加坡〕陈庆珠（Chan Heng Chee）:《独立之激情：戴维·马歇尔政治传记》（*A Sensation of Independence : David Marshall Political Biography*），新加坡，2001，第 220~223 页。参见〔新加坡〕比德（Joan Bieder）《新加坡的犹太人》（*The Jews of Singapore*），新加坡，2008，第 131 页。

② 〔新加坡〕陈庆珠（Chan Heng Chee）:《独立之激情：戴维·马歇尔政治传记》（*A Sensation of Independence : David Marshall Political Biography*），新加坡，2001，第 220~223 页。参见〔新加坡〕比德（Joan Bieder）《新加坡的犹太人》（*The Jews of Singapore*），新加坡 2008 年版，第 131 页。

以关系也开始逐渐解冻。1977 年 10 月埃及总统萨达特
访问以色列，与以色列领导人探讨和平解决埃以冲突的
途径，中国报刊热烈支持萨达特迈出的这一步，并且突
出宣传中东问题政治解决的前景。1980 年 7 月，中国外
交部副部长何英提出了中国对待巴勒斯坦问题的三条原
则，其中第三条是"中东各国应该普遍享有独立和生存的
权利"，这里的"中东各国"当然也包括以色列。1982 年，
中国领导人在访问埃及时再次表示支持埃以和解，并重申
中东各国都有生存的权利。1988 年 9 月，中国外长钱其琛
提出了中国关于解决中东问题的五点主张：中东问题应通
过政治途径解决；支持召开在联合国主持下、有五个常任
理事国和有关各方参加的中东国际和平会议；支持中东有
关各方进行合适的、各种形式的对话；以色列必须撤出所
占领的阿拉伯领土，相应的，以色列的安全也应得到保证；
巴勒斯坦国和以色列国互相承认，阿拉伯民族和犹太民
族和平共处。中国就中东问题提出的这一系列富有建设
性的主张，为中以改善关系创造了有利条件。

与此同时，以色列方面也采取进一步措施来促进对
华关系的发展。1985 年，以色列内阁专门召开会议研究
对华政策，决定由魏兹曼负责这一工作。以色列外交部
随即拨款重开关闭了 10 年之久的驻香港总领事馆，由资
深外交官鲁文·梅尔哈夫出任总领事 [①]。以政府的目标是：
利用各种途径与中国方面接触，千方百计打破以中关系
僵局，争取尽快与中国建立外交关系。这一方针得到了
当时以政坛两大政党利库德集团和工党的一致认同，也

---

① ［美］高斯坦主编《中国与犹太—以色列关系 100 年》，中国社会
科学出版社，2006，第 121 页。

受到以色列各阶层人民的支持。

香港犹太社团也在推动中国与以色列建交方面发挥了特殊的作用。中以建交前，香港便是中以两国进行间接贸易的主要中转站，一年的贸易额往往达上千万美元，而在第二次世界大战时期曾经作为难民在上海避难的肖尔·艾森伯格，便在这一间接贸易中发挥了关键作用。作为拥有多重国籍的犹太人，艾森伯格对曾经救助自己的中国情有独钟，很早就开始努力推动没有外交关系的中以两国进行间接贸易。

1978年，艾森伯格看到中国改革开放带来的巨大机遇，决心将中以间接贸易提升到更高的层次。他从以色列领导人那里获得了支持和特许，开始将高技术及其产品出售给中国 [1]，此类贸易大都是通过香港进行的。同时，艾森伯格的工作也为中以之间建立更密切的关系奠定了基础。中以两国领导人都对艾森伯格在促进中以关系方面发挥的特殊作用表示肯定和赞扬。以色列前总理拉宾就特别指出："艾森伯格先生为以色列打开了中国的大门。" [2]

第四阶段：走向建交时期。到20世纪80年代中期以后，中以之间在经济、贸易、文化、旅游、政党社团等方面的民间交往迅速发展，在中以两国政府的努力下双方重建官方联系的条件已经具备。

从1986年3月到1987年1月，中以双方官员在巴黎进行了若干次接触，商讨进一步展开官方交往的可能性，并为较高级别的官方会晤作准备。1987年3月和9月，中国常驻联合国代表李鹿野在纽约两次会见以色列外交部长办公室主任艾·塔米尔，就官方接触进一步升级进

---

[1] 美国《时代》杂志，1993年10月25日。
[2] 美国《时代》杂志，1993年10月25日。

行具体磋商。9 月 30 日，中国国务委员兼外交部长吴学谦在纽约会见了以色列副总理兼外交部长西蒙·佩雷斯，如此高级别的官员进行正式会晤，这在两国关系史上还是第一次。1989 年 1 月，中国外长钱其琛同以色列外长阿伦斯在巴黎会晤，商定由两国常驻联合国代表保持经常性接触。此后不久，根据双方协议，中国国际旅行社驻特拉维夫办事处和以色列科学及人文学院驻北京联络处先后建立，标志着中以关系不但已恢复，而且在某些方面超过了 1949~1950 年和 1954~1956 年友好接触阶段的水平。1991 年，上述两机构均已享有外交权利，使中以之间建立了事实上的领事关系。

与此同时，国际关系及中东形势的一系列急剧变化也为中以关系进一步升格提供了契机。

首先，海湾战争和苏联解体极大地削弱了中东的主战强硬派，而加强了该地区主张和平解决争端的力量。在这有利形势下，中东内外的各种支持和平的力量协同发挥作用，终于促成了马德里中东和会的召开。这样，中国作为一个安理会常任理事国，便面临着如何参与中东和平进程的问题，而要真正参与进去，与冲突的一方以色列没有外交关系显然是不行的。

其次，中东欧和前苏联地区各国，乃至蒙古等国纷纷与以色列建交，使中国这样一个大国与以色列无外交关系的状况越来越显得不正常，也使阿拉伯国家认识到越来越多国家与以色列建交的趋势不可避免，对这一发展的心理承受力有所增强。

正是在这样一种"水到渠成"的形势下，中国外交部副部长杨福昌 1991 年 12 月的特拉维夫之行和以色列副总理兼外交部长戴维·利维 1992 年 1 月的北京之行最终完成了两国关系正常化的外交程序。1992 年 1 月 24 日，中以两国外长正式签署建交公报，宣布建立大使级外交关系，从而揭开了中以两国、中犹两个民族关系史上崭新的一页。

回顾 43 年的曲折历程，我们可以看出，使中以关系的发展步履艰难的障碍主要来自于外部环境的变化和外部力量的干扰，而不在于双边关系中的问题和双方各自的内部阻力，因此当外部环境逐步改善，有利于中以关系发展的国际氛围形成之时，这些障碍便不难克服了。

二　建交以来：中以关系的全面稳步发展

建交 17 年来，中以关系全面、稳步地发展，这主要表现在以下三个方面：

第一，两国领导人互访频繁，经常就双边关系和国际问题进行有益的磋商。1992 年 9 月，中国国务委员兼外长钱其琛访问以色列。同年 12 月，以色列总统海姆·赫尔佐克访问中国。1993 年 5 月和 10 月，以色列副总理兼外长佩雷斯和总理拉宾先后访问中国。9 月份刚与阿拉法特主席签署了巴以和平协议的拉宾总理在中国受到了特别热烈的欢迎。1994 年 10 月，中国副总理邹家华访问以色列。1995 年 10 月，中国国家主席江泽民和以色列总理拉宾在纽约会晤，就进一步发展中以双边关系交换了意见。1997年，中国领导人李岚清、钱其琛、温家宝先后访以。1998年 5 月，以色列总理内塔尼亚胡访问中国。1999 年 4 月，以色列总统魏兹曼访问中国。同年 11 月，中国人大常委会委员长李鹏访问以色列。2000 年 4 月，中国国家主席江泽民访问以色列，这是有史以来第一位中国国家元首访问一个犹太人国家（见表 1）。

表1 2000～2008 年双方的重要往来

中方	年份	以方	年份
江泽民主席	2000	地区合作部长佩雷斯	2000
外交部副部长杨文昌	2002	佩雷斯副总理兼外长	2002
唐家璇国务委员	2004	卡察夫总统	2003
		奥尔默特副总理兼工贸部长	2004
		沙洛姆副总理兼外长	
外交部长李肇星	2005	外交部总司长普罗瑟	2005
中联部长王家瑞			
中国政府特使、外交部副部民吕新华			
中国中东问题特使孙必干（6月和8月两次）	2006	议会外交与国防委员会主席哈内戈比	2006
江苏省委书记李源潮		议会财政委员会主席、圣经犹太教联盟主席利茨曼	
中共中央政治局委员、北京市委书记刘淇		总理奥尔默特	2007
外交部部长助理翟隽		副总理兼运输和道路安全部长莫法兹	
中国中东问题特使孙必干（4月、7月、12月三次）	2007	副议长瓦哈比	
文化部副部长常克仁		第一副总理兼外长利夫尼	
农业部部长孙政才		副总理兼工贸和劳动部长伊萨伊	
水利部副部长胡四一		总统佩雷斯（参加北京奥运会开幕式）	2008
中共中央政治局委员、书记处书记、中宣部部长刘云山	2008	副议长阿维泰尔	

资料来源：中华人民共和国外交部网站。

第二，双边经济、科技合作迅速发展，两国之间的贸易额直线上升。1992 年 10 月，两国签署政府间贸易协定，双方互相给予对方最惠国待遇。此后，双方还签署了避免双重征税、投资保护、经贸合作、工业研发合作、海关合作、财政合作、海运合作等方面协议。中以联合经贸委员会每年召开一次会议以促进双边经贸合作。2005 年 11 月，以色列正式承认中国完全市场经济地位。2008 年 1 月，以色列副总理兼工贸部长伊萨伊访华时，双方签署了《中国商务部与以色列工业、贸易和劳动部关于进一步推动中以高技术领域合作的谅解备忘录》和《华亿创业投资基金认购协议》。

以这一系列协议作为基础和保障，中以两国在经济、科技方面的双边合作迅速发展，取得了丰硕成果，这在农业、电信、医药、矿业、建筑、能源、钻石加工、航空等行业表现得尤为突出。1993 年，两国签署农业部谅解备忘录，并先后在北京农业工程大学成立了中以农业培训中心，在北京郊区建立了中以示范农场。1997 双方正式成立"中以农业联合委员会"。近年来，两国在农业领域的合作稳步推进，由以色列援建的北京永乐店中以合作示范农场已成为中以友谊的象征，在山东、陕西、云南及新疆等地，也建立了农业培植、花卉种植、奶牛等示范基地。中以之间的摩沙夫（MASHAV，以色列集体农庄）国际农业合作交流计划进展顺利，使中国的农业技术人员有机会直接到以色列的集体农庄去实习。2008 年 11 月，"2008 中以农业合作周"在陕西杨凌举行。1995 年，中以科学研究基金成立，基金总额为 500 万美元，由双方提供。十多年来，该基金在促进双边合作科研项目的实施方面发挥了重要作用。2000 年，中以合作的上海浦东钻石交易所建立，目前已成为远东地区最重要的钻石交易集散地。

中以建交前，双边贸易额每年仅几千万美元，而到 2007 年，双边贸易额已跃升到 53106 亿美元，增长了数十倍[①]。本文完稿时获得的最新数字为：2008 年 1~10 月，中以双边贸易额为 50187 亿美元，同比增长 17%；其中中方出口 35168 亿美元，同比增长 19%，进口 15119 亿美元，同比增长 11%[②]。

第三，两国之间的文化交流和人员往来发展迅速。双方签署了多项文化、体育、旅游、教育等方面的合作协议和意向备忘录，两国的文化、艺术、体育团队进行了成功的互访，大大促进了两国人民之间的传统友谊。1993 年 5 月，两国签署了文化交流协定。1994 年 11 月，具有世界一流水平的以色列爱乐乐团访问北京、上海，受到中国人民的热烈欢迎。同时，中国的京剧、杂技等团队也在以色列受到欢迎。

1992 年 3 月，中以两国民航签订了"谅解备忘录"，同意以色列航空公司飞行特拉维夫至北京的直达包机。1992 年 9 月，以色列航空公司在北京和特拉维夫之间开始进行包机飞行。1993 年 10 月，双方签署了两国民航协定。以色列航空公司飞往北京航班改为定期国际航班，每周一次。

1994 年 6 月，两国签署了旅游合作协定，以色列国内掀起了"去中国旅游"的热潮，到以色列访问的中国人也越来越多。许多以色列城市与中国城市结成了友

---

① 中华人民共和国外交部网站，http：//www.mfa.gov.cn。
② 中华人民共和国外交部网站，http：//www.mfa.gov.cn。

好城市，如北京与特拉维夫、上海与海法等。2005 年 6
月，中方宣布将以色列列为中国公民出境旅游目的地国。
2007 年 10 月，两国签署了《中国旅游团队赴以色列旅游
实施方案的谅解备忘录》。2008 年 9 月，中国公民赴以色
列旅游首发团抵达以色列。

　　双边的教育交流也富有成果，许多教授专家不但进
行互访，还开始了合作研究或联合举办学术会议。两国
的大学和研究机构纷纷签订合作、交流协议，在以色列
的中国留学生已达上千人，以色列来华留学生也逐年增
加。2007 年 5 月，"中国文化节"在以色列开幕，特拉
维夫大学孔子学院成立 ① 。

　　17 年来，全球各地的"中国犹太人"群体在促进中
以关系迅速发展的进程中发挥了重要作用，又从中以关
系的迅速发展中获得鼓舞和利益。同时，伴随着中国的
发展和繁荣，犹太人来华再次形成高潮。在上海、北京、
广州、深圳等地又出现了新的犹太社团和犹太居民群体，
历史悠久的香港犹太社团迎来了其发展进程中最为辉煌
的时期，人数不多而十分活跃的台湾犹太社团也在稳步
发展，并从两岸关系的改善中获益。

三　规律性因素：中以关系发展的动力和障碍

　　回顾、剖析了中以关系 60 多年来的演进轨迹，我们
可以就中以关系发展的动力和障碍总结出一些规律性的
因素。

---

　　①　中华人民共和国外交部网站，http：//www.mfa.gov.cn。

1. 中以关系发展得到持续推动的根源

中以关系之所以能克服重重障碍而前进，是因为其中有着一股强劲的、可持续的推动力，其根源在于以下几方面：

第一，中犹文化的共同点和中犹人民的传统友谊。中犹两个古老文明拥有诸多共同点，如重视教育的价值，珍惜家庭纽带，善于经商理财，强调在困境中团结拼搏，等等。正因为有这些共同点儒家文化中又不存在欧洲那种反犹思潮，从古至今有许多犹太人来到中国安居乐业。当纳粹在欧洲掀起反犹浪潮之时，中国的上海成为世界上唯一敞开大门救助犹太难民的大都市。当犹太人惨遭屠杀之时，成千上万的中国人也在抗日战争中伤亡，共同的遭遇使双方在反法西斯斗争中互相支持。一些在华犹太人参加了中国的革命和建设事业，有的至今仍在为中国的改革发展贡献力量。所有这些，是这股推动力的历史、文化和感情基础。

第二，中以之间没有任何影响双边关系发展的直接障碍和冲突。如前所述，与世界上大多数国家不一样，以色列与旧的国民党政权没有官方关系。在长达 20 年的"冻结"时期，以色列也始终坚持"一个中国"政策。因此，中以之间在建立邦交问题上并无直接障碍。同时，中以在其他几乎所有双边问题上也没有直接的、根本的利害冲突。如前所述，两个主权国家在双边关系中并无直接争端而在如此长的时间里没有建立外交关系，这是十分罕见的。不过，这一特殊因素也成为推动中以关系正常化进程的有利条件。

第三，中以两国在经济全球化过程中的互补和互鉴。与前两点不一样，这是伴随着中国的迅速发展而出现的新因素。2004年，由设在耶路撒冷的犹太民族政策规划研究所撰写的研究报告提出：中国的发展将会对犹太文明的未来发展产生重要影响；作为国际化程度最深的民族，犹太人应高度重视中国和平发展进程带来的巨大机遇；犹太民族的决策者们必须要有一个全民族的对华大战略；中犹两大民族和文明的携手合作，将对世界产生深远的积极影响①。这种宏观的"中国机遇论"，代表了以色列和全球犹太精英中相当一部分人的看法，为以色列和全球犹太人参与中国改革、发展进程提供了理论依据。同时，中国的发展也可从以色列和全球犹太人的成功经验中获取经验和借鉴。可见，在经济全球化过程中互相取长补短和互相借鉴，正为中以关系的发展注入新的动力。

第四，中以在安全与反恐合作方面的密切合作。冷战后民族、宗教冲突在全球范围呈上升趋势，"9·11"事件和伊拉克战争进一步恶化国际气氛，导致极端主义、恐怖主义在全球泛滥，使中以两国均面临严重威胁。在这样的形势下，中以在打击恐怖主义，维护国家安全方面开展了富有成效的合作。例如，在组织北京奥运会、上海世博会等大型活动的安全保卫工作方面，中国就从以色列吸取了不少反恐方面的有益的经验。目前，该领域的合作已逐渐成为中以关系进一步发展的新增长点。

第五，世界的和平发展潮流与中东和平进程的推进。从长远来看，和平与发展是世界长期发展的大趋势，"9·11"事件、伊拉克战争等并没有改变这一总趋势。同时，越来越多的人已经认识到，对话和谈判是解决各类冲突

---

① ［德］所罗门·沃德（Salomon Wald）：《中国与犹太民族》（*China and the Jewish People*），耶路撒冷，犹太民族政策规划研究所，2004。

的唯一途径，也是公正解决包括巴以冲突在内的中东各种问题的唯一正确的途径。尽管中东和平进程屡屡受挫，但其步步向前推进的势头是不可逆转的。这样的发展态势逐步减少或冲淡了中以在巴以冲突和其他中东争端上的分歧，有利于促进中以关系的深入发展。

2. 中以关系发展不时遇到障碍的原因

中以关系发展过程中不时遇到障碍，今后还会有困难和问题出现，这主要是因为以下几方面的原因：

第一，社会制度和价值观念的差异。中以两国社会制度不同，价值观念有差异，走过的发展道路也不一样，必然导致对许多问题有不同看法，乃至产生分歧和争议。这是中以关系发展过程中经常遇到一些原则性、观念性分歧或意识形态型障碍的基本原因。

第二，对阿以、巴以冲突的观点不一。中以两国对许多国际问题有不同看法，但真正会对双边关系产生影响的还是双方在阿拉伯同以色列的冲突上，特别是巴勒斯坦同以色列冲突问题上的分歧。

第三，美国的干扰和"否决权"。美国的干扰曾经使中以两国失去了建立外交关系的第一个契机。不过，随着中美关系的改善和发展，美国也开始乐观地正视中以两国建立正常关系，一些美国犹太裔政治家和企业家还积极在中以之间牵线搭桥。1992年中以建交之时，美国舆论普遍表示欢迎和支持，美国对中以关系发展的干扰似乎已不复存在。不幸的是，2000年的"费尔康"预警机事件表明，一旦中以关系的发展可能产生对美国核心利益不利的后果，美国仍会对以色列的决策动用"否决权"。当然，美国也经常对其他国家动用"否决权"。

综上所述，可以得出三点结论。

其一，在中以关系演进的全过程中，动力和障碍一直是并存的。过去是这样，现在是这样，将来还是如此。正因为此，中以关系演进的轨迹一直是曲折的，经常会出现出人意料的转折。

其二，当强劲的动力推动中以关系顺利发展之时，千万不能以为万事大吉，所有问题都已解决；同样，当中以关系遭遇障碍而处于危机之中时，也不必惊慌失措，以为中以关系从此就没有希望了。

其三，要使中以关系在一个相当长的时期里得以持续长期发展，关键在于如何调动一切积极因素以增强推动力，同时在排除障碍方面更具前瞻性，更善于化解矛盾。

（原文刊载于《社会科学》2009 年第 12 期，
部分内容有删减）

中以关系大事记
（1949~2013）

成 红*

1949 年

10 月 11 日　毛泽东主席电复以色列共产党领袖米库尼斯，告以因交通不便不能派代表参加，并祝贺以色列共产党第十一届代表大会的成功。

10 月 21 日　以色列共产党第十一届代表大会召开，之前曾电邀中国共产党派遣代表参加。

12 月 10 日　亚洲妇女代表会议在北京正式开幕，以色列代表罗斯·罗碧区作为正式代表出席会议并作大会发言。

1950 年

1 月 9 日　以色列政府外交部部长摩西·萨尔特代表该国政府致电我国外交部周恩来部长，表示决定与我国

---

　　*　成红，中国社会科学院西亚非洲研究所研究馆员。

建立外交关系。

10月2日 以色列共产党书记维纳尔致电毛泽东主席，祝贺中华人民共和国成立一周年。

1951年

7月3日 以色列共产党总书记米库尼斯发贺电，祝贺中国共产党成立三十周年。

1952年

5月29日 以色列共产党召开第十二次代表大会，中国共产党中央委员会特致电祝贺。

8月1日 以色列用希伯来文出版的毛泽东著作的第二集，已由"海基布兹·海米哈德出版社"出版。

1953年

10月2日 以色列共产党中央委员会致电中国共产党中央委员会，祝贺中华人民共和国成立四周年。

1954年

9月27日 以色列共产党中央委员会致电中国共产党中央委员会，祝贺中华人民共和国建国五周年。

以色列总理兼外长夏里特致电周恩来总理兼外交部长，祝贺中华人民共和国成立五周年。

1955年

1月31日 由团长、以色列驻缅甸公使戴维·哈科汉率领的以色列贸易访问团一行6人到达北京。

10月 以色列共产党中央委员会致电中国共产党中央委员会，祝贺中华人民共和国成立六周年。

以色列总理兼外长夏里特的致电中华人民共和国总理兼外长周恩来，祝贺中华人民共和国成立六周年。

1956年

9月 以色列共产党代表团应邀到京，参加中国共产党第八次全国代表大会。团长维尔纳在大会上致辞。

以色列共产党中央委员会致电中国共产党中央委员会，祝贺中华人民共和国成立七周年。

9月30日　以色列外交部部长果尔达·梅厄致电中华人民共和国总理兼外交部长周恩来，祝贺中华人民共和国成立七周年。

1957 年

9月30日　以色列总理兼代理外交部长戴维·本—古里安致电中华人民共和国总理兼外交部长周恩来，祝贺中华人民共和国成立八周年。

以色列共产党中央委员会致电中国共产党中央委员会，祝贺中华人民共和国成立八周年。

1959 年

9月27日　应中国共产党中央委员会邀请，以色列共产党代表、以色列共产党中央监察委员会主席兹维·布莱斯坦抵达北京，开始对中国进行访问并参加中国建国十周年庆祝典礼。

1960 年

9月27日　以色列共产党中央委员会致电中国共产党中央委员会，祝贺中华人民共和国成立十一周年。

1961 年

5月27日　中国共产党中央委员会电贺以色列共产党代表大会，祝贺以色列共产党第十四次代表大会圆满成功。

9月29日　以色列共产党中央委员会致电中国共产党中央委员会，祝贺中华人民共和国成立十二周年。

1962 年

10月1日　以色列共产党中央委员会电中国共产党

中央委员会，祝贺中华人民共和国成立十三周年。

1963 年

9 月 30 日　以色列共产党中央委员会贺电中国共产党中央委员会，祝贺中华人民共和国成立十四周年。

1964 年

9 月 30 日　以色列共产党中央委员会致电中国共产党中央委员会，祝贺中华人民共和国成立十五周年。

1965 年

9 月 30 日　以色列共产党中央委员会政治局书记梅尔·维尔纳致电中国共产党中央委员会，祝贺中华人民共和国成立十六周年。

1987 年

3 月 27 日　应以色列方面希望就中东问题与安理会各常任理事国代表会晤的要求，中国常驻联合国代表李鹿野在纽约会见以方代表以色列外交部办公厅主任塔米尔。

6 月 29 日至 7 月 9 日　应中共中央的邀请，由总书记梅尔·维尔纳率领的以色列共产党代表团对中国进行访问。

9 月 30 日　应以色列方面就中东问题会晤联合国安全理事会常任理事国外长的要求，中国国务委员兼外交部长吴学谦在纽约会见以色列副总理兼外交部长西蒙·佩雷斯。

1989 年

1 月 9 日　中国外长钱其琛在巴黎会见以色列外长阿伦斯，双方就中东局势问题交换了意见。

9 月 28 日　中国外长钱其琛在联合国总部同以色列外长阿伦斯就中东局势举行会谈。

1990 年

10 月 2 日　中国外长钱其琛在联合国会见以色列外长戴维·列维，就中东问题举行会谈。

1991 年

9 月 10 日　应中共中央对外联络部邀请，以主席埃拉扎尔·格拉诺特为首的以色列统一工人党代表团即日结束对中国的友好访问。

9 月 30 日　以色列共产党中央委员会致电中国共产党中央委员会和江泽民总书记，祝贺中华人民共和国成立 42 周年。

12 月 6 日　以总书记陶菲克·图比为团长的以色列共产党代表团抵达北京，开始对中国进行友好访问。访问期间，中共中央政治局常委李瑞环在京会见了图比一行，双方就国际共产主义运动等问题交换了意见。

1992 年

1 月 22~26 日　应中国外长钱其琛的邀请，以色列国副总理兼外交部长戴维·利维对中国进行访问。利维外长是第一位正式来华访问的以色列政府官员。1 月 24 日，两国外长在京举行会谈。会谈后，两国外长分别代表本国政府签署建交联合公报。用中文、希伯来文和英文写成的联合公报说："中华人民共和国政府和以色列国政府决定两国自 1992 年 1 月 24 日起建立大使级外交关系。"同日，中国国务院总理李鹏在京会见戴维·利维，双方就双边关系、国际问题以及人们关注的中东问题交换了意见。

1 月 26 日　根据中以建交联合公报，中国驻以色列大使馆在特拉维夫正式开馆。2 月 9 日，中国驻以色列大使馆举行招待会，庆祝中以建交和开馆。

3 月 22 日　应以色列共产党和统一工人党的邀请，

中共中央对外联络部代表团即日抵达特拉维夫，开始对以色列进行为期9天的访问。访问期间，代表团同两党领导人分别举行了会谈，并会见了巴勒斯坦著名人士费萨尔·侯赛尼和巴勒斯坦中东和会代表团发言人阿什拉维。

4月5日　应以色列商会联合会和制造商协会的邀请，中国民间经贸代表团即日抵达耶路撒冷，开始对以色列进行为期6天的访问。这是中以两国建交以来到以色列访问的最大的中国民间经贸代表团。访问期间，以色列总理伊扎克·沙米尔会见了来访的中国民间经济贸易代表团。

9月15~17日　应以色列国外交部长西蒙·佩雷斯的邀请，中国国务委员兼外交部长钱其琛对以色列进行正式访问。访问期间，以色列总统赫尔佐克、总理伊扎克·拉宾分别会见了来访的中国外长钱其琛。

10月30日　中国和以色列在耶路撒冷签署一项政府间贸易协定。根据协定，两国开展互惠贸易，商品在对方市场享受优惠关税，并决定成立混合委员会。

12月6日　中国国家旅游局代表团结束对以色列为期5天的访问。访问期间，两国签署了一项备忘录，双方同意进一步开展旅游合作。

12月24~30日　以色列总统赫尔佐克一行对中国进行正式访问。这是以色列国总统首次来华访问。期间，赫尔佐克总统还访问了上海和西安。

1993年

1月6日　应以色列电影界邀请，中国电影发行放映公司在耶路撒冷举行中国电影展。这是中国电影首次在以色列举行展览。

2月14日　中国和以色列在耶路撒冷签署一项科技

合作协定，以加强两国间在科研和开发领域的合作。

5月7日　应中国共产党邀请，以哈伊姆·查多克为团长的以色列工党代表团抵达北京进行访问。访问期间，中共中央政治局常委胡锦涛在京会见了哈伊姆·查多克一行。

5月19~24日　应中国国务院副总理兼外交部长钱其琛的邀请，以色列国外交部长西蒙·佩雷斯对中国进行正式访问。访问期间，两国外长举行会谈。全国人大常委会委员长乔石在京会见了佩雷斯。

8月3日　以色列工党领袖、内阁总理伊扎克·拉宾在耶路撒冷接见了到访的以甘肃省委书记顾金池为首的中国共产党代表团。

10月10日　应时任国务院总理李鹏的邀请，以色列总理伊扎克·拉宾即日抵达北京，开始对中国为期5天的正式友好访问。这是以色列总理第一次访问中国，也是拉宾在以色列和巴解组织签署和平协议后首次访问中东地区以外的国家。访问期间，李鹏总理同拉宾总理举行了会谈。时任中国国家主席江泽民会见了拉宾总理。

10月27日　中国农业代表团抵达以色列访问。访问期间，两国签署了《中国农业部和以色列农业部谅解备忘录》。

1994年

3月11日　以色列工贸部长米切尔·哈里什一行抵达北京，开始对中国进行访问。访问期间，两国签署了《中以经贸混委会第一次会议纪要》及《中国国家进出口商品检验局与以色列标准局合作协议》。

3月14日　中国—以色列经贸合作洽谈会在北京举行。中以两国近200名工商企业界人士就通信、电子、机械、化工、生物技术和投资、轻工等方面的合作进行了洽谈。

6月18日　应中国共产党的邀请，以总书记穆罕默德·纳法为团长的以色列共产党代表团抵达北京，开始对中国进行访问。

7月1日　应中国人民解放军总参谋长张万年的邀请，以色列国防军总参谋长艾胡德·巴拉克抵达北京，开始对中国为期10天的访问。

10月3日　国务院副总理邹家华一行抵达特拉维夫，开始对以色列进行正式访问。访问期间，以色列总理拉宾同邹家华副总理举行了工作会谈。以色列总统魏茨曼会见了国务院副总理邹家华。

11月23日　国务院副总理邹家华在京会见了来访的以色列通信、科学艺术部部长舒拉梅特·艾劳妮女士一行。

1995 年

3月24日　以色列教育文化和体育部部长阿姆农·鲁宾斯坦一行应邀抵京，开始对中国进行访问。

4月12日　中国国务院总理李鹏在京会见来访的以色列财政部长肖哈特。

4月18日　应中国共产党的邀请，由尼西姆·兹维利总书记率领的以色列工党代表团抵达北京，开始对中国进行访问。访问期间，时任中共中央总书记、国家主席江泽民在京会见了兹维利一行。

5月27日　应以色列议会外交和国防委员会的邀请，由朱良率领的全国人大外事委员会代表团抵达耶路撒冷，开始对以色列进行为期一周的友好访问。

9月26日　应以色列工业和贸易部部长哈里什的邀

请，中国对外贸易和经济合作部部长吴仪一行到达耶路撒冷，开始对以色列进行正式访问。访问期间，以色列总理拉宾会见了吴仪一行。两国签署了财政议定书及经济贸易混合委员会第二次会议纪要以及有关电子通信、医疗设备、食品加工和高新技术转让等方面的 4 项合作协议。

10 月 23 日　时任中国国家主席江泽民在纽约会见了以色列总理拉宾。

11 月 5 日　时任中国国家主席江泽民致电以色列总统埃泽尔·魏茨曼，对以色列总理伊扎克·拉宾不幸遇害表示哀悼。同日，时任中国国务院总理李鹏致电以色列代总理西蒙·佩雷斯，对拉宾遇害表示哀悼。

11 月 6 日　中国国务院副总理兼外长钱其琛前往以色列国驻华使馆吊唁遇害逝世的以色列国总理伊扎克·拉宾。同日，中国政府委派正在以色列访问的国家计委副主任甘子玉作为中国政府特使出席在以色列为拉宾总理举行的国葬。

1996 年

3 月 5 日　时任中国国务院总理李鹏对近日来以色列境内连续发生几起恐怖爆炸事件，向以色列总理佩雷斯发去慰问电。

5 月 4 日　中国国务院副总理兼外长钱其琛在京会见来访的由以色列司法部长戴维·利巴伊率领的以色列司法代表团。

9 月 11 日　中以关系促进会在以色列的特拉维夫市宣告成立。

11 月 1 日　应中国全国人大外事委员会邀请，以议会外交和防务委员会主席乌兹·兰多为团长的以色列议会代表团抵京，开始对中国进行友好访问。

1997 年

1 月 2 日　中国人民对外友好协会会长齐怀远及其一行抵达耶路撒冷,开始对以色列进行友好访问。访问期间,齐怀远一行分别会见了以色列总统魏茨曼、外长利维和财政部长梅里多尔。

1 月 4 日　以色列和中国关系促进会在特拉维夫举行集会,庆祝以中建交五周年。

2 月 17 日　应以色列政府的邀请,中国国务院副总理李岚清率领中国政府代表团抵达耶路撒冷,开始对以色列进行访问。访问期间,以色列总统魏茨曼会见了李岚清副总理。中以双方签署了关于海关行政互助和合作的协议。

2 月 24~26 日　应中国国务院副总理兼外长钱其琛邀请,以色列国副总理兼外交部长戴维·利维对中国进行正式访问。访问期间,中国国家主席江泽民和国务院总理李鹏在京分别会见了戴维·利维外长。

3 月 30 日　以色列第一副总理兼外长戴维·利维在耶路撒冷会见来访的中国交通部部长黄镇东。会见结束后,双方签署了《中华人民共和国政府和以色列国政府海运协定》。

4 月 1 日　以色列工党主席、前总理佩雷斯在特拉维夫会见了来访的中国对外联络部部长李淑铮以及由她率领的中国共产党代表团。

11 月 2 日　应以色列政府邀请,中共中央政治局委员、书记处书记温家宝率团抵达耶路撒冷,开始对以色列进行为期 4 天的友好访问。访问期间,以色列总统魏茨曼会见了温家宝一行。

11 月 12 日　中国—以色列农业联合委员会首次会议

在耶路撒冷举行。中以两国签署了一项关于实施一批农业合作项目的谅解备忘录，双方同意进一步加强在农业领域的合作。

12 月 18 日　中国国务院副总理兼外长钱其琛即日离京，赴黎巴嫩、叙利亚、以色列、巴勒斯坦、埃及和南非访问。12 月 22 日，以色列总理内塔尼亚胡在耶路撒冷会见来访的中国副总理兼外长钱其琛。

1998 年

4 月 6 日　中国国务院副总理钱其琛在京会见来访的以色列前总理、以中关系促进会名誉会长西蒙·佩雷斯一行。

5 月 25~28 日　应时任中国国务院总理朱镕基的邀请，以色列国政府总理本雅明·内塔尼亚胡对中国进行正式访问。访问期间，朱镕基总理与内塔尼亚胡总理举行了会谈。江泽民主席会见了内塔尼亚胡总理。

9 月 2 日　中国国家主席、中央军委主席江泽民在京会见来访的以色列国防部长伊扎克·莫迪凯。

10 月 19 日　中国全国人大常委会委员长李鹏在京会见来访的由院长阿哈龙·巴拉克率领的以色列最高法院代表团。

1999 年

4 月 25 日至 5 月 1 日　应中国国家主席江泽民的邀请，以色列总统埃泽尔·魏茨曼对中国进行国事访问。访问期间，江泽民主席、朱镕基总理和全国人大常委会委员长李鹏分别会见了魏茨曼总统。

10 月 6 日　以色列总统魏茨曼在耶路撒冷总统府举行盛大招待会，庆祝新中国成立 50 周年。

11 月 15 日至 12 月 4 日　中国全国人大常委会委员

长李鹏应邀对毛里求斯、南非、肯尼亚、以色列、巴勒斯坦、阿曼六国进行正式友好访问。

11 月 25 日　应以色列政府和议会的邀请，李鹏委员长抵达耶路撒冷开始对以色列进行正式友好访问。访问期间，李鹏委员长分别会见了以色列总统魏茨曼、以色列议长伯格和以色列前总理佩雷斯。

2000 年

3 月 1 日　中国外经贸部部长石广生和以色列工贸部长拉恩·科亨即日在京草签了《中以工业技术研究开发合作框架协议》，并签署了中以经贸混委会第三次会议纪要。

4 月 12~27 日　中国国家主席江泽民应邀对以色列、巴勒斯坦、土耳其、希腊和南非进行国事访问。在以色列访问期间，江泽民主席会见了魏茨曼总统并与巴拉克总理举行会谈。两国政府还签署了《中华人民共和国政府与以色列国政府在工业技术研究及开发领域合作框架协议》和《中华人民共和国教育部与以色列国教育部教育合作协议》。

8 月 16 日　中国外长唐家璇在京同来访的以色列地区合作部长西蒙·佩雷斯举行会谈，双方就中东和谈特别是巴以和谈交换了看法。

2001 年

2 月 21 日　应以色列外长本-阿米的要求，中国外交部长唐家璇今天与本-阿米通电话，就中东形势和中东和平进程等问题交换意见。

9 月 10 日　应以中关系促进协会的邀请，中国人民对外友好协会会长陈昊苏及其一行即日抵达以色列，开始对其进行为期 3 天的访问。访问期间，以色列总统卡察夫会见了陈昊苏及其一行。

2002 年

2 月 27 日　以色列总统卡察夫在耶路撒冷总统府举行招待会，庆祝以色列与中国建交 10 周年。

3 月 24~26 日　以色列国副总理兼外长西蒙·佩雷斯应邀对中国进行正式访问。访问期间，中国国务院总理朱镕基、外交部部长钱其琛分别会见了佩雷斯副总理。

6 月 4 日　中国国务院副总理钱其琛在阿拉木图会见了出席"亚洲相互协作与信任措施会议"领导人会议的以色列政府代表团团长、副总理兼住房和建筑部长夏兰斯基，双方着重就中东局势交换了意见。

8 月 12 日　中国以色列旱作农业示范培训中心项目谅解备忘录签字仪式在北京举行。

9 月 15 日　正在联合国出席第五十七届联合国大会的中国外交部部长唐家璇会见以色列副总理兼外长佩雷斯，双方就双边关系和中东问题等交换了意见。

2003 年

1 月 5 日　以色列特拉维夫发生自杀性爆炸袭击事件，3 名中国工人在袭击事件中遇难。1 月 14 日，以色列外交部和内政部在特拉维夫为遇难的 3 名中国工人举行遗体告别仪式。

5 月 18~22 日　中国中东问题特使王世杰对以色列和巴勒斯坦进行了访问。访问期间，王世杰分别会见了以色列外长沙洛姆、前总理佩雷斯和巴勒斯坦民族权力机构主席阿拉法特、总理阿巴斯和外长沙阿斯。在与双方的会见会谈中，王世杰就中东和平进程和"路线图"计划提出了中方的五点主张。

10 月 18 日　中国中东问题特使王世杰大使即日起开始对叙利亚、埃及、沙特、以色列和巴勒斯坦进行访问。

12 月 14~20 日　应中国国家主席胡锦涛的邀请，以色列总统摩西·卡察夫对中国进行国事访问。访问期间，中国国家主席胡锦涛、全国人大常委会委员长吴邦国、国务院总理温家宝在京分别会见了卡察夫总统。

2004 年

11 月 25 日　中国和以色列两国政府财政合作议定书签字仪式在北京举行。

12 月 28 日　以色列总统卡察夫和总理沙龙在耶路撒冷分别会见正在以色列访问的中国国务委员唐家璇。

2005 年

3 月 30 日　中国中东问题特使王世杰即日起访问巴勒斯坦、以色列和埃及，就当前中东形势以及中东和平进程等问题与有关各方交换意见。

6 月 20 日　以色列总理沙龙在耶路撒冷会见了来访的中国外交部部长李肇星。

8 月 31 日　以色列副总理、工党主席西蒙·佩雷斯在特拉维夫会见来访的由中联部部长王家瑞率领的中共代表团。

9 月 14 日　中国中东问题特使王世杰即日起将访问巴勒斯坦、以色列、约旦、埃及和摩洛哥，就当前的中东局势、推动和平进程等问题与有关方面交换意见。

11 月 1 日　以色列政府正式承认中国完全市场经济地位。同日，中国商务部副部长魏建国与以色列工贸劳动部总司长迪努尔在耶路撒冷共同签署《关于加强经济贸易合作的备忘录》。

2006 年

8 月 6 日　中国中东问题特使孙必干即日起访问叙利亚、黎巴嫩、以色列、埃及和沙特，就地区形势特别是黎以冲突等问题与有关方面交换看法。

12月16日　中国外交部部长李肇星在京会见来华出席"巴以和平人士研讨会"的以色列前司法部长贝林。

2007年

1月9~11日　应中国国务院总理温家宝邀请，以色列总理埃胡德·奥尔默特对中国进行正式访问。此次访问是奥尔默特当选以色列总理后首次访华。访问期间，中国国家主席胡锦涛和温家宝总理分别与奥尔默特会见和会谈，双方就中以关系和共同关心的国际和地区问题交换了意见。

5月25日　为庆祝中国和以色列建交15周年而举办的"中国文化节"在以色列耶路撒冷国际会议中心隆重开幕。

7月19日　以色列总统佩雷斯在耶路撒冷会见来访的中国中东问题特使孙必干。

10月28~30日　应中国外交部长杨洁篪的邀请，以色列第一副总理兼外交部长齐皮·利夫尼对中国进行正式访问。

10月29日　中国国家外国专家局与以色列驻华使馆在北京举行仪式，庆祝中国国家外国专家局中国国际人才交流协会与以色列外交部国际合作中心开展合作15周年。

2008年

7月10日　以色列总统办公室发表声明正式宣布，以色列总统佩雷斯接受邀请，将于8月8日出席北京奥运会开幕式。

10月17日　中共中央政治局委员、书记处书记、中宣部部长刘云山在京会见来访的由以色列副议长、工党对外关系负责人克莉特·阿维泰尔率领的以色列工党代表团。

11月19日　中共中央政治局委员、书记处书记、中宣部部长刘云山应邀率中国共产党代表团即日离京，开始对伊朗、巴林、埃及、以色列和巴勒斯坦进行友好访问。

2009 年

1 月 14 日　此间正在中东地区访问的中国中东问题特使孙必干即日在耶路撒冷会见以色列总统佩雷斯，双方就当前加沙局势交换了看法。

4 月 23 日　以色列总统佩雷斯在耶路撒冷会见到访的中国外交部部长杨洁篪。

3 月 20 日至 7 月 4 日　中国中东问题特使吴思科先后对埃及、巴勒斯坦、以色列、约旦、叙利亚、黎巴嫩和俄罗斯进行访问，就当前的中东地区局势与有关方面交换看法。

10 月 28 日　以色列总统佩雷斯在耶路撒冷会见来访的由中共中央委员、宁夏回族自治区党委书记陈建国率领的中国共产党代表团。

2010 年

3 月 24 日　此间正在以色列访问的中国国务院副总理回良玉即日在耶路撒冷会见了以色列总统佩雷斯。

4 月 26 日　中国国务院副总理回良玉在京会见来访的以色列社会事务部长赫尔佐克一行。

5 月 10 日　中国国务院副总理李克强在京会见来访的以色列财政部长施泰尼茨。双方就中以双边关系和中以经贸、科技合作等问题交换了意见。

6 月 6 日　正在以色列访问的中国中东问题特使吴思科在耶路撒冷会见以色列外交部长利伯曼，双方就中以双边关系和中东和谈等热点问题交换了意见。

10 月 11~23 日　中国中东问题特使吴思科先后对约旦、以色列、巴勒斯坦、土耳其和埃及进行访问，就中东问题的最新进展与有关方面交换看法。

11月7日　以色列总统佩雷斯在耶路撒冷会见来访的中共中央政治局委员、天津市委书记张高丽率领的中共代表团。

12月13日　中国国务委员兼国防部长梁光烈在京会见来访的以色列海军司令埃利泽·马罗姆。

2011年

2月28日　以色列总理内塔尼亚胡在耶路撒冷会见率中国政府经贸代表团来访的中国商务部长陈德铭。

3月2日　以色列总统佩雷斯在耶路撒冷会见了陈德铭部长一行。

3月23日至4月2日　中国中东问题特使吴思科先后对以色列、巴勒斯坦、叙利亚、黎巴嫩、卡塔尔进行访问。访问期间，就中东和平进程和当前地区局势与有关各方交换意见。

6月14日　中国国务院副总理李克强在京会见来访的以色列副总理兼国防部长巴拉克一行。

6月21日　以色列总统佩雷斯在耶路撒冷会见了率中国政府文化代表团来访的文化部长蔡武。6月22日，以色列总理内塔尼亚胡在耶路撒冷会见了蔡武部长一行。

2012年

1月24日　中国国家主席胡锦涛与以色列总统佩雷斯互致贺电，热烈庆祝两国建交20周年。同日，中国国务院总理温家宝和以色列总理内塔尼亚胡也互致贺电。

2月19日　正在以色列访问的中国中东问题特使吴思科在耶路撒冷分别会见了以副总理兼外交部长利伯曼和以总理以巴和谈特使莫尔霍，就共同关心的重大问题交换了意见。

3月15~22日　以色列副总理兼外交部长阿维格多·利伯曼应邀对中国进行正式访问。访问期间，中国国家副主席习近平会见了来访的以色列副总理兼外长利伯曼。

4月4日　中国全国人大常委会副委员长、中国国际交流协会会长周铁农即日到访以色列。访问期间，周铁农分别会见了以色列议会副议长马贾德莱、副总理兼外交部长利伯曼、议会以中友好小组主席罗特姆等。

5月22日　中国国家副主席、中央军委副主席习近平在京会见来访的以色列国防军总参谋长甘茨。

2013年

4月29日　正在以色列访问的中国中东问题特使吴思科即日在耶路撒冷分别与以色列外交部副部长埃尔金和负责以巴谈判事务的司法部长利夫尼举行会晤，就中东和平进程等地区问题深入交换了意见。

5月6~10日　以色列国总理本雅明·内塔尼亚胡应邀对中国进行正式访问。访问期间，中国国家主席习近平会见了内塔尼亚胡总理。

5月26~28日　中国藏学家代表团对以色列进行访问。访问期间，代表团与以色列政府官员和学者进行了深入交流，介绍了西藏在和平解放——特别是改革开放以来所取得的成就。

6月17~19日　中国全国政协副主席、中国人民争取和平与裁军协会会长韩启德率团对以色列进行访问。访问期间，韩启德出席了第五届以色列总统会议，并分别会见了以色列总统佩雷斯和以色列议长埃德尔斯坦。

10月21~23日　中共中央政治局委员、中宣部部长刘奇葆率中共代表团对以色列进行访问。访问期间，刘奇葆会见了以色列总统佩雷斯。

上图	耶路撒冷国际工艺美术节特设"中国馆"（一） 新华社记者　尹栋逊　摄，耶路撒冷，2011 年 8 月 23 日
下图	"新雅乐"唱响以色列 新华社记者　尹栋逊　摄，贝特锡安，2010 年 9 月 28 日

上图	**以色列：走进孔子课堂（一）** 新华社记者 尹栋逊 摄，特拉维夫，2010 年 11 月 30 日
下图	**以色列举办能源科技展览会** 新华社记者 尹栋逊 摄，特拉维夫，2010 年 10 月 27 日

上图	**中国邮品亮相耶路撒冷国际邮票展（一）** 新华社记者 尹栋逊 摄，耶路撒冷，2010 年 11 月 22 日
下图	**中国邮品亮相耶路撒冷国际邮票展（二）** 新华社记者 尹栋逊 摄，耶路撒冷，2010 年 11 月 22 日

中国益阳市与以色列佩塔提克瓦市结为友好城市
新华社记者 尹栋逊 摄，佩塔提克瓦（以色列），2010 年 11 月 4 日

以色列举行"汉语桥"比赛
新华社记者 尹栋逊 摄，耶路撒冷，2011 年 4 月 1 日

孔子课堂走进以色列校园
新华社记者 尹栋逊 摄，特拉维夫，2011 年 3 月 24 日

以色列：走进孔子课堂（二）
新华社记者 尹栋逊 摄，特拉维夫，2010 年 11 月 30 日

上图	耶路撒冷国际工艺美术节特设"中国馆"（二）
	新华社记者 尹栋逊 摄，耶路撒冷，2011 年 8 月 23 日
下图	耶路撒冷国际工艺美术节特设"中国馆"（三）
	新华社记者 尹栋逊 摄，耶路撒冷，2011 年 8 月 23 日

上图	中国产电动公共汽车驶上特拉维夫街头（一）
	新华社记者　尹栋逊　摄，特拉维夫，2013 年 8 月 7 日
下图	中国产电动公共汽车驶上特拉维夫街头（二）
	新华社记者　尹栋逊　摄，特拉维夫，2013 年 8 月 7 日

以色列总统出席中国大使馆国庆招待会
新华社记者　尹栋逊　摄，特拉维夫，2012 年 10 月 18 日

以色列大学生角逐"汉语桥"比赛
新华社记者 尹栋逊 摄,特拉维夫,2012 年 5 月 11 日

上图	《功夫诗·九卷》亮相耶路撒冷（一） 新华社记者　尹栋逊　摄，耶路撒冷，2012 年 5 月 31 日
下图	《功夫诗·九卷》亮相耶路撒冷（二） 新华社记者　尹栋逊　摄，耶路撒冷，2012 年 5 月 31 日

上图	"南京之夜"文艺演出在特拉维夫举行
	新华社记者 尹栋逊 摄，耶路撒冷，2012 年 5 月 21 日
下图	"财神"送祝福
	新华社记者 尹栋逊 摄，特拉维夫，2013 年 2 月 20 日

中以青年举行联谊活动（一）
新华社记者 尹栋逊 摄，耶路撒冷，2012 年 12 月 14 日

上图	**中以青年举行联谊活动（二）**
	新华社记者　尹栋逊　摄，耶路撒冷，2012 年 12 月 14 日
下图	**冰雕见证浪漫**
	新华社记者　尹栋逊　摄，耶路撒冷，2012 年 3 月 5 日

中以钢琴新秀大师班在耶路撒冷举行
新华社记者 尹栋逊 摄，耶路撒冷，2013 年 1 月 1 日

Chief Editor

YANG Guang Director, Senior Researcher, Institute of West Asian and African Studies, Chinese Academy of Social Sciences (CASS); Director, professor, doctoral dissertation advisor, Department of West Asian and African Studies, CASS Graduate School; President, Chinese Association of Middle East Studies. Areas of specialty include economic development and energy security.

Modernization of Jewish Culture, A History of Jewish Religion, Israel's Path to Prosperity.

XU Xin Professor, doctoral dissertation advisor, Department of Philosophy and Religious Studies, Nanjing University; Director, Diane and Guilford Glazer Institute of Jewish Studies, Nanjing University. BA in English, Nanjing University; MA in Linguistics, Northeastern Illinois University. Has been teaching at Nanjing University since 1977. Areas of specialty include: Jewish religion, culture, history, and the history of Jewish Diaspora in China. Major publications include: *Jewish Encyclopedia* (co-editor), *Understanding Anti-Semitism, History of Western Culture, The Jews of Kaifeng, China: History, Culture, and Religion* (written in English, published in the US), and more than 50 articles, many of which written in English and published abroad.

YIN Gang   Senior Researcher, Institute of East Asian and African Studies, Chinese Academy of Social Sciences; Member, Standing Committee, Chinese Association of Middle East Studies. Has received many awards for outstanding scholarship. Areas of specialty include: Middle East international relations, Middle Eastern ethnic groups and religions, China-Middle Eastern relations, Middle East policy of major countries, Jewish societies and Muslim societies in ancient China.

FU Youde   Director, the Center for Judaic and Inter-Religious Studies, Shandong University, a Ministry of Education-designated Key Research Base for Humanities and Social Sciences; Chair, Department of Religious Studies, Institute of Philosophy and Social Development; doctoral dissertation advisor; Ministry of Education "Taishan

Scholar" Distinguished Professor; Deputy Director, Ministry of Education Pedagogical Council for the Teaching of Philosophy; Chair, Shandong Provincial Philosophical Society; Vice-chair, Chinese Society of Religious Studies in China. Editor, Jewish Studies. Areas of specialty include: Jewish religion and philosophy, comparative studies of Judaism and Confucianism, history of western philosophy. Major publications include: *Collection of Chinese Translation of Well-known Jewish Cultural Works* (editor), *History of Jewish Philosophy* (editor). Was invited by Israeli President Shimon Peres to participate in the Israeli Presidential Conference in 2008 and 2009.

PAN Guang Vice-chair, Shanghai Research Center for International Affairs; Senior Researcher, professor, doctoral dissertation advisor, Shanghai Academy of Social Sciences; Director, Shanghai

Center for Jewish Studies; Director, Center of Shanghai Cooperation Organization Studies; Vice president, Chinese Association of Middle East Studies; President, Shanghai Association for World History, and Shanghai Association for United Nations Studies; Member, Application Review Panel, National Philosophy and Social Science Fund; Expert on Soft Science, Office of Anti-Terrorism Leadership Team; member, Shanghai Expert Committee on Informatization; Deputy Director, Center for Anti-Terrorism Studies. In Nov. 2005, former UN Secretary-General Kofi Annan appointed him a member of the High-Level Group for the UN Alliance of Civilizations (AoC). Then in 2008, Kofi Annan appointed him Ambassador of the AoC. Areas of specialty include Shanghai Cooperation Organization, Jewish and Israeli studies, Middle Eastern and European issues, Russian and Central Asia, Silk Road and Asian-

European relations, ethnic religions, civilizational dialogues, anti-terrorism. He received the James Friend Annual Memorial Award for Sino-Jewish Studies in 1993, the Special Award for Canadian Studies (especially for research on Canadian Jews from China) in 1996, the Sankt Peterburg-300 Medal for Contribution to China-Russia Relations awarded by President Putin in 2004, and the Austria Holocaust Memorial Award in 2006. He has published more than 10 books and more than 100 articles on a variety of topics. His books include *The Jews in Asia: Comparative Perspective*, *The Jews in Shanghai*, *The Jews in China*, and many others, many of which have been translated into other languages.

Preface[*]

YANG Guang[**]

You are holding in your hand an edited volume on China-Israel relations, a topic that is at once old and fresh. It is old because the intercourse between the Chinese and the Jewish civilizations has a long history, going back over a millennium, and it is also fresh because both peoples have as of yet little knowledge and understanding of that history. It was not until about three decades ago when large-scale studies on this topic began in China.

Jews, in particular Jewish merchants, were

[*] Translated by Liang Fan.

[**] Director, Senior Researcher, Institute of West Asian and African Studies, Chinese Academy of Social Sciences.

arriving in China through the land and maritime routes of the Silk Road in large numbers as early as around 8th century A.D. There was a Jewish presence in many cities, including Xi'an, Luoyang, Dunhuang, Kaifeng, Guangzhou, Hangzhou, Ningbo, Beijing, Quanzhou, Yangzhou and Nanjing. A number of sizeable Jewish communities had developed by the time of the Song Dynasty, the Kaifeng Jewish community being the best-known among them. The Kaifeng Jewish community reached its peak during the Ming Dynasty, when it could claim as many as 500 families. Jews living in China at that time could be found working in a variety of trades and professions, including business, crafts, agriculture and medicine. Some even took the imperial examination and worked in the government. In this friendly and hospitable environment that ancient China offered, they learned the language, changed their names, and intermarried with the Chinese, and by the early 19th century, they had become fully integrated into the Chinese society.

More recently, there have been multiple waves of Jewish immigrants that have led to the emergence of Jewish communities in many cities across the country. Beginning in the 19th century, a group of Jews moved to China from the Ottoman Empire and India both in order to protect themselves from some of the empire's anti-semitic polices and in pursuit of business opportunities. Between 1880s and early 20th century, waves of anti-Semitism in Russia and in Eastern Europe and the outbreak of the Russian Revolution and civil war drove many Jews to cross Siberia and move en masse to China's northeast and further inland areas. The Tianjin and Harbin Jewish communities, among others, formed in this period. The rise of Facism in the 20th century was a disaster of extraordinary magnitude for both the Chinese and the Jewish people. Not only did the Chinese condemn the Nazi policy towards Jews in the most certain and harshest of terms, but also did they, particularly starting in the 1930s, admit numerous European Jews who had fled Nazi persecution and took refuge in Shanghai. Many member of the Jewish diaspora in China also directly participated in varying ways in China's war against Japanese aggression. Even though these Jews had all left China by the 1970s, and Jewish communities in China have now become a thing of the past, this history of friendship and mutual assistance between the Chinese and the Jewish people, the memories and love of China this history has left these Jews and their descendants with have been instrumental in forging a solid foundation for further development of the relationship between the two peoples.

Despite the fact that, because of the complexity

of international politics, China and Israel did not establish formal diplomatic relations until 1992, many years after the founding of the People's Republic of China in 1949, ties between the two countries have grown steadily and begun a new chapter. As of this writing, four Israeli prime ministers and four presidents have visited China. Visits to Israel have been made by Chinese presidents and chairmen of the standing committee of the National People's Congress. A series of economic and trade cooperation agreements have been signed. China exports electronics, textile, clothing, shoes and China products to Israel in exchange for potassium fertilizer, electronics, medical equipment, and electronic communications products. Trade volume grew from USD 50 million to USD 10 billion between 1992 and 2012. By 2012, the total value of construction projects in Israel that had been contracted to Chinese companies stood at USD 32 million.

Furthermore, the two countries have engaged in fruitful exchanges and cooperation in areas such as agriculture, biotechnology, IT, new materials, water resource management, nanotechnology, healthcare and medicine, renewable energy, among others. Growth can also be seen in social and cultural intercourse between China and Israel. For example, more than 50,000 Israeli tourists have visited China each year recently, and the Israeli Ministry of Education has included Mandarin Chinese in the country's middle school curriculum. China has played a positive and active role in promoting the Middle East peace process, and has designated a Middle East envoy starting 2002 who oversees the affairs of the region and assists relevant parties in finding a resolution to regional conflict.

Studies of Jewish civilization first began in

the late 19th and early 20th century in China. But complex international and domestic politics arrested the development of both research and translation work in this area until the 1970s. Very few things were published. Largely because of this, for the vast majority of the Chinese people, both the Jewish people and Israel were for a long time something of a mystery.

In the late 1970s, the ideological grip on intellectual life in China began to loosen, and the country adopted reform and opening-up policies, both of which helped to facilitate the development of the social sciences in general, and China's Jewish and Israel studies in particular. Chinese scholars have become especially interested in the Jewish people's turbulent and intriguing history, past exchanges and mutual influences between the two civilizations, and Israel's remarkable achievements in economic development. Starting in the 1980s, scholars studying Jews and Israel began to form informal groups in cities such as Shanghai, Nanjing, Beijing, Kunming and Xi'an. After 1988, a number of research centers and institutes specializing in Jewish and Israeli studies have been established, including Center for Jewish Studies Shanghai, Diane and Guilford Glazer Institute of Jewish Studies of Nanjing University, Institute of Jewish Studies of Henan University, Center for Judaic and Inter-Religious Studies of Shandong University, and Harbin Jewish Research Center. They continue to be the stronghold for Jewish research and studies in China.

Besides these, organizations such as the Institute of West Asian and African Studies, Institute of World Religions, and Institute of Foreign Literature of Chinese Academy of Social Sciences, China Institutes of Contemporary International Relations, and Yunnan University,

Northwest University, Fudan University, Shenzhen University and Wuhan University also feature Jewish and Israeli studies scholars among their faculty and research fellows. In 1985, the first Hebrew language program ever in China was launched at Peking University.

After formalization in 1992, China-Israel relations have grown rapidly, and fueled the advancement of Jewish and Israel studies in China, which have seen surges of interest. As the field of research vision expands, gaps in research work have continually been filled. While Jewish studies in China in the 1980 mostly focused on Jews in ancient China, in particular the Jewish community in Kaifeng, and introducing, often through translation, to Chinese scholars research results by international scholars, today they cover a wide range of topics, including but not limited to the Jewish communities in Kaifeng, Shanghai, Harbin,

Tianjin, Hong Kong, among other places, both in ancient and modern times, Jewish studies in the US, Jewish history, philosophy and religion, Israeli politics, diplomacy, economics, society, culture, education, military and the study of individual figures. Among these, studies in Jewish history, Jewish religion and philosophy, in Jewish literature and Israel are still more advanced both in breadth and depth. Chinese scholars in these areas have not only maintained close exchanges and collaboration among themselves, they have also been increasingly in contact with the international academic community through exchange and collaboration programs. A growing number of Chinese scholars in these areas have earned international reputation for their outstanding work. China's Jewish and Israeli studies are indeed on the cusp of an exciting era of spectacular growth.

Contributors to this volume include both Chinese

and Israeli scholars. The Chinese contributors are all leading experts in this subject as well as in the other areas of research in which they are engaged. While the limited space can hardly be expected to do justice to the scope, depth and sophistication of the results of China's Jewish and Israeli studies, the book will nonetheless provide its readers with an insightful and informative overview.

2014.3.27

Contents

Culture

Jewish Studies in China

Characteristics of Jewish Culture

A Comparative Study of Hebrew Prophets and Confucian Scholars

Notes on Israel

Visit to China Again

Jewish Studies in China[*]

XU Xin[**]

I. Stages of Study

（Ⅰ）1949-1978

Strictly speaking, because of ideological and political interference in academic research, Jewish studies had not yet begun in this period. During this time, very few books and articles on Jewish topics were published, most being reports on the situation in the Middle East and the conflict in the region. While these reports did contain some analysis, they mostly

[*] Translated by Andrew H. Keller, polished by Liang Fan.
[**] Professor, doctoral dissertation advisor, Department of Philosophy and Religious Studies, Nanjing University; Director, Diane and Guilford Glazer Institute of Jewish Studies, Nanjing University.

served political and policy purposes, and largely adhered to a Cold War mentality. Their conclusions seldom had any scholarly merit, and few articles touching on Israeli society were available. As China and Israel had no diplomatic relations, any writing on the topic was seriously wanting in objectivity and accuracy. This of course had much to do with the political conditions in China at the time. Pan Guang had summarized the situation as such: "Due to the impact of the 'decade of leftist thinking' and the Cultural Revolution, China had entered a period of closedness and isolation. The development of Jewish studies was severely restricted." [1] This was clearly a quiet period for Jewish studies in China. In view of this, little meaningful analysis of the research work during this period is possible.

(II) 1979-2009

Reform and opening-up re-launched Jewish studies and China. However, the first decade (1979-1988) was a period of recovery and served as a stage of mental preparation, personnel training, and academic accumulation. With China's deepening of reforms and further opening-up to the outside world, an academic atmosphere favorable for Jewish studies began to form in China, and scholars began to recognize the existence and significance of this topic.

In terms of research results, the first area to attract attention was the study of Jews in China. There is evidence of a

---

[1]   Pan Guang (eds), 2008. *Thirty Years of Jewish Studies in China: 1978-2008,* Shanghai: Shanghai Social Sciences Press, p. 3.

Jewish presence in China going back to the Tang Dynasty, and the well-known Kaifeng Jews have lived in China as a community since the Song Dynasty. Starting in the mid-19th century, after the gunboats of Western powers forced open the gates to China, nearly 40,000 Jews came to China and lived in different cities. Their experiences have been closely influenced by changes in these cities, something which is not lost on the Chinese people. By the 1970s, the Jews of Kaifeng had basically integrated into the Chinese society, and those that had arrived after the mid-1900s had left. But the Chinese people have not forgotten the history of the Jewish people in China in this period. Early in the recovery of Chinese academia, this was a natural focus of study. The earliest published research papers include "On Several Historical Issues related to Jews in China" by Pan Guangdan. [1] Several years later, Sidney Shapiro, a Jewish expert who had become a Chinese citizen, published "I Hope Chinese Scholars Will Study the History of Chinese Jews." [2]

Books and articles about Jews in Shanghai began to appear in considerable numbers, [3] attracting the attention

---

[1] Published in *China Social Science*, 1980, Vol. 3. It should be noted that Pan Guangdan had already passed away at this point. The article is a portion of his research from the 1950s that had not previously been published. A book of the same name was published exclusively by Peking University Press in 1983.

[2] See *China Foreign Relations Historical Society Reports*, 1983.

[3] Mainly Zhang Zhongli and Chen Zengnian's *Sassoon Group in Old China*, Beijing: People's Publishing House, 1985.

of many Chinese scholars. In a sense, we can say that studies of Jews in China opened up a new era of Chinese Jewish studies. At the same time, papers were also being published on other aspects of Jewish studies, including Yang Shen's "On Soviet Jews" (*Foreign Studies*, 1981, Vol. 3), Liu Bangyi's "The Anti-Nazi Revolt of Jews in Warsaw" (*Journal of Foreign Studies*, 1982, Vol. 7), Zhao Fusan's "Introduction to Judaism" (*Sources on World Religions,* 1983, Vol. 3), Pan Guang's "The Rise and Fall of the Ancient Jewish State" (*Historical Knowledge*, 1984, Vol. 1), Yu Chongjian's "From the Rise of Zionism to the Founding of Israel" (*West Asia and Africa*, 1984, Vol. 18), Wang Chi's "Discussion of 'Exodus'" (*Trends in World Historical Studies,* 1984, Vol. 3), and Wang Qingyu's "The Jews of Old Shanghai" (*Research Quarterly*, 1982, Vol. 2). Wang Zhongyi's *History of Judaism,* a booklet published as a stand-alone volume (Commercial Press, 1984) and Abba Eban's *Jewish History*, translated by Yan Ruisong of China's Northwestern University (China Social Sciences Press), were scholarly in nature. The publication of Abba Eban's *Jewish History* was significant for the period, and had far reaching impact. Nearly all modern Chinese scholars engaged in Jewish studies have learned the history of the Jewish people in detail for the first time from this book, an experience that lays the foundation for their subsequent research.

Of course, a number of books on the Holocaust, the Arab-Israeli conflict, biographies of famous Israelis, and so forth were published in China during this period, attesting to the range of topics in Jewish studies in which Chinese scholar were taking an interest. These books caused more ordinary Chinese, particularly Chinese youth, to become interested in the Jewish people and to begin following related issues. Several Chinese researchers who later played a key role in the field of Jewish studies grew up in this atmosphere.

Gu Xiaoming's two 1987 publications- "Jewish Studies and Its Research Field of Vision" (*Foreign Languages,* 1987, Vol. 3) and "On the Significance of Jewish Culture in Cultural Studies" (*Fudan Journal*, 1987, Vol. 3)-provide a window on the understanding and reflection among Chinese scholars of Jewish studies as an academic field. The articles called for the establishment of a system of Jewish studies for promoting the development of Jewish studies in China. Practicing what he preached, Gu Xiaoming wrote his doctoral dissertation [1] on Jewish studies.

Jewish studies, as a field of studies that is academically significant and worthy, can be said to have begun by this time in China. Specifically, we might say it began at the end of the 1980s and reached a high point after 2000. What progress had been made in Chinese Jewish studies in these 20 years? What were their distinguishing features? In what areas were the main achievements? The answers will serve as the basis for the criterion for assessing China's Jewish studies.

---

[1] See Gu Xiaoming, 1990. *Judaism: A Culture Full of "Paradox,"* Hangzhou: Zhejiang People's Publishing House.

II. The Establishment of Research Institutes

The emergence of Jewish studies academic organizations, groups and institutions is an important indicator of the maturation of Jewish studies in China. These institutions greatly promoted and deepened China's Jewish studies. They include the Center for Jewish Studies Shanghai, the Chinese Society for Jewish Cultural Studies, [1] established in 1988 and 1989, respectively, and the many Jewish cultural studies centers and institutes that have sprung up across China. [2] The formation of these institutions provided organizational guarantee and platform for exchange instrumental for further development of the field.

The Center of Jewish Studies Shanghai, at the Shanghai Academy of Social Sciences is the oldest Chinese institution specializing in Jewish studies, and it has developed into a research community with a solid research base and a distinctive academic character. [3] In 2004, the Shanghai Academy of Social Sciences labeled the center as one specializing in a "niche subject", [4] something that received much attention from the social sciences community in Shanghai and facilitated academic study and international

---

[1] The research association established its own website in the 1990s to report and introduce China's Jewish studies to the international community. Its address is: http://www.servercc.oakton.edu/friend/chinajews.html

[2] They were established in cities such as Shanghai, Nanjing, Bejing, Jinan, Kaifeng, Xi'an, Kunming, Harbin, and others.

[3] Pan Guang, *Thirty years*, p. 2.

[4] Pan Guang, *Thirty years*, p. 19.

scholarly exchanges. Researchers from the center compiled both *Jews in Shanghai* (China Intercontinental Press, 2001 edition) and *The Jews of China* (China Intercontinental Press, 2005 edition), a large book of photographs which received positive reviews. For many years, researchers at the center undertook a number of national and municipal research projects, and many of the papers and books they published proved deeply influential.

The Institute of Jewish Culture at Nanjing University (originally called Nanjing University Center for Jewish Culture) was founded in 1992, the year in which China and Israel established formal diplomatic relations. In addition to carrying out Jewish studies, the most significant feature of the institute is that it makes Nanjing University the first in China to offer a range of courses on Jewish culture, and it recruits and trains masters and doctoral students in Jewish history and culture, as well as Judaic studies. The institute has held three Jewish history and culture summer courses, training more than 100 teachers, researchers, and graduate students from universities and research institutions around China. In addition, the institute is home to what may be China's largest Jewish studies library, which holds more than 10,000 English-language books covering all aspects of Jewish culture. The library provides ample supply of books and references needed for Jewish studies.

The Shandong University Institute for Jewish Culture was established in 1994. In 2004, its application with the Ministry of Education to become a key research base for humanities and social sciences was approved and was renamed "Shandong University Center for Judaism and Inter-Religious Studies." The center has built a research team for Judaism and inter-religious studies that is fairly comprehensive in scope. It has a masters and a Ph.D. program, and leads the country in the study of Jewish philosophy.

Although the Chinese Academy of Social Sciences, China's largest and highest-level research institution, has not established an institute specializing in Jewish culture, its Institute of Western Asian and African Studies, Institute of Foreign Literature, and Institute of World Religions all have researchers dedicated to Jewish issues. Research communities and institutions specializing in Jewish studies have also strongly promoted Jewish studies and exchanges between Chinese and foreign researchers, and helped China better meet international standards for Jewish studies.

III. Voluminous Publications

According to incomplete statistics, over the past 20 years, More than 600 books on Jewish culture and more than a thousand articles have been published in China. [1] This reflects the healthy growth of Jewish studies in China. Some of the most influential and representative publications from the 1990s include:

---

[1] For specific works, see Pan Guang, *Thirty years* Index.

(1) The *Jewish Culture Series,* edited by Gu Xiaoming and published by Shanghai SDX Joint Publishing Company. This was the first series published in China on Jewish culture. Sixteen titles have been published in this series.

(2) *Jewish Encyclopedia* edited by Xu Xin and Ling Jiyao and published in 1993 by Shanghai People's Publishing House. It stands at more than 2 million words and contains some 1,600 entries, and offers the Jewish studies community in China a large, authoritative source of reference on Jewish culture.

(3) *Collection of Chinese Translations of Well-Known Jewish Cultural Works* edited by Fu Youde et al and published by Shandong University Press. The collection has ten volumes. While they are all translations, the selection covers only those works that have "generated a significant impact in the West, especially exceptional academic works in their respective fields." [①] Its academic value is significant.

These works to a certain degree show China's achievements in Jewish studies. If the vast majority of books relating to Jewish studies published in China before the 21st century were translations with new introductions, then the mainstream for Jewish studies within the 21st century is made up of rigorous influential academic works written by Chinese scholars. Among them are *The Arab-Israeli Conflict: Problems and Solutions* edited by Yin Li (International

---

[①] Fu Youde (eds), 1995. *Collection of Chinese Translations of Jewish Cultural Works,* General Preface, p. H.

Cultural Publishing Company, 2002), *Hardship and Rebirth——The Modernization of Jewish Culture* by Zhang Qianhong (Jiangsu People's Publishing House, 2003); *Key Points of Jewish Culture* by Liu Hongyi (Commercial Press, 2004), *Study of Contemporary Israeli Authors* by Zhong Zhiqing (People's Literature Publishing House, 2006), *History of Jewish Culture* by Xu Xin (Peking University Press, 2006), *The Enigmatic Jew* by Xiao Xian (China Workers Press, 2007), *Text of the Hebrew Bible, Historical and Ideological World* by You Bin (Religious Culture Press, 2007), *History of Jewish Philosophy* by You Bin (China Renmin University Press, 2008), *History of the Social Life of Shanghai Jews* by Wang Jian (Shanghai Dictionary Publishing House, 2008), *Jewish Women in Medieval Western Europe* by Wang Shuqing (People's Publishing House, 2009). These are all studies with high academic standards, representing the best of domestic Jewish studies.

In addition, the journal *Jewish Studies* started by Shandong University Institute of Jewish Culture in 2002, and the journal *Jewish and Israeli Studies,* edited by the Shanghai Academy of Social Sciences Shanghai Center for Jewish Studies [1] have become the two chief journals for Jewish studies in China.

---

[1] These two publications are published in the form of serial publication, currently published once a year. The Journal *Jewish Studies* has for several years been named a core academic publication in China.

IV. Jewish Studies at Universities and Colleges

Another important mark of the deepening of Jewish studies in China is the level of research done in and classes offered on this subject in Chinese universities. Almost no Chinese university offered courses on Jewish studies or carried out Jewish research until about 20 years ago. Since then, progress in this area is most prominently reflected in the in the growth in the offering of Jewish studies courses and advanced degrees.

In the mid-1980s, Peking University's Hebrew Language department produced China's first group of young people who had mastered Hebrew. Several years and much training and further education later, some of the graduates of the program have completed their Ph.D. degree and are now active in various Jewish studies institutions across the country. In addition, Nanjing University Institute of Jewish Culture and Shandong University Institute of Jewish Culture have been dedicated to training masters and doctoral students with research focus oriented toward Jewish studies. Over the past decade, each year, these two institutions have selected several MA and Ph.D. students to travel to Israeli or American universities for advanced studies and do research for their doctoral dissertations. Many of the graduates have joined the faculty at various universities, making Jewish studies a new growth point. A "Nazi Holocaust Education and Training Seminar" has been held annually between 2005 and 2009. ^① It was initially sponsored by the Nanjing University Institute for Jewish Culture, and other universities would later join in organizing it. The seminar gives Chinese students an opportunity to form a deeper understanding of the massacre that occurred in World War II and helps combat Holocaust denial. Much can be learned from it for dealing with Japan's denial of the occurrence of the Rape of Nanking. Other Chinese universities are offering education and research opportunities in Jewish history and culture, such as the Jewish history course Henan University Institute of Jewish Studies has been offering to MA students since 2002. The course has distinguished itself by specializing in the study of recent Jewish history and general Israeli history. Yunnan University, Qilu University, Henan Normal University, Northwestern University, Fudan University, Nankai University, Heilongjiang University, Tongji University, Changchun University, Shenzhen University, and Wuhan University all offer courses in Jewish studies. Their research is constantly being published.

V. International Exchanges of Jewish Studies

Another sign that Jewish studies in China are growing both broader and deeper is increasing participation by Chinese scholars in international academic activities and exchanges. Over the past 20 years, Chinese Jewish studies researchers

---

① The symposium has been funded by European and other Jewish research institutions and its teachers are mostly international experts specializing in the Holocaust.

have frequently visited North America, Europe, and Israel. In particular, the heads of the various Jewish studies research communities have been invited to conduct academic research abroad, attend international conferences, organize exhibitions, and give lectures in English. Researchers like the Shanghai Institute of Jewish Studies Director Pan Guang have visited several dozen countries. The Nanjing University Institute of Jewish Culture director Xu Xin has given more than 300 lectures abroad in English. Shandong University Institute of Jewish Culture director Fu Youde travels abroad nearly every year to lecture and conduct exchanges. At the same time, China's Jewish studies institutions invite international Jewish studies scholars each year to China on academic visits. Through these exchanges, Chinese Jewish studies scholars have established wide-ranging and close relationships with Jewish academic circles, institutions, and societies worldwide.

Organizing international symposiums is another important aspect of China's international exchanges in Jewish studies. Large conferences that have been organized include: The First International Symposium on Jewish Culture (1996), International Conference on Diaspora Jews in China (2002), and International Symposium on Judaism (2004) all held in Nanjing; the International Conference on Judaism and Inter-Religious Studies (2006) at Shandong University; Jews in Shanghai (1994) and Jews in Asia: A Comparative Study (2006), Harbin International Conference on Jewish History and Culture (2004), Harbin Jewish History and Culture International Forum (2006), and Harbin International World Jewish Economic and Trade Cooperation Forum (2007) have all featured the participation of a large number of Chinese and foreign scholars. Such activities have helped pushed forward the development of Jewish studies in China and accelerated exchange and cooperation among Chinese and foreign scholars. All this shows that Jewish studies in China have received the attention of the international academic community, in which China can now claim its own voice.

VI. Academic Contribution and Social Impact

（I）Contribution to Middle Eastern Studies

Advances in Jewish studies have allowed the Chinese people to have a better understanding of the Middle East and to develop their own judgment and perspective on the complex conflicts, wars, politics, economics, and cultures of the region. The ability to better understand Middle Eastern cultures and society has established a firm foundation for China's participation in international activities relating to Middle Eastern issues. A number of scholars engaged in Arab studies have also joined in Jewish studies. Many scholars engaged in Jewish studies undertake leadership roles in the Chinese Association of Middle East Studies. Becoming Chinese experts in Middle Eastern issues and giving advice and suggestions for Chinese Middle East policy is the greatest expression of this contribution. Jewish studies have also promoted the specific study of Israel. The books published on Israel cover many aspects of Israeli society, such as *Israeli Politics* edited by Yan Ruisong (Northwestern University Press, 1995), *Israel's Agricultural Development* by Zhao Zhihao (China Agricultural Science and Technology Press, 1996), *The Study on the Economic Development of Middle Eastern Dragon Israel* edited by Yang Guang (Social Sciences Academic Press, 1997), *State of Israel* by Sun Zhengda (Contemporary World Press, 1998), *The Israeli Economy* by Zhao Weiming (Shanghai Foreign Language Education Press, 1998), and *Israeli Education* by Qiu Xing (Chinese Literature and History Press, 2004).

(II) The Promotion of Studies on the History of the Jewish Diaspora in China

The development of Jewish studies in China has promoted the study of the Jewish Diaspora in China. For 20 years, Center of Jewish Studies Shanghai at the Shanghai Academy of Social Sciences has carried out fruitful and rich research through national and provincial research projects. Besides the activities mentioned previously, the "Jews in Shanghai" exhibition curated by the center became an important sightseeing destination for visiting foreign leaders. Since its establishment in 2000, the Harbin Jewish Research Center of the Heilongjiang Academy of Social Sciences has actively carried out research on Jews in Harbin, undertaking multiple national and provincial-level research projects. *Harbin Jews,* a picture book compiled by the center and the "Harbin Jewish History Exhibition" curated by the center are both first-class. Many works have been translated into other languages. They include, among others, *The Jews of Kaifeng, China: History, Culture, and Religion* written in English by Xu Xin and published in the U.S. [①] and Liu Shuang's *A History of the Jews of Harbin* (Chronicles Press, 2007). These works focus specifically on the history of the Jewish diaspora in China.

(Originally published in *West Africa*, 2010, Vol. 4.)

---

①   Xu Xin, 2003. *The Jews of Kaifeng, China: History, Culture, and Religion,* Jersey City: KTAV Publishing House, Inc.

Characteristics of Jewish Culture[*]

ZHANG Qianhong[**]

Jewish culture has a distinctive ethnic dimension. "It is not difficult to see that since ancient times, Jews have always been able to adapt to the challenges of the times without destroying core Jewish values." [①] In other words, in exchanges with other cultures, Jewish culture has constantly adapted, transformed, and improved itself without losing its unique identity. This article provides a summary and analysis of the basic characteristics of Jewish culture, from three perspectives: its religious, national, and global dimensions.

---

[*]   Translated by Andrew H. Keller, polished by Liang Fan.

[**]   Vice-President, Zhengzhou University; Deputy director, Institute of Jewish Studies, Henan University.

①   Adam Garfinkle, 1997. *Politics and Society in Modern Israel-Myths and Realities*, M.E. Sharpe, Inc., New York, p.282.

I. Religious Dimension

Jewish culture has historically been strongly religious in nature. The core tenets of Jewish culture, in a complete sense, reflect the history of the formation of religious doctrine. A significant feature of Jewish culture is the use of religious concepts in its explanation of social and cultural phenomena and of religion through social and cultural phenomena. That the Jewish people, while missing a key element in forming a national history - stable geographic boundaries - have still been able to live tenaciously as a national community and create the historical and cultural phenomenon of being geographically dispersed yet closely linked is to a large extent attributable to religion. Religion has become an indispensible cultural tool to ensure the integration and coordination of Jewish society, and religion inevitably restricts and impacts all aspects of Jewish social life.

The formative process of Judaism is still an unresolved academic issue, but one fact is indisputable: In ancient times, even when polytheism prevailed, the Hebrew people created the world's oldest monotheistic religion. Moreover, it was thoroughly monotheistic; by making their own god the sole god, they denied the sacredness and legitimacy of other gods.

Judaism is constantly developing and evolving. It has passed through a number of development stages, including the Biblical Period, the Pre-Rabbinic Age, the Rabbinic Age, the Middle Ages, the Period of Transition, the Emancipation, and Contemporary Judaism. [①] In the Pre-Emancipation Period, Judaism dominated Jewish culture. With the rise of the Emancipation movement and the impact of modernism, the status of Judaism waned, and Jewish secular culture flourished. But today, Judaism still has a strong influence on the Jewish cultural system. This influence has been maintained through the adaptation of Judaism to world trends and the constant reform of its teachings and customs.

The close relationship between Judaism and Jewish culture can be seen in the connotation of the word "Judaism". The word was first used by Greek-speaking Jews to refer to faith and canon. In Christian literature of the Middle Ages, it was used to refer to the Jewish religion. In recent times it has been widely used by Jews. "Judaism" is indeed intended to refer to the Jewish theological system, and so many dictionaries translate it into Chinese as *Youtaijiao*, or "Jewish religion," and many Chinese-language works today still understand it as the religious beliefs of the Jews. Because Judaism emphasizes everyday behavior rather than the doctrine itself, it is more of a reflection of a Jewish code of conduct and way of life. Many modern Jewish scholars believe that Judaism is more accurately described as a cultural system. In the words of Daniel Jeremy Silver, "We no longer strictly understand Judaism as a creed, rules of conduct, or system of worship. Judaism covers all these elements, but is not confined to them. It includes all the ideas and culture of the

---

①   *Encyclopedia Judaica*, 1971. Jerusalem: Keter Publishing House Ltd., Vol. 10, p. 383.

Jewish people and the phenomena that profoundly affect the inner lives of the Jewish people." [1]

In this sense, the impact of Judaism on Jews is no less significant than the impact of Confucianism on Chinese in traditional Chinese society. It far surpasses religious beliefs narrowly construed in terms of both scope and depth. Thus, just as we do not recognize Confucianism as a religion, we should not look at Judaism as a pure faith. The English edition of the *Encyclopedia Judaica* explains Judaism as "the religion, philosophy, and way of life of the Jewish People." [2] Rabbi Mordecai Kaplan, the founder of Reconstructionist Judaism, has always held that Judaism is not a religion but a culture in the broadest sense, which should include all aspects of culture, such as Jewish theology, history, literature, philosophy, language, science, art, architecture, clothing, social organizations, and ethics.

As an ideology, Judaism became the basic element in the culture of the Jewish people and its main vehicle for dissemination and inheritance. This was for a long period of time the mainstream and distinguishing feature of Jewish culture. One cannot fully understand Jewish culture without understanding Judaism. Even in modern society, Judaism is still an important part of the Jewish spiritual and cultural system. On the one hand, as the main body of Jewish tradition and in

---

[1]   Daniel Jeremy Silver & Bernard Martin, 1974. *A History of Judaism from Abraham to Maimonides*, Basic Books, Inc., New York, vol. 1, p. 10.

[2]   *Encyclopedia Judaica*, 1971. Jerusalem: Keter Publishing House Ltd., vol. 10, pp. 387-395.

its contact with modernism, it restricts the development of Jewish society through the cultural role it plays. On the other hand, it performs its cultural function through its influence on other cultural phenomena. In Israel today, Judaism is not only the spiritual pillar of the Jewish people, but it also serves as the reference by which they identify themselves as such. It is both the essence and the distinctive feature of the Israeli national culture. Orthodox Judaism imposes serious constraints on the country's politics, economics, culture, education, and art. Religious holidays are state holidays mandated by law. Religious taboos permeate all aspects of society. So despite its positive function, the adverse impact of religion is also vividly on display. Its conflict with and hindrance of modern cultural and social trends have become a thorny issue.

II. Ethnic Dimension

Its ethnic identity is another characteristic of Jewish culture. In ancient times, Hebrews were nomadic, moving around in search of pastures, water, and grass. They relied on the strength of their communities to contend with nature. Although Jews established their own kingdom, and the period of David and Solomon was glorious, the majority of their existence - from the time of their settlement in Canaan to the time when they were conquered by Rome - was spent under the repression of neighboring powers. During this period, the Jewish people struggled with different tribes: contending with a ruthless Pharaoh when leaving Egypt; engaging in repeated battles with the Canaanites and Philistines in the Haji era; losing to the Assyrians and Neo Babylonians in the kingdom period; and later, enslavement by Persia and Rome. In this difficult and tortuous course of history, the Jewish people formed a strong ethnic consciousness with religion at its core. In the later Diaspora, cycles of anti-Semitism strengthened the Jewish ethnic identity. Shaped and developed within this macro context, promoting its ethnic identity is naturally one of the leitmotifs of Jewish culture.

The covenant is one of the basic teachings of Judaism. The Bible records on numerous occasions the covenant between God and the Hebrews. In Genesis, after the "rainbow covenant" with Noah, God established covenants with Abraham and Moses. Thus, the special relationship between God and the Hebrews was established by way of the Chosen People. In this relationship, God is the highest expression of the will of the group. This dominates the fate of Hebrews (i.e. individuals). But in addition to the requirement that man should devoutly revere and obey God, God also undertakes a commitment and responsibility to man that cannot be overlooked. The Jewish concept of the covenant endowed new qualities on the relationship with God for the first time in history, breaking the long-standing fatalism in which man was in an absolutely passive position. Only in the Kingdom Period did kings, in order to strengthen their own rule, fully emphasize the unilateral binding role of the covenant, even as they gradually lose sight of God's responsibility. In the concept of the covenant, God's covenants with Abraham, Moses, and others were not individual covenants, but covenants with the entire Jewish community and

Jewish people.

Because the harsh environment at the time forced individuals to rely on the community for survival, this gave rise to the urgent need to establish a healthy relationship between the individual and the community that could both advance collective interests and ensure individual survival. It was such a requirement that facilitated the emergence of the notion of the covenant. After the division of the kingdom, the Sages of Israel assumed the point of view of the entire people and used the degree to which the people's "covenant" had been complied with as the criterion for judging the merits and demerits of Northern Israel and Southern Judah. The collective interests clearly take precedence.

As a type of "ethical monotheism", many unique rituals and customshave formed over the long course of history of Judaism. They are both a crystallization of the life experiences of the Hebrew people, as well as the main symbol of the difference between Jews and people of other tribes. Jewish religious festivals are numerous. Although the origins and meanings of these festivals are different, none of them simply commemorate the achievements and life of an individual. Rather, they originate from the experience of the entire Jewish people and are a subtle blend of history and festive and religious rituals. This is a reminder for the Jewish people not to forget their suffering, to enhance cohesion, and to prevent assimilation by other tribes. In other words, religious festivals, as cultural markers, whether somber or joyous, are all epitomes of the historical trajectory of the entire Jewish people. For example,

Passover commemorates the ancient Hebrews casting off the persecution of the Egyptian Pharaohs; Sukkot exhorts people always to remember the difficult years in which the Israelites wandered the Sinai desert; Purim is a celebration to commemorate the defeat of Haman's plot to massacre the Jews; Hanukkah expresses the Jewish desire for light and cherishes the memory of Maccabi's heroism against the rebels; Yom Kippur encourages Jews to engage in introspection and exert themselves to make the nation prosperous. These unequivocally efficacious national holidays have played an important role in maintaining Jewish culture. Among the world's civilizations, very few have such a prominent ethnic character.

Since the 19th century, some reformist thinkers deeply influenced by modern thoughts have staunchly denied the ethnic nature of Jewish religion and culture, holding that Jews should abandon their ethnic identity and blend into mainstream society. In their view, the ethnic nature of Judaism has made it a cult that is behind the times, and Jewish culture a "constrictive culture" that lacks vitality. They argue that Jewish culture will become a mainstream culture like Christian culture only if the "ethnic barrier" is broken. Some respected scholars of modernity have gone further to say that "[m]odernity tends to accompany universalism. Modern Jews tend to see Jewish particularism as a narrow mentality." ① German reformist thinkers deleted the concept of the Messiah from prayer books,

---

①   Moshe Sharon, 1993. *Judaism in the Context of Diverse Civilization*, Johannesburg: Maksim Publishers, pp. 21-24.

generalizing the concept of "mission of Israel" so as to render it universally, i.e., globally applicable. The intention and goal was to enhance the position of Jewish religion and culture and attract those who have converted to other religions to "return to the faith." However, facts show that the universalization of religion and culture cannot be achieved by the inspiration and passion of a few, but requires deeper societal forces.

After its rise in the United States, Reform Judaism for some time denied and rejected the ethnic nature of Jewish culture. But the rise of modern anti-Semitism shattered the "Emancipation Dream" of many and revived in them an ethnic consciousness. The rise and achievements of the Zionist movement have prompted reformists to rethink their advocacy against Jadaism's ethnic dimension and against traditionalism. The "Columbus Programme" of 1973 symbolizes Reform Judaism's approval and acceptance of the ethnic character of Jewish culture.

After the founding of Israel, a large number of emigrants began to return, and cultural differences became "a more thorny issue than arranging for basic necessities and employment." Integrating these cultural differences was called the "key factor in turning Jewish immigrants into true Israeli citizens" and a "basic condition for Israel to complete its mission of national integration" . [1] In the process of constructing a new national culture, the integration of Israeli society and the realization of "the gathering of the exiles in the land of Israel" are only

---

[1]   Eleazar Laserson, 1951. "Turning Immigrants into Israelis," *Jewish Affairs*, Johannesburg, p.12.

possible when people are united around their commitment to traditional Jewish culture. But the Jewish community of the second half of the 20 century is different from that of the Pre-Emancipation Era. A great change occurred in Jews who have gone through The Enlightenment and been exposed to modern thinking on nationand democracy. Religious fervor waned overall, and the number of secular Jews grew. Although they have drifted away from the religion, they still firmly believe in their national identity. This has produced a large number of "secular Jews." To accommodate this phenomenon, the Israeli government has laid particular stress on the ethnic dimension of Jewish culture to make the idea of an "ethnic home" appealing, and to elevate the status of Israel in the hearts of Jews around the world and to win much-needed aid for the social development of Israel.

III. Global Dimension

Jewish culture is a typical ethnic culture, but the ethnic nature of this culture does not negate its "universal/global nature." In other words, the difference between Jewish culture and other ethnic cultures is the former is also a "culture with universal/global properties." Of course, "universal/global properties" and "universal/global culture" are two different concepts. The former only possesses some qualities and features of the latter. Some of the main "universal/global qualities" of Jewish culture are as follows.

First is the global nature of cultural exchanges. From a

historical perspective, the Jewish people may well have engaged in more cultural exchanges than any other people. In ancient times, Jews had wide ranging exchanges with the Canaanites, Assyrians, Philistines, and Babylonians of West Asia. In the process of these exchanges, Judaism distinguished itself among the many regional religions in the world and became the world's oldest monotheistic religion. Thereafter, Jews had exchanges with Greek and Roman cultures after being conquered. After prolonged exposure, integration, and trials, Hebrew culture and Greek culture ultimately converged and spawned Christian culture. In the 1st century A.D., Jews were expelled from Palestine. The "Diaspora" forced them into a myriad of exchanges, and "the earth became their homeland." These particular historical circumstances meant that the Jews far exceed other peoples in terms of cultural exchange.

From the mid-18th to the 19th century, the Jewish Enlightenment can be seen as a huge exchange of far-reaching historical significance. The Jews for the first time had the courage to break the ethnic barriers of their culture, and they threw themselves into studying and absorbing modern science and culture. With slogans such as "re-building Judaism" and "cultivating the spirit of science," they strove to turn Jewish culture into a "malleable, organic national culture always able to adapt to the environment." Neither the starting point nor stopping point of The Enlightenment, with its modern characteristics, would have been possible without historical exchanges. That the enlightenment should have so propelled the Jewish people is precisely because of the unprecedented sense of crisis they felt when they became exposed in historical exchanges to the rapidly advancing culture of the west, especially when it was compared with their own. And the enlightenment movement in turn helped broaden and deepen historical exchanges between Jewish and Western culture.

Frequent historical exchanges had a profound impact on Jewish culture. First, historical exchanges not only ensured that Jewish culture would be passed on from generation to generation, it also enriched it. Historical exchanges are one of the basic forms of human existence and development. Any civilization must maintain a kind of openness so as to ensure the development of productive forces and the consolidation and continuation of the achievements of civilization in the process of exchanges. Jewish history is powerful evidence that historical exchanges are the driving force behind social progress and development. It is hard to imagine how Jewish culture could ever have become a deeply influential culture with global characteristics had Jews been confined to their tiny piece of Palestine and engaged in no exchange with other people or nations.

A significant feature of Jewish history is continuous migration and dispersal. In this process of continuous displacement, Jewish culture has drawn extensively from the elements of other cultures. Upon entering the Diaspora era, exchanges between Jews and other cultures broadened. The blending and integration of Jewish and Arab - Islamic culture in the Mediterranean region, particularly on the Iberian Peninsula, gave birth to a gem of Jewish culture - the Sephardic culture - that was most alive from the 8th to the 13th centuries. The inter-penetration of Jewish culture and Germanic and Slavic civilization produced yet another Jewish cultural branch, namely, Yiddish culture.

Since modern times, Jewish culture has adapted to the modernization process and a distinctive American Jewish culture came to being in the United States. Since the Mid-20th century, with the establishment of the nation of Israel, the moral center of Jewish culture has returned to Israel, and it became a spiritual pillar of the new national culture of Israel. One can see that from its earliest origin and throughout its later historical evolution, Jewish culture has continued to enrich itself and to develop both within conflict and through its contact with other cultures. Jewish culture has thus become a broad and profound philosophical and cultural system with global characteristics. In short, through its contact with other cultures, Jewish culture has managed to maintain a kind of exchange relation that allows conflict, absorption, fission and fusion all at the same time. And it is precisely through this relationship that the achievements of Jewish culture have been maintained and renewed. Seen in this light, its global nature is not only a characteristic and manifestation of Jewish culture, but it also helps guarantee that Jewish culture can constantly surpass itself, stay vital, and influential.

Second, historical exchanges promoted the formation of an ethnic identity and the Jewish spirit. The Jewish spirit is a relatively stable value system and ideology with which the majority of the Jewish people identify. It was gradually formed from the daily experience and social practices of the Jewish people over centuries. The emergence and development of this spirit cannot be separated from a wide range of historical exchanges. On the one hand, exchanges provided a broad field of vision and nourishment from cultures of other areas, which led to the emergence and condensation of a national spirit. On the other hand, exchanges themselves were an important force that drove the realization of national spirit. The formation of the Jewish business mentality confirms this.

Before the ancient Hebrews entered Canaan, they lived a nomadic life. It was the unique environment of Canaan that bred their entrepreneurship and business acumen. Located to the east of the Mediterranean Sea, Canaan is bordered on the east by two river basins, on the north by the Eurasian hinterland, on the southeast by the Arabian Desert, and on the southwest by the African continent. It is the earliest intersection of trade routes in history. When Abraham led the Hebrews into Canaan, the local culture was far more advanced than Hebrew culture. Canaanites of every shade and description had established small city-states and mastered agricultural and smelting technologies. The handicraft industry was also quite developed. The cities and castles built by each city-state were each trading centers. The frequent trading activities of the Canaanites profoundly influenced the Hebrews, who had not yet settled down. Some abandoned animal husbandry and agriculture and became involved in local trading activities. Thereafter, Jewish trade expanded with the development of

Canaanite society.

By the Solomon era, the Jews were trading with businessmen from all over the Arabian Peninsula, Mesopotamia, India, and Africa. Thus, the historical interaction with the Canaanites played a very important role in the formation of a merchant culture among the Jewish people. The settlement process of the Hebrews in Canaan was not simply a transformation from nomadic to settled lifestyle. It was "a process of the merchant genes of the Hebrews adjusting to local Canaanite commerce." If the Jews of ancient times only engaged in trade activities in a certain fixed area, then we might say that the Diaspora truly drove them into the world market.

Overall, the Jewish people are no longer closely related to any particular market in any particular place. Their dispersion to the four corners of the earth means that they were going to take up international trade. Before flowing into Europe, the vast majority of Jews lived within the Arab empire. One could say that the rise of Islam gave Jewish merchants a rare opportunity for development. Due to the long confrontation between Christianity and Islam, and in particular to the emergence of two empires in the core region of East-West trade along the coast of the Mediterranean - the Christian Frankish Kingdom and the Arab Islamic Empire - the two sides often went to war over commercial interests. Merchants of different religious backgrounds were thus afraid to enter each other's territories, and trade between Europe and Asia basically broke down. The Jews naturally played the role of intermediaries in East-West trade. They were at the time active in Spain,

France, Italy, Byzantium, Palestine, Egypt, Tunisia, and other places. "They played a very active role in Mediterranean and intercontinental trade, and as international merchants emerged for the first time in Western Christian nations." [1] They had their own "representatives" in major ports, making up a huge, exclusionary, self-contained, commercial network that ensured the smooth operation of long-distance trade.

One can see that it is in the long history of exchanges that the Jews obtained opportunities one after another to nurture their business expertise. And it is also in the process of interaction that they developed a special sense and cognition of money, which became for them a "defense mechanism," "survival insurance," and "ticket" to the outside world.

The second global quality of Jewish culture is the openness of its content. A valuable lesson the Jews have learned over their long history of exchanges with others is that as an ethnic entity they are able to resist both strong pressures from outside societies and the temptations of various charms and to maintain their ethnic identity.

On a cultural level, despite lacking "geographical boundaries", the Jewish people have rather successfully guarded their own "cultural boundaries" while at the same time continuously enriching the content of their culture, thereby achieving a unity of cultural closedness and cultural openness. "Closed" and "open" are mutually exclusive categories, and

---

[1] H. H. Ben-Sasson, 1976. *A History of the Jewish People*, Harvard University Press, p. 394.

present a paradox that any people or nation will have difficulty avoiding in its development. For a people lacking a "foundation" but determined to stay viable and strong, it is important for Jewish culture to be closed. Only by maintaining the tradition of "keeping their" ethnic culture closed can mainstream Jewish culture continue to thrive, the ethnic idiosyncrasies of the Jewish people be sustained, and the Jewish people, widely dispersed as they are, maintain integrity under the pressure of assimilation. If the "closed" nature of their culture is lost, the Jewish people would be like so many others who have lost their culture to assimilation, decline, and demise. This is why the Jewish culture has long been thought of as being conservative. This view is in fact one-sided, as it only sees the "closed" side of Jewish culture while overlooking its open side.

Prior to the 2nd century A.D., the main achievements of Hebrew culture were embodied in the Bible. Because the Bible came about under specific historical conditions, and also because of the need to establish the esteemed status of the people, Hebrews strove to make the Bible a sacred and classical text, so as to turn it into a closed and literal "holy book". But the more "holy" the Bible became, the wider the gap became between it and real life. Therefore, the Jews, who have always pursued development, urgently needed a "quasi-Bible" that could function as a bridge between God and man and provide a code of conduct for future generations. Thus, between the 2nd and 6th century A.D., the Jewish community in Babylon brought its religious sages and intellectual elites together and had them compile the "Babylonian Talmud," an impressive oral law records of 2.5 million words. In addition to an interpretation of traditional Jewish laws, the Talmud also covers a wide range of topics, including myths, ancestral legends, customs, astronomy, geography, medicine, mathematics, botany, and history. The Talmud, popular, simple, and practical, and the Bible together constitute the blueprint for Jewish education.

The completion of the Talmud reflects the openness of the way the Jewish people think.

Jewish cultural openness is also clearly reflected in their attitudes toward different cultures. Early Hebrew culture was formed by drawing from neighboring peoples. During the period of Babylonian captivity, the Hebrews came into contact with the more advanced Babylonian culture, and learned from their lifestyle and educational system. After coming into contact with Greek culture, Jewish intellectuals studied it with fervor, and advanced the synthesis of ancient Greek and Hebrew philosophy and helped form a new school, known as "Jewish Hellenistic Philosophy". [1] This school later profoundly influenced Western culture. During the time of the European Diaspora, although Jewish and Christian cultures had irreconcilable incompatibilities, the blending of cultures could still be seen in numerous areas. In modern times, with the rise of scientific and technological revolution and education, Jews have suddenly found themselves facing a challenge that was

---

[1] Julius Guttmann, 1964. *Philosophies of Judaism——The History of Jewish Philosophy from Biblical Times to Franz Rosenzweig*, New York: Rinehart & Winston, Inc., pp. 18-29.

given rise to by new knowledge, a challenge that cannot be ignored. If the Jewish people want to make sure their culture continues to be respected in its spirit, they must incorporate modern philosophy must into their thinking on issues such as God, the world, rationality, and human nature. The Jewish people must draw extensively from new knowledge that was beyond the traditional and allow themselves to be swept up by the wave of modernization.

In response, a number of Jewish intellectuals strongly advocated for a secular philosophy, attempting to help the Jewish people understand Western culture and grasp modern science and technology through the implementation of a system of education that was multi-level, modern and secular. Also necessary was a profound reflection on Jewish culture, the refinement of the Jewish faith, the elimination of the falsehoods and fabrications that have permeated Jewish religious doctrine since the Middle Ages, and the dispelling of cultural isolationism, and the bridging of spiritual and cultural gap with Western civilization and society, and "ultimately molding a new Jew that can adapt in thinking and culture to the whole of European society." It was in this context that Jewish Enlightenment and Reform Judaism emerged, and the Jewish secular culture rose rapidly.

The third indicator of the global character of Jewish culture was the universality and generality of its cultural influence. While retaining its character of openness, the culture of the Jewish people has had considerable influence over other cultures. The genetic lineage among the three major monotheistic religions in terms of doctrines, rituals, and the norms of conduct for followers illustrates this best. Not only has Hebrew culture adequately negotiated the delicate balance among what is sacred and what is secular, faith and utility, tradition and reform and managed to enrich and improve its own culture, it has also set a good example of how to handle exchanges between one's own culture and other cultures.

Hebrew culture has had a large impact on the European intellectual life. In the period of Renaissance and Reformation, Britain, France, Italy, Germany, and other countries were in a craze to study Hebrew culture, and almost all the religious reformers, such as Desiderius Erasmus, John Calvin, and Martin Luther studied Hebrew diligently. This was an era of convergence of different ideologies and a miracle of human cultural exchanges, in which numerous Jewish scholars took on the roles of mediators and facilitators of cultural exchange.

In modern times, the emergence of Jewish elite in different countries and different professions is also a reflection of the global nature of Jewish culture. Because the Jewish people are scattered around the world, Jewish culture is often manifested as a stateless culture. On the one hand it possesses important markers and specific content of an ethnic culture, but on the other hand, in terms of form, content, and influence, it clearly transcends ethnic boundaries. Jewish literature offers a good example. Not only are there large numbers of Jewish authors writing in Hebrew and Yiddish, there is also widespread use of English, French, German, Russian, and other languages not traditionally spoken by the Jewish people. Therefore,

Jewish authors writing from different countries and in different languages can also be classified under different ethnic and national literary categories. Their works are at once Jewish literature and the literature of their place of residence.

Jewish culture has been able to have a prominent position in human culture and history, and the source and vitality of its influence can to a large extent be attributed to its global quality. The Polish Jewish thinker Isaac Deutscher (1907-1967) used Marxist views to trace and analyze the formation process of the thinking of Jewish greats such as Baruch Spinoza, Heinrich Heine, Karl Marx, Rosa Luxemburg, Leon Trotsky, and Sigmund Freud. He said that although these people have been called heretics, Jewish tradition had laid an indelible mark on them, and their mode of thinking and way of doing things were "very Jewish." They did not belong to an ancient tradition that may be ignorant, old, or decayed. Instead, they were urgently seeking ideas and undertakings that would transcend Jewishness, and were trying to find and accept the newest thinking in the philosophy of the modern world, sociology, and political science. He wrote, "As Jews, their being 'advanced' consists in their living on the border lines of different civilizations, religions, and ethnic cultures and in their being born and living during the transition from one era to the next. Their ideas matured under the influence of cultures that learned from and nourished one another in complex and intricate ways. They lived in the remote nooks and crannies of the countries in which they reside. They each were at once part of the societies in which they live and apart from it. This peculiar mode of existence explains how they have managed to create ideas that transcend everything: society, country, time and their contemporaries, and how their minds and spirits can travel freely on the vast horizon and into the distant future." [1]

(Originally published in *West Africa*, 2000, Vol. 3.)

---

[1]   Paul R. Mendes-Flohr and JehudaReinharz, 1980. *The Jew in the Modern World*, Oxford University, p. 231.

A Comparative Study of Hebrew Prophets and Confucian Scholars[*]

FU Youde[**]

It is widely lenown that the Jewish religion is based on the word of the prophets, and in China, Confucianism attaches great weight to individuals with special gifts of wisdom and insight. In ancient Israeli society, the prophets, acting as spokesmen for Yahweh, played an especially important role in the society's religious, political and moral life. In China, the Confucian intelligentsia understood and interpreted the Will of Heaven, and their words and spirit had a strong influence on the individual, the family, the society and the nation. It is easy to see that as major actors in the founding and early development of their respective civilizations, the Hebrew prophets and

[*]   Translated by Paul M. Denlinger, polished by Liang Fan.
[**] Professor at the School of Philosophy and Social Development, Research
      Center for Judaism and Inter-Religious Affairs, Shandong University.

Chinese sages are worthy of comparison. The aim of this research paper is to promote mutual understanding between the two peoples, and during this phase of globalization, enhance mutual respect between these two old and great civilizations.

I.

The origin of the Hebrew word for prophet comes from navi (plural: naviim), which means "the fruit of the lips". What is this "fruit of the lips"? In the view of the ancient Hebrews, there was a close relationship between the lips and speaking, the speaking was literally the fruit of the lips. So, for this reason, the prophets were literally people who were good at speaking. In the Book of *Isaiah*, before becoming a prophet, Isaiah was referred to as a "man with unclean lips". In a dream he sensed the presence of Yahweh, and a six-winged angel appeared before him, and put a burning red coal to his lips saying "As this burning coal touches your lips, your sins will be taken away and forgiven." [1] Here, the reference to a "man with unclean lips", is to someone who cannot speak well.

This etymological analysis is not sufficient to express the concept of prophets, and requires further explanation. Here is how it is explained in the most recent edition of the *Encyclopedia of Judaism* [2] : "The prophets were charismatic individuals, believed to have the divine gift of receiving and

---

[1]   Book of Isaiah 6: 5-7

[2]   Geoffrey Wigoder (ed), 1989. *The Encyclopedia of Judaism,* Jerusalem, The Jerusalem Publishing House, p. 571.

sending the revelations of Yahweh. Revelations were how information was sent, and were not necessarily prophecies of the future. Prophets acted as the intermediaries between the will of Yahweh and the people." [①] From this definition, we can understand four points. First, the prophets had a special divine gift which enabled them to send and receive the word of Yahweh, making them charismatic individuals. Second, their divine task was to transmit the will of Yahweh to the public. From a functional perspective, they were the spokesmen for Yahweh. Third, in terms of their social position, they acted as intermediaries between Yahweh and his followers. Prophets were humans and not divine, but because of their special responsibilities as transmitters of the will of Yahweh, they occupied a social position higher than ordinary people, putting them between Yahweh and ordinary people. Fourth, their prophecies could refer to future events, or they could choose not to refer to future events; their sole role was to transmit the true word of Yahweh.

The roles of the early Confucian scholars were in many ways similar to the early Hebrew prophets. This is described in *Mengzi-Wanzhang Shang* when the King of Shang, Tang, tried to recruit Yi Yin to become his advisor. In the beginning, Yi Yin declined the offer, preferring instead to stay in the mountains to study the original teachings of Yao and Shun. But in the end, he changed his mind after three tries by Tang. thinking that much good can be achievet if Yao and Shun's teachings can be put to

---

[①] Geoffrey Wigoder (ed), 1989. *The Encyclopedia of Judaism,* Jerusalem, The Jerusalem Publishing House, p. 571.

practice. Since Yi Yin knew first the original teachings of Yao and Shun, if he did not perform this task, he asked himself, then who would? Eventually, he advised and helped the King to create the Shang dynasty and helped several members of nobility after Tang, and became remembered in history as a loyal minister.

Among Confucian scholars in subsequent generations, there were discussions of those who knew the Will of Heaven first, and those who understood it later. Zhu Xi, the famous Neo-Confucian scholar from the Southern Song Dynasty, said: "All people are essentially good, and there are those who understand the Will of Heaven first, and those who understand it later. Those who understand it later must follow those who understand it first, so that they can follow the Good." [1]

The Confucian scholar Mengzi not only said that there were those who knew first, he also offered the opinion that those who knew first were comparable to prophets. On this point, Mengzi commented: "Boyi was the model for pure and incorruptible behavior among prophets, and Yi Yin was the model for strong capabilities and getting things done among prophets. Liu Xiahui was the model for moderating and controlling his emotions among prophets, and Confucius was the model of the prophet who came at the right time, collecting the wisdom of all previous generations and opening a new era." [2] According to Mengzi, these were all important prophets who had their own individual and unique abilities.

---

[1]   Zhu Xi 1986, *Si Shu Ji Zhu*, Changsha; YueLu Shushe, p. 70.

[2]   Liu. Fangyuan, 1985. *Modern Translation of Mengzi*, Jiangxi People's Press, p. 197.

According to the Chinese etymological dictionary *Ciyuan*, the definition for 圣 ("sheng" or "holy person") is someone who knows everything. Reflecting this thinking in *Guodian Chujian-Wuxing* Mengzi had this quote: "He who hears and understands is a holy person. The holy person knows the way of Heaven. He knows the source of the rites, and the five virtues of benevolence, righteousness, propriety, wisdom, and holiness." [①] Mengzi understood that the sages knew the way of Heaven, and conceived of Heaven as the source of all rites on earth, and these were encapsulated in the Five Heavenly Virtues of charity, righteousness, propriety, wisdom and holiness. From this we know that the prophets, or sages, acquired this wisdom first, and it was their task to spread this wisdom and knowledge among the wider public, so that they too could be transformed into people with wisdom and virtues. This means that the Chinese sages not only had the role of understanding the Will of Heaven, but also of spreading this word among the common people.

In the Hebrew scriptures, Yahweh is the highest substance, and is not only the Creator of all living beings, but also the source of all truth and law. Yahweh is also the source of all of the Word brought to humanity by the prophets. As for what Confucian scholars meant by heaven, we have different interpretations including, the Heaven which determines everything, the Heaven which is the source of all truth, and the Heaven which is the source of all natural things. Working with

---

all sources currently available, we still cannot find an interpretation of 天 ("Heaven") which is acceptable to everyone. One thing we can all agree is that following the Zhou dynasty, all Chinese scholarly literature accepts that Heaven was the supreme substauce. This means that in the Confucian interpretation of Heaven, it occupied the same stratum in the hierarchy as the Hebrew Yahweh. Extrapolating from this, the Way of Heaven is on the same level as the messages of the Hebrew prophets to their people. One could also say that the Chinese sages were on the same level as the Hebrew prophets. This is the sense in which, the British scholar H.H. Rowley said very clearly that the Hebrew prophets and Chinese sages played the same role in transmitting the message of Heaven to their respective societies. In this respect, China's sages were not weaker than the prophets of ancient Israel. According to this interpretation, even though there were significant differences between the Chinese sages and Israel's prophets, the Chinese sages could still be seen as prophets, and can be placed on the same level as the prophets of ancient Israel. In some places, their words can even be directly compared with each other. [1]

Moreover, similar to the prophets of Ancient Israel who were endowed with special talents, Confucian sages also had special gifts which were related to their mission. In the Chinese classics, Confucius, Mengzi and others mention that their talents were related to the special mission they were on. In *Lunyu*,

---

[1] H.H. Rowley, 1956. *Prophecy and Religion in Ancient China and Israel,* New York : Harper & Bros, pp.20 -21, 26.

Confucius said that Heaven has provided the necessary virtues, indicating that he was aware that his special talents were given to him so he could accomplish these tasks. He also said that in order to accomplish the tasks given to him, he had to act like a wooden hammer, which meant that his role was to give warning to the rest of the world, and to put it on the right path. According to Mengzi, when heaven assigns one a task, it must put that person's will to test, and his body through strenuous exercises. Mengzi meant that all the historical sages of previous dynasties had been given a huge task by heaven, and achieved their status as sage by accomplishing the enormous tasks they faced. It could be said that these sages were given special talents to accomplish their missions, and that these talents were innate to them. Without this condition, they would have been unable to accomplish their tasks and become sages.

In Judaism, the prophets occupied a special place lower than Yahweh, but higher than ordinary mortals. Although they had special divine capabilities, they were still human and not divine, and would never become divine. They could do what was beyond the capability of ordinary mortals, which was to accept divine will and transmit the divine message. In Confucian teaching, the sages were also special humans endowed with special talents to promote the Will of Heaven, but were also human and not divine. They were special people who represented the best of the best, and occupied a position higher than ordinary mortals. In this respect, they were also very similar to the prophets of ancient Israel.

Prophets were an important element of Judaism. According

to Hebrew tradition, as the founder of Judaism and the leader of the Israelis, Moses occupied a special position as the pre-eminent Jewish prophet. Following Moses, a large number of prophets appeared in ancient Israel. The appearance of these prophets and their activities formed the prophet movement in Jewish history. Before the Kingdom of Israel, Samuel was the most famous representative of that period. Following the founding of the Kingdom of Israel but before the appearance of the biblical texts there were Elijah, Elishah, Nathan, Micah, Ahijiah and so forth. [1] In the period from the 8 century BCE to the 5 century BCE, with the Kingdom of Israel in the north and the Kingdom of Judah in the south, followed by the Second Temple period, there appeared Amos, Hosea, Isaiah, Micah, Zephaniah, Nahum, Habbakuk, Jeremiah, Ezekiel, Obadiah, Haggai, Zechariah, Joel, Jonah, Malachi and others. These prophets especially drew the attention of western philosophers. The famous 20 century German philosopher Karl Jaspers said that the Hebrew prophets were just as important as Socrates and Plato were in ancient Greece, Sakyamuni in India, Laozi and Confucius in China, and set the foundation for a new golden age of social and political thought. Together, they formed what Jaspers called the 'Axial Age'.

In ancient China, in different periods and different schools of thought there were different understandings of the Chinese sages. Sometimes they were believed to refer to the kings, other

---

[1]   Huston Smith, 2006. *The World's Religions*. Trans. Liu Anyun. Haikou; Hainan Press, p. 310.

times to people with special talents. When it comes to naming the sages, most Confucian scholars accept the list in the last section of the Book of *Mengzi*, *Jinxinxia*. Among the sages on the list were Yao, Shun, Yu, Gaotao, Tang, Yi Yin, Laizhu, King Wen, Taigongwang, Sanyisheng and Confucius. Elsewhere, *Mengzi* also mentions Boyi, Fu Shuo, Bailixi, Liu Xiahui, King Wu, and Zhou Gong, making the number of sages, at least according to Mengzi, nearly two dozens. The number of Chinese sages were about the same as the Hebrew prophets.

II.

While there were many similarities between the Hebrew prophets and the Chinese sages, there were also significant differences, which manifest their respective uniqueness.

In the Jewish scriptures, we often come across phrases such as: "Yahweh said to Moses", "Yahweh told Moses to say", "the king of kings and leader of Israel said", "when the words of Yahweh reached me and said", "Yahweh thus spoke", "this is what Yahweh said" and so forth. According to the Jewish interpretation, *the Five Books of Moses* tell the Jews about the Ten Commandments which are of divine origin, along with other laws. Amos, Isaiah, Jeremiah and other prophets then transmitted the message of these laws to all the Jews. The prophets were very clear that their message came directly from Yahweh. This was why in Judaism, they were regarded as the messengers of god.

This is very different from the Chinese classics where we see "Yao said", "Shun said", "Yin Tang said", "the teacher said" , "the poem said" and so forth. There is no mention of "Heaven said" . In each classic, a different lead speaker speaks. But what they all have in common is that, the author of the book speaks his own words, or quotes a past emperor. For example, when Confucius described something, he would frequently refer to what were for him, ancient classical sources. In his classic, *Lunyu*, he said that "For something trustworthy, refer to the ancient source, otherwise just avoid it." In *Zhongyong*, he said "Describe the ways of (the ancient sages) Yao and Shun, promote their ways of literature and warfare". Whether it's something the sages themselves said, or something the sages quoted other sages from ages past, it is always "word of man". This is very different from what the Hebrew prophets did, who always ascribed what they said to a divine source. This fundamental difference is very important, as it highlights the differences between how prophets and sages obtained extraordinary knowledge, and in their characters.

The prophets received their knowledge from Yahweh in the form of revelations. Revelations were Yahweh's way of showing his existence, nature, goal, plan or objectives. From the *Torah*, we know that Yahweh made his revelations by communicating with the prophets. For example, Yahweh spoke to Abraham, giving the land of Canaan to him and all his descendants (*Genesis* 17: 1-8); he spoke to Moses, revealing the Ten Commandments (*Exodus* 20: 1-17); he predicted the fall of Jerusalem and the fall of the kingdom of Judah (*Isaiah* 3: 4-13). These revelations appear repeatedly in the Jewish scriptures. Not only this, according to traditional Jewish interpretation, *the Five Books of Moses* were the words of the Lord as received and written by Moses at Mount Sinai. In the books of the prophets, the contents were also the revelations of the prophets. Regardless of whether Moses heard it while awake, or they were dreams of the prophets, they were all revelations from Yahweh. In short, everything the Hebrew prophets received were divine revelations. In theology, spoken revelations were an important form of special revelations.

The way Confucian sages received their messages were more complicated, and need some explanation. One thing is clear, and it is that the way of Heaven did not refer to a divine revelation. This is because in the early classics such as *Shi, Shu, Li, Yi, Chunqiu, Lunyu* and *Mengzi,* there is no narrative about the ancient sages speaking to the heavens. The early sages, which included Yao, Shun, Yu, Tang, Wen, Wu and Kong, never said that their messages came down to them from the heavens, or some divine source. Another thing that is clear is that the message was not something innate to them. Confucius said this clearly in his quote: "No one is born with such knowledge." If this knowledge did not have a divine source, and the sages were not born with this knowledge, the only way left for them to acquire this knowledge is through learning and experimentation. Confucius said in *Lunyu*: "I was not born with knowledge. I studied the past as a student." He also said: "Only deep wisdom and extreme stupidity can never change." We can say that Confucius and the other sages achieved what they did because of a combination of extra - ordinary gifts and hard work.

In Chinese traditional culture, there is no clear, systematic theory of knowledge. Because of this, we do not have a clear idea of how Chinese sages used sense, thought, reason or instinct to understand the way of heaven. From research which is available to us now, we know that the two main ways the Chinese sages used to get knowledge were to find the way or to sense the way through sudden insights. The traditional Chinese character for a sage or holy man is 聖, which includes the elements for ear (to listen), mouth (to speak) and king. From "*Guodian-Wuxing*" we have the saying "A holy man is someone who knows by listening". In *the Mawangdui Hanmu Silk Books*, the saying was found: "Being a good listener is the beginning of the path to becoming a sage." [1] The Chinese characters for "to listen" (闻) and "to ask" (问) are related, because the actions are. For Confucius, the way to find the truth was to ask the ancestors, who were full of ancient wisdom. In *Lunyu* Confucius said: "If I hear the truth in the morning at sunrise, then it does not matter if I die in the evening". This highlighted the importance of finding the truth for him. In the last section of *Mengzi*, we learn that the sages learned by listening and asking the ancient sages, beginning with Yao, Shun and then ending with Confucius, and that sometimes, there would be a break in the knowledge of several generations. There was a constant process of asking and listening from these ancient sages and sources.

The other path to knowledge was through insight, usually by

---

[1]　Mawangdui Hanmu Boshu, 1980. Beijing: Cultural Rilics Press, p. 20.

personal experience. While asking and listening for knowledge usually involved dealing with contemporaries, or previous generations, insights were usually derived from observing nature and society. In *Mengzi*, there is the phrase "heaven doesn't speak". Still, for momentous matters such as the changing of dynasties, e.g. Shun receiving the position of king from Yao, they were determined by heaven. But the will of heaven was not communicated in the form of spoken orders, and was simply manifested in the smooth transfer of government duties. For example, Mengzi noted that Shun was put in charge of rites, and the different gods came and feasted. This showed that heaven approved of the change. Shun became the head of political affairs, and government continued smoothly, and the people were happy. This, in turn, showed that the people approved. Although heaven does not speak, it shows its will through social and natural harmony. While ordinary people cannot fully comprehend its will, the sages such as Yao, Shun and others can through observation, contemplation and insight. In a broader sense, revelation through actions and events is very different from revelation through direct and explicit words, as in the case of Yahweh. Because the former is less clear, it is harder for ordinary people to understand its meaning. Because it is subtle, those with wisdom had to strive to understand the will of Heaven. This process of gaining insight to this hidden meaning was an important part of what made one a sage. Through gaining insight, sages could then interpret the will of Heaven.

From the point of view of western epistemology and

epistemic psychology, "listening to the truth" and "gaining insight to the truth" do not perfectly match any epistemic categories. They may involve sense, reason, introspection, experience, instinct, and other ways of gaining knowledge, but they are all human ways of learning, and are not divine revelations. While the Chinese sages had special human talents, they were not as lucky as the Hebrew prophets, in that they could not directly receive the word of Heaven through revelations. Instead, they had to constantly think and observe and seek proof for what the will of Heaven was. In this respect, they were devout truth seckers, learning about how to observe and interpret the Will of Heaven, so in that respect one could call them prophet-philosophers. The Hebrew prophets never needed to seek out the will of Yahweh actively, since they were very clearly told what it was. They only needed to communicate his will, as it came to them either in dreams or while they were awake. In this respect, they were prophets only, not philosophers.

Those who have read the Jewish scriptures know that the Jewish god has emotions, will and can speak and give orders, and can directly reward and punish his followers. In these respects, he is just like humans. At the beginning of *Genesis*, we are told that this god can speak, and that he can will things into existence. Whatever he wills comes into being as soon as he wills it. In the book of *Exodus*, the Ten Commandments were revealed to Moses on Mount Sinai, along with other laws and commandments, and he communicated these revelations to his followers. The reason he was able to transmit the Word was because be had directly received it as a revelation from Yahweh. Unless the Jewish prophets received their revelations in word form, they would not have been able to communicate his will and revelations to their followers, and Judaism would have had a completely different form. This means that the reason the Hebrew prophets have the standing they have was because the Jewish god was a human god who could speak in language form.

In contrast to the language-speaking Jewish god, the heaven for the Chinese sages did not. [1] This characteristic is best illustrated in the Confucian classic *Lunyu*: "Why doesn't heaven speak? The four seasons change, and all living things continue to grow. Why doesn't heaven speak?" The conclusion is that heaven does not need to speak, because nature continues to go through its cycles without the god speaking. The sage then fills the role of attempting to receive, then interpret, the will of heaven. In order to understand the will of heaven, a sage must learn the wisdom of previous sages by asking, then gain insight through observation. This is why the Confucian sages are philosophers. In contrast, because the Jewish prophets could directly receive revelations from their god, they do not need to be, and are not philosophers.

---

[1] Chinese scholars have long been debating whether the Chinese god/s had human form. The author believes that up to the time of the Chinese philosophers of the Qin Dynasty, the belief that he/they did had been unquestionable. However, these writings in the Chinese classics were never collected together in a systematic fashion. In this article, I only discuss heaven's not speaking, and I will not discuss whether heaven has humanity.

III.

Another characteristic of the Hebrew prophets is that they did not fear social rejection and criticism. The ancient prophets strongly criticized the corruption of the kings, and criticized the people for turning their backs on Yahweh by worshipping false gods and following false prophets and their lies. They also criticized immoral behavior and unfair practices, and predicted the fall of the kingdoms of Israel, Judah, Assyria, Babylon, Tyre and Egypt, and the rise of the kingdom of Israel, and announced that Yahweh would punish the unfair and unjust. They called on the people to repent for their sins and to stay away from evil. "He has shown you, O mortal, what is good. And what does the Lord require of you? To act justly and to love mercy and to walk humbly with your God." [1] These prophets lived in different periods, some before the Assyrians defeated Israel, some before the fall of the kingdom of Israel, some before the fall of the kingdom of Judah, some during the period of Babylonian exile, and some at the time of the Persian kingdom. They also lived in different kingdoms and regions, some in Israel, some in Judah, some in Babylon, and some in Jerusalem, and so forth. They were all linked though by their rejection and loud criticism of political corruption, and social moral decay. At the same time, they urged the society to shift to a path to righteousness. Frequently their messages supported the poor and less fortunate

---

[1] *Micah* 6 : 8.

in society and their needs, and they represented the conscience of society. In Judaism, the prophets played a very important role, and their influence was profound. Even in modern times, the prophets represent thesocial conscience.

The Chinese sages would also criticize society. Confucius criticized how the music and rites of society had collapsed. His criticism was " Virtues not followed, studies not learned, hearing lessons but not applying, the bad not improved, these are my worries." [1] and he also said "Bad government is worse than a fierce tiger." [2] Mengzi also criticized saying that "People lived and prospered when they were challenged, but if times are too easy, then they become lazy and die." [3] However, when compared with the unforgiving criticism by the prophets of ancient Israel, those by the Chinese sages were much weaker. This was because the sages were kings, ministers, advisors or functioned in some capacity in the court, and wanted to be able to influence the ruler. As members of the ruling class, it would have been impossible for them to target their criticism at themselves or their own administration and society. Some philosophers, such as Confucius, did not hold official positions, but wanted to influence the kings. While they may have voiced their criticisms of contemporary society every now and then, it would have been impossible for them to oppose the ruler or his administration. In the Chinese classics there is mention of "good rule and happy kingdom" . This is a reference to an

---

[1] *Lunyu: Shu'er.*

[2] *Liji: Tangongxia.*

[3] *Mengzi: Gaozixia.*

ideal kingdom where the ruler is beneficent, the ministers are virtuous, government is clean, and the citizens live simple and happy lives, in short, an almost perfect society. In the classic *Mengzi*, Shun advised Yao for 28 years, and Yao turned his kingdom over to Shun. Yu advised Shun for 17 years, then Shun turned his kingdom over to Yu. Yi advised Yu for seven years, then Yu turned over his kingdom to Yi, but the people did not want him, wanting the son of Yu instead, who was named Qi. So, Qi became the king, bringing an end to the non-hereditary transfer of power. From then on, all kings would transfer their power to their own eldest son. [①] Yao, Shun and Yu had all adopted the principles of benevolence government, and practiced compassion, rituals, love, and respect in their rule, which was why they were all loved by their subjects, and the society under their administration prosperous. The fact that the king could give his kingdom away to anyone of his choosing showed that he was virtuous and trusted in his decisions by his own people. In this golden age of politics and society, there was no need for strong criticism.

Behind the weak criticism by the Chinese sages, and the strong, even barbed, criticism by the Hebrew prophets, we can see two completely different political systems and methods of rule.

In the Chinese classics, Yao, Shun and Yu lived during the formative period of the early Chinese Huaxia culture. This could be described as the beginning of the golden age of

---

① *Mengzi: Wanzhangshang.*

Chinese social development. In this period, rulers and ministers sought to rule by setting an example of virtue, instead of ruling through harsh government. Shun was the best example for ruling by virtue. According to the book *Mengzi*, Shun's father had a strong dislike for his son, and tried to kill him on several occasions. On one occasion, he sent Shun to clean a granary roof, then took away the ladder and set the granary on fire. On another occasion, he told him to go clean up a well, and then covered up the well. But after becoming king, not only did Shun not turn against his father, but he treated him kindly. [1] Shun's younger brother had taken upon himself the task of killing Shun, but after becoming king, not only did he not turn against his younger brother, he made him the king of Youbei kingdom. [2] Not only did Shun not retaliate against the two people who had tried to kill him, he treated them with genuine kindness. For this reason, Mengzi and other Chinese sages respected Shun as a model for virtuous rulers.

After the Xia and Shang dynasties, the Zhou Dynasty had a very complete system of rites. The purpose of these rites was to clearly define human and social relations. Special emphasis was placed on the king-ministers and father-son relationships. On these foundational relationships, all other relationships were based. The basis for all these relationships was virtue, which was instrumental for ruling the kingdom. For this reason, Confucius strongly supported the rites and model of virtue used

---

[1]   *Mengzi: Jinxinshang.*

[2]   *Mengzi: Wanzhangshang.*

in the Zhou Dynasty. Confucius said: "Government should rule by virtue, just as the north star rules in the sky with other stars around it." He also said: "If government is guided by politics, and order is maintained through punishment, then the people will have no shame. If rule is by virtue, and order is kept through rites, then the people understand shame and have character." [1] Another Chinese classic, *Daxue*, starts by describing the three rules and eight clauses, and also focuses on ruling by virtue.

Generally speaking, Yao, Shun, and Yu's passing the throne to a competent successor, and rule by virtue during the Qin Dynasty, all exemplified the power of humanity and virtue as instruments of govenance. These Chinese sages - Yao, Shun, Yu, Tang, Wen, Wu, Zhou Gong, and Confucius - all embodied these characteristics of rule of virtue.

In the history of ancient Israel, there is no similar period dominated by the Chinese model of rule of virtue. Moses and his followers essentially adopted divine rule. In this period, the laws were set by their lord, and Moses was the spokesman and representative for the divinity. All the other high priests and ministers were in charge of executing those laws. All their duties revolved around obeying the will of this divine ruler. In peacetime, they handled civil affairs, but at wartime, they would lead soldiers into war, but ultimately all served the divinity. [2] Later, during the kingdom period, the divine power

---

[1] *Lunyu*: *Weizheng*.

[2] J. Maxwell Miller and John H. Hayes, 1986. *A History of Ancient Israel and Judea,* Philadephia: The Westminster Press, pp. 111 – 112.

and the power of the king ruled side by side, executed by the prophet and the king, respectively. In theory though, the divine ruler was still Yahweh, and the divine power was higher than the earthly ruler, and just like his people, he needed to follow the will of his divine lord. In practice though, the power of the king often trumped that of the divine lord, and sometimes acted disrespectfully toward the divine lord. These included encouraging idolatry, which tended to lead to moral decay. Many of the prophets spoke during these periods, seeking to arrest this trend. The existence of prophets had to do with the political system they lived in, which was based on the concept of divine rule. In this kind of system, the prophet acted as the spokesman for the divine lord and introduced the divine laws. Acting as the divine spokesman, he acted as a critic and check on the earthly king.

IV.

Confucian scholars have the tradition of following the Chinese sages. This was because in the eyes of the Confucian scholars, the Chinese sages were not only prophet-philosophers, they were paragons of virtue. In the Chinese etymology dictionary *Ciyuan*, the definition of a holy man is someone with the highest moral character. In Judaism, the prophet does not have such a high moral character, nor is prophethood the goal of moral education.

Confucius divided people into different ranks based on their moral character. At the top were the sages and gentlemen (君

子), who were considered to be morally exemplary. In daily life, "the gentleman acts quietly and speaks carefully" . [1] When it came to duties and benefits, "the gentlemen honors his duties without seeking benefits for himself" . [2] The gentleman was also someone who could enjoy life. [3] Mengzi went even further, claiming that, becoming a sage was not only a goal, it was an attainable goal, which was captured in the saying "anyone could become Yao, Shun" . Mengzi said that the way to become a sage was to practice constantly, to focus on being good, and to build on one's innate goodness until it defined every aspact of one's being. Because Confucius and Mengzi set this goal, and after the Han Dynasty, the sages were the most highly respected, becoming a sage became the goal for all Chinese intellectuals, and devotion to the sages became a main part of Chinese social pursuit. In the eyes of the Chinese, Yao and Shun were the earliest and best Chinese sages, and Confucius was the "uncrowned king" , the "high holy man and highest teacher" , and "the model for all teachers forever" . These were the highest exemplar of virtue and the best teachers in Chinese society and history.

Beginning with Confucius, Chinese intellectuals recognized the power of a good example. He said: "If the example is straight, then the walk will be straight. If the example is crooked, then the walk will be crooked." [4] Another quote was: "With good rites,

---

[1] *Lunyu: Xu'er.*

[2] *Lunyu: Liren.*

[3] *Lunyu: Yaoyue.*

[4] *Lunyu: Zilu.*

the people will be respectful. With good justice, the people will obey the laws. With good trust, the people will be honest. If you follow this good example, people from all over will bring their families to come to live in your kingdom." [1] Mengzi said: "If the king is benevolent, then everyone will be benevolent; if the king is righteous, then everyone will be righteous; if the king is moral and straight, then the nation will be at peace." [2] . In following periods, all Confucian intellectuals would follow this, and put special emphasis on the power of good moral leadership.

Prophets were different. In the time of the Jewish scriptures, prophets were those who stood on the side of the divine lord to criticize the king and society, and all social behavior which ran counter to divine teaching. Because of this, the prophet represented the social conscience and was respected by the public. The Jewish scriptures did not call upon the people to copy the prophets, and did not call them a model for moral behavior. Because Yahweh was the divine lord, and it was up to them to follow the divine word. In this religion, humans were "made in the form of God, and they should follow the word of God". This god is all powerful, and had made a contract with humanity, and had given his laws to the people so that they would have a way to follow him by following his laws. Prophets where the spokesman for god on earth, but they were not divine, and could not become divine. For this reason, they could not become a model for ideal thought and behavior. Also, one could not become a prophet through

---

[1]   *Lunyu: Zilu.*
[2]   *Mengzi: Lilouxia.*

study. According to the Jewish scriptures, the prophets were chosen by god. Since they were divinely chosen, there was no way someone could study to become a prophet.

In Judaism, a person of high moral character was considered a righteous man. Unlike a prophet, who did not necessarily have to be a person of high moral standing, the righteous man was noted and respected for the devotion to his faith, and devotion to his god, and willingness to obey all of the laws and commandments. In the Jewish scriptures, examples of righteous men were Abraham, Noah and Job. Even though they were described as models of good behavior, their social position was much lower than the prophets, and much lower than the Chinese sages among Confucian intellectuals. This was because in a society ruled by divine law, which ancient Israel's was, the influence a righteous man could have on a society was minimal. By contrast, in ancient Chinese society, which was ruled by kings who were using virtue and setting a good example, sages were very important as model rulers and advisors for the whole society.

V.

All religions and cultural traditions advocate benevolence and justice. If we compare the Jewish prophets and the Chinese sages who were venerated by Confucian intellectuals though, we can see that there is difference in emphasis. To the extent that the Hebrew prophets were the embodiment of justice, the Chinese sages were the embodiment of charity.

In the Jewish scriptures, there is the love of the lord, and love of each other. In *Deuteronomy* 6: 4 -5, the text reads: "Hear, O Israel: the Lord our God is one. Love the Lord your God with all your heart, with all your soul, and with all your strength." This is the commandment which must be recited by all devout Jews every day. In *Leviticus* 19:34, the text reads: "The foreigner residing among you must be treated as your native-born. Love them as yourself, for you were foreigners in Egypt. I am the Lord your God." This is about love and compassion for others, and is Judaism's contribution to humanity.

Standing in contrast to love and compassion is justice. While love and compassion stand for care, devotion and other emotions, justice largely stands for fairness and equity in the social and psychological sense. Justice is impartial, fair and unselfish, and treats everyone the same. In Judaism, justice is frequently what the prophets talk about when discussing the poor and the disenfranchised in society, when they are struggling against the powers that be to look for support. If one were to ask whether the prophets preferred love and compassion, or justice, it would have to be justice. In *the Five Books of Moses*, there are many laws about fair punishment. The most attention-grabbing rule is "A life for a life, an eye for an eye, a tooth for a tooth, a hand for a hand, a foot for a foot." ① Not only should the laws be just, but

---

① *Exodus* 21:23-25. One interpretation is that this does not necessarily mean that one must get the same in return for a loss, but rather that one should seek an equivalent value for a loss. No matter what is the correct interpretation, it should be close in value.

the judicial system should be just. "You should not give false testimony against your neighbor" [1] "Do not follow the crowd in doing wrong. When you give testimony to a lawsuit, do not pervert justice by siding with the crowd." [2] "Keep far from a false charge, and do not kill the innocent or the righteous, for I will acquit the guilty. You shall not take a bribe, for a bribe blinds the clear-sighted and subverts the cause of the just. You shall not oppress a stranger, since you yourselves know the feelings of a stranger, for you also were strangers in the land of Egypt." [3] There are many examples of prophets standing up for the weak. There is the famous story of King David, who coveted the wife of Uriah the Hittite, Bathsheba. After making her pregnant, David sent Uriah to battle, where he was killed. When the prophet Nathan learned of this, he denounced King David, and the king confessed and repented for his sin. In addition, shortly after birth, his new son died of illness, which David took to be punishment for his sin. If we were to say that most of the prophets mentioned first directed their criticism at certain individuals, later on, they directed their criticism at whole peoples, such as the Israelites, the Ephramites, the Aramites, and the Assyrians, or at whole classes, such as high priests, or whole countries, such as Israel, Judah, Jerusalem, and there was more criticism of "corrupt and oppressive practices which challenged social order." [4] The

---

[1]   *Exodus* 20:16.

[2]   *Exodus* 23:2.

[3]   *Exodus* 23:7-9.

[4]   Huston Smith 1991. *The World's Religions: Our Great Wisdom Traditions* (orginally titled: The Rigilions of Man.) New York: *Harpercollins*, p.312.

prophets'struggle for social justice is most clearly expressed in this phrase: "But let justice roll on like a river, righteousness like a never-failing stream!" [1]

The greatest scientist of the 20 century, Albert Einstein, was Jewish, and in his memoirs, he noted that social justice was a core value for the Jewish people. "The pressure of several thousand years of history has forced the Jewish people ever closer together, and to develop our philosophical beliefs. First is our desire for social justice, and then there is our mutual help and forgiveness. Even in our oldest scriptures, these are mentioned, and reveal our dreams for a just society. These ideals have influenced Christianity and Islam, and have had a positive social influence on many societies. Such major figures as Moses, Spinoza and Karl Marx, even though very different in their beliefs, all sought social justice, and were willing to sacrifice themselves in the process. Their ancient beliefs were what brought them on this path." [2]

Confucianism has its own theory of justice. For the confucian sages though, the core value was benevolence, from which, everything else flowed. Confucius said that "Do not do unto others, what you would not have them do unto you", this was a way of implementing benevolence. Rites and manners were for implementing benevolence: "Controlling oneself and honoring the rites are benevolence." Other virtues which were

---

[1]   *Amos* 5:24.

[2]   Albert Einstein 1979, *Collected works of Einstein* Vol.3, Translated and edited by Xu Liangying, Zhao Zhongli and Zhang Xuansan. Beijing: Commercial Press, p.164.

related to charity are warmth, compassion, respect, thriftiness, magnanimity, filial piety, loyalty and trust. All of these virtues are specific ways of being benevolent. Confucius thought that gentleman of high moral values had to have three virtues: wisdom, benevolence and courage. He said: "The wise man is never confused, the charitable man does not worry, and the courageous man is never afraid." [1] Within these three virtues, the most important is benevolence. By this he meant that a benevolent person would have charity at the core of his moral character, and can understand, and become a wise person who practices charity. This was why he said: "A benevolent person must have courage, but a courageous person need not have charity." [2] Mengzi, who frequently talked about the ancient Chinese sages, including Yao, Shun, Wen Wang, Zhou Gong and Liu Xiahui were all exemplary of benevolence and filial piety. He strongly supported the concept of virtuous government. To sum up, Confucius and Mengzi placed benevolence at the core of their systems of values.

As mentioned before, the prophets functioned as social critics. We have discovered that they must have a standard for judgment, and a goal. This goal is justice. Anything which departs from the standard of fairness, departs from the will of god, should be criticized and rejected. One could say that the Hebrew prophets were using justice as a mirror to criticize

---

[1] *Lunyu-Zihan.*

[2] *Lunyu-Xianwen.*

the unjust and unfair. In comparison, Chinese sages acted as role models for society. Their words and behavior were all supposed to manifest the core principle of benevolence. The prophets' core principle of justice, and the sages' core principle of benevolence served as the basis of the social and political systems for their respective people.

VI.

We have been discussing the Chinese sages and Hebrew prophets from about 2,500 years ago. In terms of time, they belong to the past. But their words and thoughts transcend time. The influence of the Hebrew prophets continues to this day in Jewish communities all over the world, and also on Christian and Islamic thought. When comparing the Hebrew prophets and Chinese sages, therefore, we should not only compare dead materials in the forms of books and archives; we should also compare their values and spirit that are still alive today. In modern times, it would be inconceivable for us to think of prophets receiving the word of god, and communicating it to the rest of society. However, they had many qualities which are worth following even today, such as their fearlessness and commitment to justice. As modern Chinese society changes and strives to adopt the modern values of democracy and justice, these qualities are needed now more than ever. Now, although the traditional social relationships promoted by the Chinese intellectual class seem outdated, there is a continued need for benevolence, righteousness, manners, wisdom, trust, warmth,

234 / CHINA AND ISRAEL: Through the Eyes of Scholars and Journalists

kindness, respect, frugality, and other traditional virtues. Even more important, there is a greater need now, more than ever, for the core Confucian value of benevolence in contemporary China.

We can also see how the Hebrew prophets and Chinese sages complemented each other. The prophets' fearlessness and strong commitment to social justice help compensate for the Chinese sages' weakness in this area. At the same time, the Chinese sages' core principle of benevolence and their high moral standard, and keenness in making virtue an instrument of governance, may also help Jewish society, and the western societies that have been deeply influenced by Jewish values. In fact, no society is perfect, and every society needs role models. This is especially true of modern societies, which all need democracy and rule of law, including limits on the power of the rulers, criticism and oversight. In this sence, this comparison of the Hebrew prophets and Chinese sages with respect to their functions, characteristics, values and characteristics is bound to have genuine value and significance.

(Originally published in *Social Sciences in China*, 2009,

Vol. 6.)

Notes on Israel[*]

HUANG Heng[**]

In 2008, before the Beijing Olympics, I went to work in Israel. In spring of 2012, I left. In China, not only in China really, but also in Italy, France, England, Spain, Japan, etc, everyone who knew I had lived in Israel for some time asked me, "What kind of a country is it?"

In fact, as a professional reporter, I have to say that this is a very normal but also very poor way of asking a question. A responsible person would have a hard time using a few simple words to describe a whole country, unless he is arrogant and prejudiced. Therefore, every time I was faced with this question, I thought hard, and finally choked out one word: amazing.

---

*   Translated by Andrew H. Keller, polished by Liang Fan.

**   Reporter from the Xinhua News Agency.

Israel is an amazing place.

Its amazingness lies not in what it has created or destroyed, but its very existence. In the era of globalization, nothingness is increasingly a sociological issue. But in Israel, the existence of actuality, conflict and compromise, clamor and silence, mosque minarets, tourists walking Jesus' path to crucifixion bearing crosses on their backs, constitute everyday life rather than words in academic books.

I. Damascus Gate

Driving through Damascus Gate in Jerusalem is like crossing between two worlds.

One side is orderly, where one can see Jewish scholars dressed in black clothes with black hats and pale faces. Seeing them standing under traffic lights waiting to cross the road is one thing. Watching them walk under the white stones of the Old City wall frequently invites the illusion of being several thousand years back in time.

The other side is chaotic, but also full of life. During the day, truck after truck bring vegetables and daily necessities, and brawny, dark and rough-skinned Arab men and children busy themselves unloading them. A shop owner taps on a calculator rapidly. A girl holding an English book makes her way quietly through the streets. At night, on the wet ground, vegetable leaves and wrapping paper are everywhere. Young people driving cars, windows rolled down, dance music shaking the ground.

One day, at dusk, I was sauntering through the Old Town area inhabited by Arabs. I had just crossed through Damascus Gate when I suddenly saw a rabbi passing through the narrow streets and walking toward Mediterranean Inn, where Mark Twain once lived. Today, the Mediterranean Inn is a Jewish religious school, with the property rights to the rooms belonging to different Jews. Former Israeli Prime Minister Ariel Sharon bought one, which was considered a gesture, like the large Star of David banner flapping above. All sounds seemed to disappear at that moment. The same look was written in the eyes of the rabbi and the other Arab passers by. The rabbi, with a stiff back, walked on and away. Everyone soon recovered their gaze, and someone again made a move on a chessboard.

This is normal life in Israel, life no tourist can find. Many backpackers take the light rail in and out, not realizing that the section of the road that extends north before Damascus Gate was the "green line" before the Middle East war of 1967. In political news in various languages, things repeatedly appear that most viewers do not understand.

Yet Jerusalem does not just have the Old City and Damascus Gate. Even under the 1948 United Nations partition boundaries, Israel has other life within its borders, mixing problems and happiness.

II. Israel's Fashion

In Israel, Ultra-Orthodox religious people, it goes without saying, wear black suits and black pants, white shirts and black shoes from morning to night. They all look very much the same. If we look closer, most people's outer coat is of a decent quality; the shoes are heavy bottomed, round, of rough, black leather and with thick laces. In the rainy season they become stained with grass clippings and mud, giving one a flavor of life in Israel.

Women in Orthodox religious families do not wear bright-colored clothes. They wear mostly black and white, and occasionally blue-gray, all very tidy and clean. When I first arrived, Israel seemed to offer a refreshing kind of aesthetic enjoyment, especially to someone who had been exposed to the neon-lit debauchery of other cities for too long. The appearance of Jewish girls aged fourteen to fifteen is rather unique, they are mostly petite, with thin frames, thin color, plus shy eyes and pale faces.

The last few summers in Israel, Crocs were popular in the summer - those plastic sandals with lots of holes. From old ladies to babies, almost every pair of feet had a pair of Crocs on them. In the winter, UGGs, those Eskimo-style deerskin boots, were popular. Neither young girls nor middle-aged women wanted to be seen as behind the times, or others, fashion-wise.

When going to a synagogue on the Sabbath - an important social occasion - fashion is reflected in dignity. You can see numerous big-brand basic models shirts, ties, vests, and jackets-no gaudy decorations and tailoring, only ironed, straight lines and meticulous cuffs, hats, and brooches.

III. The Reality Show "Big Brother"

"Big Brother" is a reality show originating in the Netherlands. In 2009, the show's ratings actually hit a new record, reaching 30 percent. Newspapers said that it was Israel's most successful television program ever, earning about 25 million US douars in advertising and receiving over 6 million text message votes. The telecom company earned about 500,000 US douars from these text messages.

A pensioner lady buying vegetables on the street told me that she liked watching this show. She would get online to watch the live stream on the Internet as soon as she woke up, and watch the featured-clip broadcast version on television at night.

A veteran columnist I admire explained that the program is popular because it shows the conflict among Israeli Jews. Contestants naturally fall into two camps based on their backgrounds. One represents the descendants of Jews that had previously lived in the Middle East and North Africa. The other represents Ashkenazi Jewish immigrants from Europe.

IV. The Archaeologist and the Poet

In Israel, media publicity permeates every place and is on all the time, not only in the office of the Prime Minister or the Facebook and Twitter feeds of the Israeli Defense Force, but in each discovery and report of archaeologists. They are attempting to convey a message: Jews, not Palestinians, have lived on this land since ancient times. Even though the Roman Empire and 19th-century Britain-appointed rulers called it Palestine, it is a place in concept by name only, not in concept by ethnicity.

When Poet Laureate Mahmoud Darwish was buried in 2009, a group of the Arab world's most famous intellectuals issued a petition calling for him to be returned safely home to what is today the Galilee region of northern Israel.

To understand Israel, one needs a sense of time. And only with enough time would one be able truly to understand Israel's reality. Of course, this is not a distinguishing feature of Israelis or Israeli Jews. The rest of the world is similar. There is no qualitative difference between two people because one does or does not believe in the Five Books of Moses. As Hendrik Willem van Loon wrote, "The Jews of 3,000 years ago, 2,000 years ago, and today are all ordinary people, like you or me. They are neither as they sometimes claim, so much better than others, nor are they as their enemies often criticize, so much worse than others."

This is a change that the so-called experts in international affairs that are stuck with issues of theoretical system would never imagine. Time is like a pendulum, swinging calmly to the vertex, ultimately falling with the collapse of the left wing in Israeli elections in 2009.

(Originally published in *Tong Zhou Gong Ji*, 2013, Vol. 4.)

Visit to China Again

Sondra M. Rubenstein*

I. First Visit to China

Did you ever have the experience of realizing that your beliefs were out of touch with today's reality? Normally, that would lead to the uncomfortable feeling of cognitive dissonance, unless, as in my case, you were thinking about China and about how good it felt to have been proven wrong.

---

* Professor Sondra M. Rubenstein is a media expert, who was born and educated in the United States.She chaired the Department of Journalism & Mass Media Studies at Hofstra University in New York until her retirement in 2001, when she and her husband moved to Israel.Her first visit to China was on a Hofstra Exchange Program in 1986.Her second visit was on a joint Sino-Israeli program in 2004, when she saw great changes in China. She was deeply impressed by them.

The first time I was in China was back in the fall of 1986, when I was on an Exchange Program from Hofstra University (New York), assigned to teach in the Foreign Language Department of East China Normal University, in Shanghai. My decision to apply for my University's program was based on my love of China, its history, culture, and my excitement over the economic reforms that were being introduced by China's then leader, the late, beloved Deng Xiaoping.

By the time I arrived in August 1986, I was primed to expect a greater degree of "openness" than actually existed. It took a while, but I came to realize that there was merely an illusion of friendliness. Most of the "foreign experts," as we were then called, were kept at arms' length by our Chinese colleagues, who feared appearing "too friendly."

In the second week on campus, I purchased a bicycle and often went riding on the streets and in the alleyways of Shanghai. There was very little auto traffic in those days, and at night the city streets were almost all dark, except for an occasional dim streetlight. During our daytime rides, another professor and I often stopped in local shops for a bowl of noodles or dumplings, especially on cold days. I remember feeling the friendliness of these hard-working people, who always made room for us to sit amongst them.

Besides biking all over Shanghai, I was able to do some sightseeing with the help of the University's Foreign Affairs Officer. I visited Nanjing, Hefei, Beijing, Xi'an, Guangzhou, and other more local sites. Although I enjoyed my work and loved my students and the one or two Chinese colleagues who befriended me, I experienced a constant tension in the air.

When I was preparing to leave Shanghai in mid-January 1987, I felt a deep sense of sadness. Students came individually to say goodbye the night before my flight out of China. All brought some gift and warmly wished me well. One student, a sensitive poet, asked me why I seemed so sad. I answered, "I am sorry that I may have spoken about unrealistic goals regarding the future of your country." He understood and, taking my hand, said "You and other foreign professors have helped to sow the seeds of a better future. It will take time."

II. Revisiting China

Although I read about China's development with real interest in the years following my first visit, I had apparently held on to my "old baggage," which was packed with skepticism and with a certitude that not much had changed since 1986. In August 2001, I retired from Hofstra University and my husband and I moved to Israel, where I began to teach in the Communication Department of Haifa University. I also began to lecture, on an occasional basis at the Mount Carmel Center for International Training in Haifa.

When the Carmel Center and the Foreign Ministry of Israel sent me to Nepal and to Ethiopia to work with journalists in those countries, I was very pleased. And, when I was given the opportunity to do a two-week course in Beijing, I was delighted. I had already met some Chinese journalists who participated in seminars at the Center, and I was struck by their openness and by how well informed they were. As I prepared to return to China to teach a two-week seminar in August 2004, I thought of the words my Chinese poet had uttered on my last evening in China, back in 1986, "It will take time." I told myself not to expect too much.

The Sino-Israel Workshop on Media Strategies for Social Change was sponsored by the Women's Foreign Language Publications of China, the Golda Meir Mount Carmel Center for International Training and by the Foreign Ministry of Israel. My colleague, Rafi Mann (Senior Editor, Maariv and Lecturer at Hebrew University's Department of Communication and Journalism), and I were extremely proud to represent our country, Israel, and we were anxious to do the best we could in our professional efforts and in helping to cement our country's friendship with China.

From the moment we arrived at the new and beautiful Beijing International Airport and were greeted so warmly by the course organizers, I began to realize the immensity of the changes that had been taking place. As we were driven to the lovely Jianguo Garden Hotel, I was amazed at what I saw through the car windows:The fashionably, well-dressed pedestrians; the huge number of cars; the magnificent buildings; and the laughing, smiling, happy-looking people. Beijing had become a "world-class" city.

That first afternoon, we were introduced to the four young women who were going to be our translators. They were delightful, self-confident, out-going and extremely bright. To me they came to represent the best of what has been changing in

China.I thought back to 1986 and remembered all the unhappy young women students who had approached me, seeking help to leave China. Most of them didn't care where they went; they merely wanted out.

The first week of our course sped by. We enjoyed interacting with our participants. Their questions and comments were excellent and challenging, and their sense of humor delighted and warmed our hearts. Again, I thought back to my passive and mostly silent students in Shanghai. Comparing the two teaching experiences reminds me of the comparison between night and day.

III. A New Shanghai

Having heard of the massive construction that had taken place off the Bund in Shanghai, I felt I had to see it to believe it. As they say, seeing is believing! Several times a week (back in 1986) I had ridden my bicycle from the University to this area, which fronted on the bay. The old "Peace Hotel" was still there, along with its staid neighboring buildings. However, a new promenade - filled with early local risers and many tourists from around the world - faced a view that had not existed eighteen years ago.

"Think of the view of lower Manhattan and imagine it dozens of times more beautiful, more graceful, with architectural styles more imaginative," I later wrote to friends in Israel and in the United States. My mouth fell open as I gaped across the bay. The old bridge that I had ridden over from one side of the city to the "old" side of the city had been replaced by a more sturdy structure. While the old Seamen's Inn was still there, cleaned up and proudly standing among its new neighbors, it looked like what it was, an interesting relic of China's past when its trade was dominated by foreign merchants. The new magnificent skyscrapers announced China's new age and new growing economic power.

Later that evening, we walked around a bit on the brightly lit streets of Shanghai, where we saw Chinese people of all ages enjoying themselves in the many restaurants or shopping or just sitting or standing and talking to each other. Everyone seemed freer, more open, and definitely happier than anything I remembered.

IV. Beijing Impression

Back in Beijing for the last week of the course, I tried to see as much of the city as possible, and, of course, I was extremely impressed with the old and the new. I considered the tremendous economic development that had occurred and that was still in progress. However, as impressive as the beautiful new buildings, the huge number of cars, the well-lighted streets, the enormous presence of cell phones and the many other modern technologies, the biggest change, the change that touched my heart, was the absence of fear and the presence of smiles on people's faces. For me, this was the most profound change of all.

I have no memory of having seen young couples holding

hands in the streets in 1986. Nor do I remember hearing laughter, or seeing people hugging, young people joking around in public, or old people smiling. I'm not saying it didn't happen. I am saying I never saw it public.

One evening I walked around Tian'anmen Square. I saw many couples and children flying colorful kites of various sizes. As I watched, I felt the old images slip away, and experienced a wave of happiness as children laughed excitedly to see their colorful kites sailing in the skies far overhead.

On my last Saturday in Beijing, I spent a few hours strolling around the huge Beihai Park, after revisiting the Temple of Heaven. The park was filled with people of all ages. Some were involved in a large group activity; others sought out quiet places to be alone or together with a loved one. People were exercising to music, singing in a large group while standing in the shelter of the beautiful pine trees, playing games, listening to amateur opera singers, picnicking or just sitting and enjoying a beautiful day in a lovely park.

Yes, the physical and economic changes in the two major cities I returned to visit are profound. However, the changes that most warmed my heart, that forever laid to rest old perceptions and fears, can be seen in the faces of the people, from those wonderful journalists and editors who participated in our workshop, to those I met or simply observed going about their daily business or enjoying a day in the park.

(Originally published in *Women of China*, 2005, Vol. 3.)

Economy

Agricultural Challenges in Western China: Sino-Israeli Partnership

Comparative Analysis of Chinese and Israeli Water Strategy

Economic Development and Environmental Protection in Israel

Agricultural Challenges in Western China: Sino-Israeli Partnership[*]

Itzhak Shelef^{**}

The development of western China means first the development of agriculture in the region. As a diplomat detailing to the experts seated here the difficulties and challenges faced by Chinese agriculture, I may not be an expert. But as a national representative who understands Israeli agricultural technology, I hope I am able to provide some useful advice and information to this respectable forum. I will concentrate on four main points.

(1) The water scarcity issue and the necessity of introducing water-saving technologies;

(2) The role of advanced agricultural technologies in

---

    *   This article is adapted from a speech given at the "2001 Western China Forum". Translated by Andrew H. Keller, polished by Liang Fan.

    **   Israeli Ambassador to China.

sustainable agricultural development, especially in western China;

（3）The importance of the technology promotion process and the successful application of technology;

（4）Israel's role in increasing efforts to develop western Chinese provinces.

I. Water Scarcity and Water-saving Technologies

Drought plagues not only China, it is a global problem. Water scarcity is a major factor restricting the economic development of any country, including China. Rational allocation of water resources and the application of water-saving irrigation technologies have become the basis for agricultural development. This is suitable for the arable regions that account for a quarter of China's total land area.

In order to make sure my questions have sufficient foundation, let me provide some facts.

China's annual per capita water consumption is 2,440m^3, which is less than a quarter of the world average. Twenty years ago, agriculture accounted for 88% of China's total water consumption. Today this has dropped to 72%.

Population explosion and continued urbanization will reduce this ratio to 52%.

The area of farmland affected by drought has increased progressively from 11 million ha in the 1950s to 20.6 million ha in the 1990s.

China is one of 13 countries in the world facing critical water shortages.

China has 130 million hectares of arable land, of which 53 million hectares can be irrigated. But only 5% of irrigable land can use water-saving irrigation technology.

Saying China's water use efficiency is low would not be wrong. The following examples illustrate this point. On average, it takes 1 cubic meter of water to produce a kilogram of grain in China. In some developed countries, it takes only 0.2 to $0.3m^3$ to produce as much.

From the aforementioned facts, we can conclude that China must promote the efficient use of water.

I intend not to use the generic term water-saving technologies because water conservation is only one component of the integrated system of efficient water use. Water conservation is one manifestation of efficient water use.

The ultimate goal of advanced agriculture is high quality and high yields under the premise of water conservation.

The basic standard should be to get the highest yield from every drop of water.

II. Advanced Agricultural Technologies

China's accession to the World Trade Organization will enable Chinese agriculture to meet the challenges of low-value foreign crops.

For example: Corn planted by Chinese farmers cannot compete with what will be imported from North America in quality or price.

The way to cope with this new situation is to introduce

new, advanced agricultural technologies. The upgrade process integrates different elements: irrigation, fertilization, qualified seeds, and other elements play important roles here.

III. Technology Promotion

People often make the mistake of thinking that the transfer of technology from developed to developing countries will solve most problems. In some cases, they might be right, but not in the case of agriculture.

The key to the sustainable development of agriculture is to strengthen technology originating from research and to transform the transformation process among the targets of the technology.

In many situations, the development of a country's specialized technology originates from disconnects among the targets of technology application. What forms these disconnects is a lack of an intermediary agent to convey research to farmers and train them in the use of innovative technologies and techniques.

An intermediary agent is a professional technology dispatcher. People call it a "technology promotion broker" or simply a "training system." Technology can originate from abroad or at home, but if there is no intermediary agent, any existing technology will lose value.

IV. Israel's Role in China

Severe water shortages, the necessity of introducing efficient water use technologies, as well as the need to train experts and farmers in western provinces in new technologies all make Israeli willing to share with China the experience we have accumulated over the years.

The project the Israeli government has put forward based on the aforementioned considerations is to create a center for agriculture in arid areas. The center attaches importance to developing effective irrigation agriculture in arid areas. The Chinese government has decided that the center will be located in the Xinjiang Uygur Autonomous Region.

The center will carry out three tasks: training, research and development, and production.

(1) Training. The goal of the center is to train technicians and farmers from all regions in western provinces to introduce effective water use methods in order to achieve high yields and high quality.

(2) Research and Development. Research and development, including planting high-value vegetables, fruits, cash crops, and flowers with advanced irrigation, fertilization, and management will be done in cooperation with local research institutions. It will also pay attention to the planting of "green" organic vegetables.

(3) Production. The project will demonstrate the potential goals that adopting advanced, effective water use technology in arid zones will reach. The demonstration is aimed at encouraging other groups and companies to strengthen the implementation of innovative practices in additional agricultural projects. Israel will provide necessary equipment for the center and dispatch experts to provide technical support in the form of exchanging experiences with local experts and farmers.

The expected goals of the China-Israel Center for Agriculture in Arid Zones are as follows:

(1) The production and use of quality cultivars and qualified seeds appropriate for areas with large temperature swings, high-salinity soil, and drought conditions.

(2) Demonstration of technologies increasing the efficient use of water and fertilizer, including the use of brackish water and treated wastewater.

(3) Domestication of new desert crops and guidance of large-scale cultivation.

(4) Improvement of post-harvest storage methods.

(5) Demonstration of applications for crop protection technologies (including plastic and net-membrane coverage).

(6) Demonstration of the benefits of soil exposure, crop rotation, and topsoil cover.

(7) Demonstration of selective plant protection measures and application methods for bio-pesticides.

(8) Demonstration of how business beginning with agriculture can sustain the development environment of the arid zone economic system.

China and Israel hope this joint project will strengthen agriculture in western China and increase its standards.

(Originally published in *Western China's Development*,
2001, Vol. 10.)

Comparative Analysis of Chinese and Israeli Water Strategy[*]

HUAN Ji[**]

Water is a basic natural resource and a strategic economic resource. It provides important support for economic and social development, plays a key role in shaping the ecological environment, and an indispensable part of a country's comprehensive national prowess. Water is the sine qua non for the presence of life on earth. The world consumes 3 trillion tons of fresh water annually, more than it does any other forms of resource. The significance of water for a country's development is even greater than that of crude oil. This necessarily calls for treating water as a strategic resource. Water matters are regarded with utmost seriousness in Israel, whose government

---

* Translated by Andrew H. Keller, polished by Liang Fan.
** Professor, Zhengzhou University, Zhengzhou, Henan.

has attached to them national security strategic importance. The Israeli government uses legislation to strengthen water management and use. Indeed, it leads the world in this area, and other countries should learn from Israel's valuable experiences.

I. Comparative Analysis of Chinese and Israeli Geographic and Climatological Characteristics

China is located in eastern Asia on the west coast of the Pacific Ocean. It is bordered by both land and sea. Most areas are located in the northern temperate zone, featuring four distinct seasons, and suitable for human habitation. Israel is located in western Asia, on the east coast of the Mediterranean also bordered by both land and sea. Its central and northern regions are made up of hills and rift valleys. The south is covered in deserts. Thi is a harsh living environment, and it belongs to the Mediterranean subtropical climate zone.

(I) Similarities

China and Israel are countries in the northern hemisphere bordered by both land and sea. We might for purpose of simplicity treat Beijing and Jerusalem as the geographic center of the two countries. Since Beijing is located at 39° 9' N, 116° 3'E, and Jerusalem at 31° 47'N and 35° 13'E, the two countries are also close in latitude.

China is dry in the northwest and wet in the southeast, cold in the north and hot in the south. Water distribution is geographically uneven, with much more precipitation in the southeast than in the northwest. In comparison, Israel is wet in the southeast and dry in the northwest, cold in the north and hot in the south. It has a significant north-south precipitation gradient, with average annual precipitation of 800 mm in the north, 600 mm in the center, and less than 50 mm in the southern Negev desert region. Distribution of water is uneven between the north and the south.

(II) Differences

The Chinese territories span a vast range in terms of both latitude and longitude. Topographically speaking, it is more elevated in the northwest than in the southeast. It has a complex and diverse climate, and a notable monsoon climate. Rivers in southern China have large volumes of water, long flood seasons, no ice season, and little sediment. Rivers in the north feature much less water volume, shorter flood seasons, periods of ice, and significant sediment content. The east features mainly forests and grasslands, while the west is dominated by deserts and grasslands.

Israel is territorially much smaller, in terms of both latitude and longitude coverage. It is more elevated in the northeast than in the southwest. It has a subtropical climate. The rainy winter season goes from November to March of the following year. The dry summer begins in April and ends in October. Because Israel is situated between ocean and desert, there are significant regional variations in climate, which reflect the elevation of different places and their distance from the sea. The Jordan River is the only major river in all of Israel, making it a country with a single water source. Between the desert climate and the Mediterranean climate is a transitional area of semi-arid climate.

II. Comparison of Water Resources in China (Yellow River Basin) and Israel

Precipitation across the Yellow River Basin is uneven, generally showing a decreasing trend from southeast to northwest. Average annual precipitation is 466 mm. According to data from 1956 to 2000, the annual natural runoff of the Yellow River was 53.5 billion m^3, the total volume of surface water resources was 59.5 billion m^3, and that of total water resources was 70.7 billion m^3, which would amount to per capita water resources of 647 m^3 in the watershed.

Israel also has uneven rainfall distribution across its territory, decreasing southward. Average annual precipitation is about 360 mm. Surface freshwater resources are concentrated in the northern region. The Jordan River and Galilee Lake are the main water systems. The Jordan River has annual natural runoff of 600 million m^3. Israel has total freshwater resources of approximately 200 million m^3, or less than 370m^3 per capita.

(I) Similarities

Similarities between the water resources of the Yellow River Basin and in Israel include: uneven distribution of rainfall, large differences in water resources within each region, and low levels of per capita water resources by international standard.

The Yellow River's runoff accounts for only 2% of the country's total water resources, but it the source of water supply for 15% of China's arable land and 12% of its population. The runoff per unit of area for this watershed is only 15% of the national average. With the acceleration of urbanization, water use in the basin has increased sharply, and the mismatch between the supply and demand for water is becoming increasingly prominent. Moreover, water quality is deteriorating and its ecological function is either decreasing or lost.

Two-thirds of Israeli land requiring irrigation is located in the south, but that area has only 20% of the nation's water resources. Israel's water environment has faced increased consumption, reduced supply, pollution, falling water tables, among others.

(II) Differences

The Yellow River Basin has one of the better watershed management systems in China. China began implementing water use permits in 1987, but this program is a macro allocation indicator based on multi-year averages, and no allocation programs or restriction suggestions have been formulated for different water supply situations. Thus, the system does not perform as well as it might. [1] Uneven distribution of water resources persists within the basin area. There is a lack of a scientifically sound and

---

[1] Ma Jianqin, 2009. "Comparative Analysis of Management of the Yellow River Basin and Australia's Murray-Darling Basin," *Henan Agricultural Science*, No.7: 69-73.

standardized control mechanism for urban, industrial, and agricultural water use. Agricultural water use is still extensive and inefficient.

The Jordan River runs approximately 300 km through Israeli territory with a total watershed of 15,000km^2. Surface water accounts for one third of Israel's water resource, and groundwater for two-thirds. Galilee is the largest freshwater lake in the country, with a surface area of 160km^2. It is also the source of the Jordan River. Since the 1960s, Israel's agricultural water use has remained steady at 1.3 million m^3, while agricultural production has increased five fold. Agricultural output value has increased even more. Israel is more than self-sufficient in agricultural products, it exports USD 1.3 billion worth of agricultural products annually. [1]   Israel has managed well the relationship between water resources and economic development.

III. Comparative Analysis of Israeli and Chinese Water Strategy

In contrast to the Jordan River in Israel, the entire course of the Yellow River is within the Chinese territory, making the water resource environment relatively strategically secure. For Israel, the Jordan River is a trans-boundary river, and as such more strategically insecure. Israel is located in the Middle East,

---

[1]   Wei Changlin, 2001. "Israel's North-South Water Diversion Project," *World Agriculture*, No.10: 29-30.

and water-related conflicts with its neighbors are becoming increasingly prominent.

(Ⅰ) Similarities

China and Israel both include water resources among the list of items subject to national macroscopic management by the central government. And they both use legal instruments to strengthen the management and use of water resources. For example, the government stipulates that water resources are public property controlled by the state, and that individuals have only the right to use, but not own water resources. The two countries also use laws to set the priority ranking in water allocation. First priority is given to residential use, followed by industry, agriculture, and other uses, in that order.

(Ⅱ) Differences

1. Laws and Regulations

The goal of Israel's water strategy is clear. In the early days of the nation, Israel gave full consideration to the special nature of its geographic environment and natural conditions, seeing water as the lifeblood of the country's existence and economic and social development. Since 1959, Israel has introduced *Water Law, Water Measurement Law, Well Drilling Control Law, Rivers and Streams Law,* and other laws and regulations, and law enforcement agencies have a clear division of labor. The *PRC Water Law* went into effect in 1988, and has been through numerous revisions and amendments since. But its operability is still poor. In addition to inadequacy and deficiency in supplementary laws, compliance is weak and enforcement lax. This is particularly evident in cross-regional and cross-industrial enforcement.

2. Water Pricing Mechanism

As a law enforcement agency, the Israeli Water Commission provides the government with the legal basis for water supply management and water supply charges. Using legal instruments, the government requires all sectors and citizens to use water in ways that are rational and scientifically sensible. Israel applies a fee-based water supply system that is based on water licenses and quotas, and implements a tiered water pricing system for urban residents and farmers. Excessive water use results in steep price increases. At the same time, the government collects sewage treatment fees from urban residents, and employs a preferential pricing policy for the use of recycled water.

China only recently began to incorporate water resources into commodity pricing management, but the water pricing mechanism is still seriously wanting. Water prices are generally too low even to cover the cost of supply, and there are few institutional constraints on urban, industrial, or agricultural water use. Due to a lack of clear policy direction and pricing mechanisms for its development and use, water recycling technology is only in its infancy in China. Most reusable water is wasted.

3. Water Conservation Awareness

Through law enforcement and publicity, a general awareness of the importance of water conservation exists among the Israeli public. Conservation is awarded and waste published.[①] State and local governments actively promote water conservation among residents. The "don't waste a drop" slogan is a household phrase in Israel. Every citizen knows that Israel's existence is dependent on extremely limited water resources.

By contrast, there is a much weaker awareness of water conservation among the Chinese public, which is reflected in the absence of a market mechanism for regulating water use. Water prices are too low, and most people have little appreciation for the severity of China's water situation. Despite serious water stress in China, urban landscaping and greening projects are nonetheless allowed to compete with residential water use, something that is strictly prohibited in Israel. Water wastage is also an acute problem in China. Agricultural water use efficiency is only about 40%-50%, industrial water recycling rate lies between 20% and 30%, and water use per unit of economic output can be as high as ten times that for developed countries.

4. Technological Measures

Israel has used scientific and technological measures, including recycling, rainwater use, desalination, and drip irrigation to bring water resource utilization to an advanced level by international standard. Israel's rainwater utilization rate is as high as 98%, its recycled water utilization rate as high as 72%, and more than 80% of farmland uses drip irrigation technology. Israel's water management is highly automated,

---

①   Zhu Jianmin, 2008. "Israel's Water Management and Its Inspiration for Beijing," *Beijing Waterworks*, (2): 1-5.

where computers control water storage, delivery, and supply. Above a certain scale, systematic control is employed for urban landscape and greenery water supply. It is essentially a "smart" system that customizes water supply according to the different needs of different types of greenery in both quantity and timing. The urban domestic water supply system is also fully "smart" controlled.

China lags far behind Israel in the use of modern technology for improving its utilization of water resources. The distance is so great in some areas it is beyond comparison. In terms of rainwater utilization, farmers in many arid, upstream areas of the Yellow River have constructed water storage caverns, which have basically solved their water shortage problems. But these are just pilots and are not yet applied on a large scale. In downstream urban and rural areas, rainwater use is almost nonexistent. During the flooding period in the Yellow River Basin, rainwater is abundant. If fully utilized, it would greatly improve the water situation.

IV. Conclusion

Through the above analysis of the water resources strategies of China and Israel, it is easy to see that there are major differences between the two countries in the development and utilization of water resources. The core issue is water resources management, and at the core of that is legislation. In order to ensure that China's water resources can meet the needs of sustainable development of the national economy, the country must employ a strict legal system to manage water resources. By educating the public about the *Water Law*, China can enhance national awareness of water security and elevate the position of water resources in its national security strategy. China should improve its water pricing mechanism, promote water conservation, and combat waste. It should introduce advanced technologies, learn from international experiences, and do its utmost to improve the utilization of water resources.

(Originally published in *Yellow River*, 2010, Vol. 32, No.7.)

Economic Development and Environmental Protection in Israel*

Amram Pruginin**

Israel has a population of approximately 8.1 million as of the end of 2013 and is one of the countries with the highest population density. Israel's area is roughly 27,000km² and nearly half of the land is covered by desert or semi-desert causing periodic water shortage problems. Over the last forty years after statehood, Israel has realized agricultural self-sufficiency and becomes a high technology products powerhouse serving markets across the globe. Israel has maintained an average economic growth rate of 9% and its gross national income per capita is nearly 8,000 US dollars,

*   Excerpted from "Environmental Quality In Israel: A Forty-year Perspective" , in *The Proceedings of the Third International Symposium of Biopolitics, BIOPOLITICS,* Vol. 3 (1991).
**   Deputy Director General of the Israeli Ministry of Environment.

making it the fastest growing economy of all the non-natural resources dependent countries in the Middle East.

Economic and population growth are often accompanied by environmental deterioration. The Ministry of Environmental Protection, which was established in December, 1988, upon the consolidation of several relevant agencies, is responsible for the protection of the environment. The ministry has passed 13 environmental protection laws and plays an active and effective role in monitoring and administration.

To protect the public and the environment from pollution and nuisances and to improve Israel's natural environment, the ministry has adopted various measures for the protection of nature (air, water, and soil), the abatement and prevention of environmental nuisances (air, noise, water, and marine pollution), and the safe treatment of contaminants and pollutants (hazardous materials, radiation, and solid and liquid waste).

I. Strict Emission and Fuel Standards

The serious pollution incurred by the massive use of fuels in various sectors has constituted one pressing concern along with economic development. Demand for electricity in Israel has grown from 543 million kilowatts in 1950 to 6,610 million in 1970, and 18,761 million in 1988. Today's installed capacity stands at 4,062 megawatts (1988) and, according to demand forecasts, will increase to 11,200 megawatts by the year 2017. The ministry had formulated several regulations to address the problem. Thus, for example, growing numbers of industries are required to burn low-sulfur fuel, and the fuels used in electricity production and oil refining have come under similar restrictions. According to some scenarios, requirements such as these will soon apply to a growing number of users, and the terms of the requirements will be toughened, i.e., the maximum permitted quantities of pollutants in fuels allowed for use will be reduced. The burning of heavy fuel oil will stop gradually, and the Reading power station in Tel Aviv will be shut down and not replaced. Meanwhile, the scenario envisages 3,200 installed megawatts produced at inland facilities using indigenous energy sources, oil shale, solar energy, wind, and pumped storage, to reduce fuel pollution.

There were an estimated 800,000 registered motor vehicles in Israel. With the rising living standards and the population growth, the number of motor vehicles is expected to grow by an annual average of 5.9% until the year 2000 and 2.5% in 2000-2025. Consequently, 3.74 million motor vehicles will be plying Israel's roads by 2025, a figure 4.5 times greater than the present number. As for transportation fuels, tough lead standards were recently approved and are being enforced, and unleaded gasoline is expected to become compulsory soon. This industry will be affected inter alia by legislation and standards enacted in the developed countries and by anti-pollution (air and noise) technological improvements devised by overseas motor vehicle manufacturers. The changeover to lead-free fuels in Israel was precipitated by changes in the structure of motor-vehicle engines.

In recent years, environmental protection departments have

exerted strict control over the pollutant content in the fuels used in transportation, industrial sectors and energy industries as well as the total emissions of air pollutants through laws, regulations, administrative orders, and bylaws, and have obtained favorable results.

II. High air quality standard

Total emissions of the major air pollutants (sulfur, carbon and nitrogen oxides) will increase from three major sources, energy production, transportation and industry. Some of the increase, however, will be offset by technological solutions and changes in the composition of fuels. The Israeli environmental standards for several pollutants, including sulfur dioxides, carbon monoxide, lead particles and ozone, are in the final stages of stringent revision which, if approved, will force various polluters to comply. For example, the maximum emissions permitted at the first four units of the power plant in Hadera (1,400 megawatts) are less than half of the Israeli standard, and this maximum was not modified when, in 1989, an expansion of capacity at the site to 2,500 megawatts was approved. Air quality in Haifa, for example, will improve when the quantity of sulfur in the fuels consumed at the existing power plant and oil refineries is reduced; this will happen when the new orders go into effect. Plans in the Ashdod area call for the extension of smokestacks at the local power plant. Here, too, the possibility of implementing a program for the use of lower-sulfur fuels in critical periods is being explored.

III. Rising volume and proportion of sewage impounded

The number of incidents of drinking water contamination has been rising in the past few years. The most salient of these incidents occurred in the summer of 1990, when the entire population of the Dan area (metropolitan Tel Aviv) was ordered to boil its drinking water for several days. Acute manifestations of the public's attitude are the growing use of various home water purification appliances and, above all, the tremendous increase in consumption of bottled drinking water. Research results from various studies on Israel's water source protection, accompanied by the public opinions and criticisms, also promote the sewage treatment and water source protection.

Currently, this trend of increase in the proportion of sewage impounded manifests itself chiefly in the establishment of impoundment systems for domestic and industrial sewage in several locations. In the rural areas, the discharge of a certain quantity of sewage (accounting for 1% or 2% of all sewage country-wide) by way of septic tanks will evidently continue in the long term. The overall quantitative manifestation of this trend is the growing proportion of treated sewage relative to all sewage generated each year country-wide. This proportion has grown from 26% in the early 1970s to 81% in 1987, and the trend will undoubtedly continue until the rate approaches 100% between 2000 and 2025.

Household and urban water consumption will continue to increase, as a result of population growth and the expected rise in standards of living, from 460 million m^3 in 1985 to 610-710 m^3 in the year 2000 and 910-1100 m^3 in 2025. Industrial consumption, too, will continue to grow, from 104 m^3 in 1985 to 120-160 m^3 in 2000 and 150-200 m^3 in 2025. In other words, the two sectors together will account for about half of all water consumption in Israel in 2025. Therefore, the expansion of the sewage treatment capacity has become an overwhelming problem. Activities today include the expansion of the treatment plant serving Metropolitan Tel Aviv and the connection of additional municipalities; the construction of new facilities in Jerusalem and a plant for treatment of the sewage of Nahariya and Acre; and the improvement and overhaul of existing facilities, such as that of Kiryat Gat. In all, the process will presumably culminate in the intermediate future, meaning that most impounded effluent in Israel will be treated in a modern engineering facility.

This trend will create a growing shortage of water for agriculture because, as stated, the natural sources have been almost fully exploited. The major source of additional water supplies in substantial quantities will be treated sewage, which will increasingly replace fresh water in irrigation. It is predicted that the growth of total sewage used for irrigation will grow from 60 million m^3 in 1985 to 260-300 m^3 in 2000 and 430-500 m^3 in 2025.

IV. Better waste disposal management

Trash collection has improved in the past 15 years, as

manifested in the introduction of modern containment devices such as collection tanks and dumpsters of various sizes, all adjusted for modern collection technologies. This ensures a more orderly collection and prevents the environmental nuisances that typified the more diffuse methods previously used. A major change has taken place in the transport of wastes, with the establishment of transfer stations where garbage is unloaded from municipal collection vehicles into regional transport vehicles, from where it is hauled in concentrated form to regional burial sites. Further improvement has occurred in the covers for of waste transport vehicles, making incidents of garbage flying from these vehicles increasingly rare. The greatest change in this regard, one with substantial environmental implications, is the changeover to a small number of official regional disposal sites, replacing the local garbage dumps that had caused major environmental degradation. The garbage at these sites is covered with a layer of soil every day, and additional measures such as separation and compression to prevent environmental hazards are taken. Approximately 30 such sites have been selected within the framework of a national garbage disposal master plan, with careful attention paid to the minimization of potential groundwater degradation. However, much remains to be done until the objectives are attained in full. The most troubling problem in this area is the disposition of garbage from Metropolitan Tel Aviv and Haifa, and also the quality of operations at the dumps.

V. Improve the environment for the public

Trash receptacles have been installed, growing use is made of special vehicles to clean sidewalks and streets, and "cleanup campaigns" in open areas are increasingly frequent. All of these, and changes in the public's habits in its treatment of public spaces, have improved the level of cleanliness in the public domain. An increase in standards of living, the public's demand for a better-kept environment, educational and informational activities, and stepped-up enforcement of the *Cleanliness Preservation Law* ensure the maintenance of these achievements and a strengthening of the trend in the future. Improvement has also been noted in the disposal and recycling of junked or wrecked cars.

VI. Improving city and trourism environment

Tourism is one of the most profitable industries in Israel and plays a significant role in its national economy. The number of tourists entering Israel in 1985 was 1.2 million, with a total income of 1.2 billion US dollars. Israel's great tourism potential originates in its tremendous variety of historical and archaeological sites of universal importance, holy places of the three monotheistic religions, and a broad range of unique natural and recreation attractions, which attract both domestic and foreign visitors. According to some statistics, the number of tourists may rise to 7 million in 2025. The boom of tourism adds pressure on sustainable environmental protection. The local authorities are acting in various ways to help improve the appearance of the urban landscape, e.g., by creating stylized pedestrian malls, paving promenades such as those along the Tel Aviv shore and near the Abu Tor and East Talpiot neighborhoods of Jerusalem, and designing and beautifying town entrances. Cleanup campaigns for house facades, the setting of visual criteria for business signs, and the installation of street furniture (benches, trash receptacles, direction and business signs, bulletin boards, bus stops, street-lighting, street flowerpots, and architectural floor tiling) are attracting greater lay and professional attention, thus making a maximum contribution to the improvement of street appearance. Perceptible progress has also been made in the quality and extent of public gardens. Great visual progress has also been made in public and private residential building, as manifested in new residential neighborhoods and construction areas. The planning of neighborhood structure and public gardening, the diversification of architectural styles and building materials, and the quality of construction, all combine to contribute to the total visual impression of these built environments.

The facades of commercial buildings, including signs and display windows, show major improvement in the quality of architectural design and levels of cleanliness and upkeep. This is most evident in the urban areas. Individuals, too, are doing much to improve the appearance of the cityscape. Resident involvement in the revitalization of residential building facades is growing, the quality of private gardening is improving, and "hanging" rooftop gardens are becoming more prevalent. Awareness of the visual blights caused by various rooftop appliances, such as the tanks of solar water heaters, is growing; the practice now is to conceal them. The "forest of antennas" phenomenon on condominium rooftops is gradually disappearing as central antennas come into greater use.

These positive trends are most evident in city centers, new neighborhoods, and major travel arteries, which constitute the towns' display windows.

In the most visited areas, chiefly in the northern part of the country, local agencies on one hand continue to build communication towers, wind electricity generators and other infrastructure, on the other hand, they employed strict environmental impact assessment and planning systems to protect the key tourist landmarks.

These new norms, including indicators of the public's demands, rising standards of living, and the urge to emulate and compete, ensure that this trend will continue into the future.

VII. Improving beach environment and water quality

The Mediterranean shore was once beset for protracted periods by grave oil and tar pollution, coupled with high levels of chemical and microbial contamination originating in raw sewage dumped into the sea in large quantities, along with industrial wastes. The disposal of domestic and construction waste along the shores, compounded by maritime refuse, completed the sad picture. The beaches were in critical condition. Some were closed for recreational use because they failed to meet sanitation standards; others were exceedingly unpleasant. In all of these regards, substantial improvement has occurred in the past ten years. The quantity of tar on the beaches has decreased by a factor of 150, the discharge of the sewage into the sea has largely stopped, and the dumping of refuse onto the beaches has diminished significantly. The rehabilitated beaches again serve the public on an appropriate level of environmental quality and cleanliness, meeting international water-quality standards. As for industrial wastes, an improvement is expected in the near future when the *Prevention of Effluent Discharge from Land-Based Sources Law* goes into effect, and the dumping of refuse on the beaches should stop altogether when the regional disposal sites and the special construction-waste sites are brought into use.

VIII. Expanding and enhancing toxic waste treatment

The National Toxic Waste Treatment Site at Ramat Hovav began to operate in the early 1980s. At first the facility was used for collection and storage, but by the mid-1980s various treatment and neutralization activities began to take place there. Increasing quantities of waste are gathered at the site each year, and a growing proportion of all such waste generated in Israel is brought there. However, because of the massive growth in total quantity of toxic waste generated in Israel, the volume of uncontrolled discharge is increasing. It appears today that the Ramat Hovav site, after its protracted birth pangs, is on the way to success. This development, perhaps the best guarantee that today's positive trend will continue, as manifested in the transfer of responsibility for the site, and for the issue in general, to the Environmental Quality Services Corporation, ensures future growth in the number of Ramat Hovav users. The installation of new facilities is expected in the near future, including an incinerator that will permit the site to treat substances that have merely been stored thus far. The *Toxic Waste Law*, presently being drawn up, will also help strengthen these trends once it goes into effect.

IX. Establish emergency response agency for chemical disasters

In the past few years, decision makers on the highest government echelons have become increasingly aware of the need to devise frameworks to cope with chemical accidents, and coordinated activity for the establishment of such frameworks is under way. Action has been taken to define the various agencies' spheres of responsibility, databases of hazardous substances have been improved, and alert systems for immediate response have been constructed.

The past decade has witnessed substantial improvement in Israel's readiness to handle pollution caused by small-scale marine accidents and mishaps; in this regard, it may be said that Israel is adequately girded. By contrast, no real progress has been made in the country's readiness to deal with marine pollution on a large scale. Therefore, Israel's coasts are unprotected against large-scale chemical or oil pollution, and the only avenue that offers prospects of success in coping with this problem is international cooperation. Activity in this regard is expected to develop further.

X. Expansion of nature conservation areas

With the implementation of the *National Parks, Nature Reserves, and National Sites Law,* 1963, the process of declaring protected areas under this law has begun and is in full swing; the map of Israel's protected areas is augmented each year with new parks and reserves. Once all the proposed reserve and park areas are declared as such under the law, approximately 25-30 % of the country's land area will be protected, if planted and natural forest areas tended by the Jewish National Fund are included. As stated, the trend is expected to continue and reach completion within ten years. The greatest change is expected when the large reserves in the Negev are declared.

No long-term downward trend in the quality of the water of Lake Kinneret is evident. An equilibrium seems to have been reached among the activities in the Kinneret drainage basin, environmental measures taken to reduce the flow of pollutants into the lake, and the ways in which the lake is used as a reservoir. The use of planning tools such as the National Kenneret Coast Master Plan, organizational tools such as the Kinneret Administration, and follow-up and monitoring tools applied with respect to the lake, such as the Kinneret Research Laboratory, will apparently sustain this equilibrium in the coming years as well.

In order to restore wildlife in erstwhile parts of the natural ecosystem, Israel has established two wildlife preserves: one for desert wildlife (Yotvata) and one for typical Mediterranean wildlife (Carmel). No fewer than 54 species and vertebrates have been designated as being at risk of extinction in the Mediterranean part of Israel; another 29 have been so defined in the desert area. The intent is to restore the natural habitats of the wildlife and encourage reproduction as a way of maximizing the survival prospects of this wildlife.

XI. Restoring Mediterranean woodlands and forests

After a protracted period of felling, overgrazing, and burning that brought the natural ecosystem to a nadir, natural vegetation in the Mediterranean hill areas is making a comeback. This process actually began in 1940s and 1950s, when sheep grazing was brought under control (including an absolute ban in certain protected areas) and when the uncontrolled felling of trees was prohibited. Thus areas that had been laid bare, along with other areas that were covered with bush and scrub forest, are now profusely vegetated with scrub or, in certain cases, mature forest. These processes have transformed the appearance of the landscape in many areas of Galilee and the Carmel range. Revitalization in most of the country's mountain areas will continue, and initial attempts to create a management system channeling the process onto more desirable paths will be made in some locations.

XII. Promoting afforestation

The planted area will grow by 15,000-20,000 dunams per year (a common area unit used in Israel). Future planting will focus on urban outskirts and strips of forest along coastal-plain rivers. These will serve as interurban buffers, obstructions to urban sprawl on the coastal plain, and parks for active recreation by city dwellers. Additionally, emphasis will be placed on afforestation in the northern and western Negev for land preservation purposes. Greater use will be made of planted buffers between major focal points of environmental hazard such as quarries, roads, and industrial areas. Afforestation will serve purposes other than the traditional ones, e.g., rehabilitation of various kinds of landscape degradation, including the revitalization of quarries and the stabilization of wandering dunes and the banks of rivers and gullies.

The disadvantages of the traditional approach, based mainly on homogeneous, densely planted pine forest have been acknowledged. The comprehensive three-dimensional planting structure of multiple layers and species is employed, and evident progress has been made in recent years. Despite the fact that the area of cultivated farmland has reached 4.4 million dunams, the current cultivated farmland may be damaged and reduced due to non-sustainable use, erosion, salinity damage and desertification.

Though great achievements have been made by now, the environmental protection department in Israel still needs to carry out many tasks, to strengthen internal management and domestic investment on environmental protection, promote international cooperation and communication and spare no effort to protect "Our Common Earth".

(Excerpted from *Pollution Control Technology*, 1992, Vol. 3, No.4.)

Technology and Education

Sixty Year's of Support: Israel and Its Soft Power

Characteristics of the Israeli Education System

A Comparative Study on Vocational Education in China and Israel

Sixty Year's of Support:
Israel and Its Soft Power[*]

YIN Gang[**]

Israel has survived and prospered for a number of reasons.
A powerful military and the strong support of the United
States have been crucial. But the key has been its soft power.
The strengths of Israel's soft power can be found in a sense
of ethnic identity that has persisted for a millennium, its
unrelenting sense of crisis, a high degree of national cohesion,
as well as a rigorous legal system.

I. Ethnic existence sustained by faith

Israel is the world's only "resurrected" country, reestablished

[*] Translated by Andrew H. Keller, polished by Liang Fan.
[**] Senior Researcher, Institute of East Asian and African Studies, Chinese Academy of Social Sciences.

from land returned from various countries 1900 years after the Jews lost their country. This fact alone illustrates the strong cohesion of the Israeli people and nation. After the Roman Empire destroyed the ancient Jewish state, the surviving Jews began a Diaspora that dispersed them around the globe. Throughout a millennium of racial discrimination and religious persecution, the Jews resolutely adhered to their faith. Under harsh living conditions, they tenaciously survived and multiplied. The key to this ability was the adhesive effect of Judaism.

Judaism is the world's oldest monotheistic religion, which features not only belief in one god who created all things (God), but also a firm belief that the Jews are his "Chosen People," and that Canaan (today's Palestine) was granted by God to the Jewish people to enjoy for all time. Obviously, Judaism is an ethnic religion. Of course, there are many other ethnic religions in the world, and Judaism is unique in that it is not only the religion of the Jewish people, but also the foundation and origin of both Christianity and Islam. It is because Judaism, Christianity, and Islam share a common attribute - belief in the same supernatural being - that the "orthodox dispute" has run through the past 2,000 years of history.

In this orthodox dispute, others do not accept the status of the Jews as the "chosen people," nor do the Jewish people acknowledge the authority of other ethnicities and other religions that are in dominant positions. For the Jewish people, a weak and small community, discrimination and persecution are almost a matter of fate. At the same time, discrimination and oppression have continuously strengthened the Jewish identity and the cohesion of the Jewish people. At the end of the 19th century, yearning to end the oppression and slaughter of the Jewish people once and for all, the Zionist movement took hold, eventually leading to the birth of the State of Israel. In order to restore their homeland, the Jewish people persisted for half a century in purposeful, organized, and strategic preparation. By the 1947 United Nations General Assembly debate on the partition resolution, Jewish land-owning farmers and Zionist organizations had selectively dispersed and purchased 6.8% of Palestine's land and established 300 settlements, illustrating the truth that "there is strength in number" . The funds to purchase the land came not only from wealthy Jewish merchants, but also from weekly donations from ordinary Jews around the world, including pocket money saved by Jewish children. Under the strict management of the Jewish National Fund, these funds were used to purchase land that became the common property of the Jewish people. Capitalizing on such small area of land and some 500,000 settlers and the outpouring of sympathy worldwide for the millions of Jews massacred during World War II, the Jewish people miraculously secured the legal basis for the restoration of their homeland.

II. Cohesiveness as an invincible force

The Jewish Zionist-controlled areas in Palestine prior to the restoration of the nation were called the "Jewish homeland." In this homeland, Jews mainly lived communally. Through Zionist determination, a communal spirit, organized construction of the homeland, a rainy day mentality that governed armed training, and savvy and persistent diplomatic efforts, the Jewish people were able to concentrate all their strength, to withstand the joint siege of neighboring countries and to achieve victory in war for survival.

"Kibbutzim," which scrupulously abided by the concept of collectivism, was the most important grassroots organization of the Jewish homeland. Among the nearly 300 settlements prior to the founding of the State of Israel, kibbutzim accounted for half. Nearly all of the early Jewish immigrants from around the world lived in such collective farms. The kibbutzim were a product of the combination of socialism and Zionism, the purpose of which was to establish an ideal society of "common labor, common ownership, common life, equality, harmony, and democracy, without exploitation or oppression." In such collective farms, Jewish immigrants had no concept of private property, only those of collective interests and individual responsibilities. Drawing from such an organizational form, Jewish immigrants not only achieved strong cohesion, but also provided excellent conditions for the establishment of an effective operation for Jewish Zionism and underground armed forces. The Israeli army was born in the kibbutzim, and the majority of early soldiers and generals in the Israeli army were trained in kibbutzim. The well-known, one-eyed general Moshe Dayan who served as the first commander-in-chief of the Israeli army- was born in a kibbutz. The various factions of Israeli military born in kibbutzim successfully defended the Jewish settlements and played a crucial role in the war of independence.

The conflicts between different religious sects and political factions among the Jewish people can be spectacularly confounding. But when it comes to ethnic destiny and national interests, there are no evaders, and no traitors. There is only the difference between good sense and extremism. When faced with a formidable and common foe, the Jewish people have worked together. Once a war has broken out, no one would flinch or abandon their comrades. At the beginning of the War of Independence in 1848, able-bodied Jewish men and funding from around the world flowed into Palestine to aid compatriots and their homeland, in the hope of ensuring the survival of the State of Israel. When war broke out in 1973, Jewish youth in America and Israeli tourists in far-away India and Nepal rushed back to fight in the war within a matter of a single day.

A high degree of cohesion and a shared sense of crisis are the most critical and valuable sources of strength that has made Israel's survival and growth possible.

III. Forging a unified national army at all costs

The early Jewish armed forces were divided into different factions: The Haganah, led by the Workers' Party of the Land of Israel (a predecessor to the modern-day Israeli Labor Party) and the radical nationalist "Irgun." Haganah, which contained Zionist revisionist influences, was the rational and pragmatic half-legal, half-underground body of the Israeli armed forces. The Irgun position was radical, ready and willing to resort to extremism and terrorism to achieve its aims. When Mandate authorities confronted Arab armed forces, Irgun displayed strong combat effectiveness, but its extreme measures harmed the Zionist voice, and also intensified enmity between Arabs and Israelis. Haganah did its utmost to oppose Irgun's extreme acts. In order to curb the Irgun forces, Haganah went so far as to arrest non-essential Irgun members and hand them over to British Mandate judicial authorities for discipline.

In the War of Independence, although Haganah and Irgun fought side by side, Israel's founding Prime Minister David Ben-Gurion was determined not to allow two armies in Israel. After the promulgation of relevant laws, Irgun's actions were brought to an end with an iron fist.

On June 10, 1948, just as Israel was using a second ceasefire to prepare for war, an Irgun arms smuggling ship carrying 5,000 rifles, 250 machine guns, 3,000 bombs, hundreds of tons of explosives, 3 million bullets, and a large number of rocket-propelled grenades and mortars, along with more than 800 new immigrants, arrived in the Tel Aviv port to support the war. The government ordered the confiscation of all arms. Irgun leader Menachem Begin insisted that 20% of the arms be allocated to his own armed forces for use. After a tense confrontation, Ben-Gurion, after reaffirming that "one country could not have two armies" and asserting that "these 5,000 guns would be enough to ruin the whole country," personally ordered the "rebel" arms ship destroyed. The shelling resulted in dozens of casualties and the destruction of a large number of arms urgently needed by the Israelis. The ceasefire with the Arabs instead became an Israeli civil war. Although Ben-Gurion was reproved for the move, Irgun ultimately submitted to government authority and joined the national army.

Of course, as long as one plays by the rules, they enjoy equal opportunity as any other. Begin, head of the Irgun, and once called a "terrorist leader," legally set up a political party after the war, ultimately leading the Likud party to victory in the election of 1977 and becoming the supreme commander of the Israeli army. As prime minister, Begin signed a permanent peace treaty with Egypt.

The Israeli government's determination to unify the country's armed forces at all costs laid a strong foundation for victory in the War of Independence and long-term domestic stability in the future.

IV. Accumulation of wealth in the mind

"Wealth begins in the mind" is a mantra of the Jewish people, and the foundation upon which the Jewish people acquire and achieve wealth.

It is well-known that Jewish people take education extremely seriously. During the millennium of Diaspora, most Jews were not allowed to own real estate such as land, mines, and factories, and their means of subsistence were extremely limited. Relying on wisdom and knowledge for survival became quintessentially Jewish. Education is the source of knowledge, and Jewish education is first and foremost education in Judaic knowledge and then an education in survival skills. Because they were not permitted to own "hard assets," "soft assets" shaped by knowledge became the main form of wealth possessed by the Jewish people. So far as their "soft assets" were concerned, the Jews had an advantage in fields such as commerce, finance, law, medicine, art, and theoretical thinking. Their considerable presence in these fields allowed Jews to have significant control over a nation's economy and that region's political development. "Soft assets" cannot easily be taken away, and they are also the form of assets that the highly educated Jewish people are able to transfer and re-accumulate. It is this characteristic of the Jewish people that allowed them to revive family businesses and restore communities in a short time after having been stripped of their property and driven out of their homes time after time in Europe.

The high premium the Israelis have placed on education is a major reason for their success. Both before and after the founding of the State of Israel, Zionist organizations and the Israeli government invested an inordinate amount of effort and money toward education. Israel's educational expenditures as a percentage of GDP are in the 8% - 9% range, double the world average. There are twelve years of compulsory free education nationally, from kindergarten through high school. Over 60 years, Israel's per capita GDP has grown from less than 300 US dollars at the time of the country's founding to some 20,000 US dollars today, which is comparable to that for Gulf oil-exporting countries. The high level of universal education has allowed Israelis to accumulate great wealth on their small parcel of land. The country is a world leader in science and technology, and their national wealth has provided a foundation for building hard power and military force.

V. Legal construction as a priority

Israel's political and legal systems are also distinctively Jewish. The country does not have a constitution, but it has a large number of "basic laws" that guarantee the operations of state apparatus and social life, including "The Knesset," "The People's Lands," "The President of the State," "The Judiciary," "The State Economy," "The Army," "Human Dignity and Liberty," and others. In Israel's early days, taking into account the huge effect that Judaism had on holding the Jewish people together, the Israeli government and legislative organs honored the wishes of the strongly religious among the population and allowed religious forces to have an impact on the country's politics and social life. While Israeli's legislative and electoral systems are not the "best," and there were obvious drawbacks once they were up and running, after all, Israel is "Zionist," and setting the country's legal in such a way was inevitable at that early stage.

Israel's parliamentary system, the name of its parliament, and the number of its members all comply with the ancient system. The electoral system of proportional representation in individual districts makes for a multitude of small political parties, with frequent and complex political battles. In such a system, every 40,000 people elect a member of parliament, achieving a political party. Under normal circumstances, each parliamentary election has more than 30 candidate groups competing, of which 20 or so would gain seats in the parliament. No single party has ever had a parliamentary majority, resulting in unreliable coalition government. Seldom are elections held on time after the completion of a full governing period.

But it is precisely such a system that has ensured that all groups in Israel have the opportunity to participate in governance, and it has provided safeguard for the basic interests of Israeli Arabs, which account for roughly 20% of the population of this "Jewish state". Fierce and complex power struggles also help enhance oversight over the government and government officials, resulting in outstanding achievements in the construction of a clean government. Some have even seen this as a kind of over-achieving. Numerous examples can illustrate this.

Because the State of Israel was established on the foundation of a Jewish homeland implementing a Jewish communal system, Israeli cities have a keen sense of ownership and oversight. Possession of public property, corruption, and malpractice are absolutely not tolerated. Even in joint-stock enterprises, there is intensive oversight. For example, in Israel, it is not uncommon to see ticket inspectors suddenly board a bus to check tickets. No special treatment for friends and relatives by the driver and conductor is permitted.

Israel's military prowess and the existence of steady flow of external support are undoubtedly important factors in the country's continued survival and development in a turbulent environment.

(Originally published in *Contemporary World*, 2008, Vol. 6.)

Characteristics of the Israeli Education System[*]

ZHANG Qianhong[**]

The Jewish people have the fine tradition of valuing education and educators highly. Education has long played a significant role in helping them maintain cohesiveness, preserve their traditions, shape their distinct character, and enrich their culture. Since its founding, Israel has viewed education as the fundamental wealth of Israeli society and the key to its future success. Even as it found itself in a situation of continuous conflict and with much else to be done, Israel invested enormous human, material and financial resources toward building a relatively sound education system

---

[*]   Translated by Lu Caixia, polished by Liang Fan.
[**]   Vice-President, Zhengzhou University; Deputy director, Institute of Jewish Studies, Henan University.

within a short period of time. This has made education an indispensable tool in raising the general caliber of its people, promoting social integration and transforming a resource-based economy into a knowledge-based economy. I hope this article can provide some inspiration for China's own modernization through an examination of the various characteristics of the Israeli education system and its successful experience in nation building through education.

I. A flexible education policy

Long before the founding of the State of Israel, the Zionist movement had used education as a means to support the creation of a Jewish nation-state, with schools being the first Jewish organizations to be established in the Palestinian region. Jews have been passionate about education since the early days when living conditions were harsh. Even before Israel was established, the school enrollment rate for Jewish children was already as high as 85%. From the early years of nationhood until the 1950s, the Israeli government focused on implementing compulsory education and instituted a uniform national education system. The Ministry of Education and Culture was established in April 1949 and its responsibilities were to maintain and develop the educational system, ensure consistent educational standards, train and guide teachers, promote education plans and curricula, improve the conditions for teaching and learning, and organize and promote educational and cultural activities for adults. Soon after the ministry's establishment, the *Compulsory Education Law* was passed and went into effect, and it required the provision of free and compulsory education for all children between the ages of 6 and 14 and all youths between the ages of 14 and 17 who had yet to complete primary education. In 1953, the Israeli government passed another important piece of legislation, the *State Education Law*, which helped promote the nationwide adoption of compulsory education and transformed the pluralistic nature of the education system that had existed in the period of the Yishuv and the early years of nationhood. It also introduced a State education and State-religious education system and put schools run by some political parties, groups and social organizations under uniform state supervision. The new legislation also established the basic principles of Israeli education, which were "to base education on the values of Jewish culture and scientific achievement, love of the homeland and loyalty to the State of Israel and the Jewish people, skills training in agriculture and other trades, the principle of creativity and the commitment to building a society that is free, equal, tolerant, compassionate." In order to realize a uniform system of education, the education and culture ministry set some guidelines for issues such as educational content, curriculum and examinations. Large numbers of immigrants had moved to Israel since the 1950s as it achieved political stability and economic development, and the country received close to a million immigrants from 1948 to 1960.

These new immigrants came from 103 different countries and regions around the world and they spoke more than 70 languages and had different cultures. The Israeli government thus used education as a means to eliminate these differences and promote social integration, aiming to create a new model of "Israeli culture" that blended the agricultural traditions of the East and industrialized culture of the West. The government also began to adjust its education policy from the 1960s in order to strengthen collective identity and social integration. With the principle of equal opportunity in education as the basis, and the promotion of diversity in education as the objective, the government introduced several key measures.

First, reforming the structure of the education system. Israel's education system was initially built with reference to the Western model, but many Jewish children of non-Western origin could not adapt to it easily. As such, in 1968, the government reformed the entire school structure from a system of kindergarten (3-5 years old), primary school (6-13 years old) and secondary school (14-17 years old) to a system of kindergarten (3-5 years old), primary school (6-11 years old), junior secondary school (12-14 years old) and senior secondary school (15-17 years old). The purpose of adding a junior secondary education phase was to allow primary school children from different backgrounds to become familiar with the new system before moving to senior secondary grades within the same school. An obvious result of this reform was a 20% increase in the number of students who made it to the senior secondary level in the first decade of its implementation.

Second, running remedial classes that gave immigrants a new education opportunity in their adopted homeland. As the number of immigrants increased, Israel made immigrant education part of its formal agenda. The central government and local administrative departments, unions as well as communities and enterprises worked together to provide remedial classes and training courses at various levels which taught language, general knowledge and vocational skills to people from different backgrounds. According to statistics, there are 150 places in Israel where new immigrants can learn Hebrew, in addition to the hundreds of centers for literacy and remedial training that provide all kinds of education opportunities. The central and local governments also worked together to establish a system for settling immigrants and gave priorities in employment to many who had completed their re-education.

Third, creating the conditions conducive for educating students of African and Asian origin. Considering that these students usually had lower levels of pre-existing educational attainment compared with their European and American Jewish counterparts, the Israeli government implemented many preferential policies to facilitate their enrollment in public school, such as adjustments to the admission requirements. All primary school graduates in Israel take a national qualifying examination known as the Seker, and the passing mark is 80. But students of African and Asian backgrounds pass if they earn 68. These students could also enjoy tuition reduction or exemption depending on family income, due to government subsidy. In 1978, Israel began collecting education taxes based on income, and students of African and Asian backgrounds from low-income families enjoyed the same education opportunities despite paying lower taxes. In addition, the government and schools provided various types of scholarships and boarding school arrangements for these students. As a result of these measures, the average number of years spent in education for these students rose rapidly to 9.7 years in 1981 from 5.9 years in 1961.

Fourth, promoting specialized education for children. Israel has a special training program for gifted children designed to help them realize their full potential. Children who are in the top 3% of their cohort can attend an elite school or extra classes after passing a qualifying examination to gain specialized knowledge and receive skills training. And for those who are learning impaired and handicapped, there are also special education programs to assist them, with measures such as extra time and individual counseling. The responsibility of educating children with special needs is shared by schools, parents, medical and healthcare professionals, special education professionals and community support groups. The aim of these measures is to make Israeli society and citizens responsible for every child and see them as the wealth of the whole society.

Israel's economy entered a golden age from 1948 to 1973, and it not only established relatively robust industrial, agricultural and defense sectors but also achieved high-speed economic growth at 10% per annum. The Israeli economy was transitioning from extensive growth to intensive growth to become a knowledge-intensive economy. Economic development placed new demands on education, and general universal education could no longer keep up with the needs of development. As such, in the mid-1970s, Israel once again adjusted its education policy. In addition to increasing the number of years of free education and developing education in poorer areas, the government had two new emphases in its education policy: developing vocational training and supporting higher education.

In order to train large numbers of skilled workers, the government set up all types of vocational schools and encouraged students and adults to enroll in courses that imparted skills urgently needed for the country's economic development, such as computer skills, business administration, and market strategy. In 1974, the government passed a resolution to raise the industrial capabilities of its citizens (regardless of age or educational level). The education and culture ministry established an Open University with 25 teaching centers nationwide. The university accepted students without a secondary level education, those with a secondary level education and those at the university level. Every student had the opportunity to be guided by a mentor. The teaching centers were fully equipped with libraries, laboratories and other teaching facilities and provided more than 80 types of degrees and vocational training. The Open University helped nurture large numbers of talented people who would later contribute to the country's economic development.

Israel began planning for the creation of high technology industries in the 1970s. By the 1980s, high technology industries were very much a part of Israel's industrial structure. The government placed great hopes on higher education in the development of these industries. The universities played an important role in supplying qualified industrial engineers and skilled workers. In 1972, Israeli universities produced a total of 11,500 such workers, and the number increased to 30,800 in 1984. In 1965, there were 8 engineers for every 1,000 people in the industrial workforce, and there were 33 in 1982. By 1984, as much as 13% of Israel's total working population was made up of university graduates, up from 7.6% in 1973. By 1992, one out of every 353 people in Israel had a doctoral degree. In short, the flexibility of Israel's education policy made education more adaptive to the needs of the country and the characteristics of its people, and more effective in facilitating social progress and economic development.

II. A unique education system

In its decades of educational practice, the Israeli government, with practicality in mind, established a comprehensive education system consisting of the following components:

preschool education, primary education, secondary education, post-secondary education and higher education. In 1978, it implemented the system of 12 years of free education (including one year of preschool). The uniqueness of Israel's education system is reflected in the following ways:

First, it is noted for the consistency between centralized leadership and local management. Education in Israel is led by the central government, with the education and culture ministry in charge of formulating education policy, allocating education funds, setting educational standards and instituting the syllabus, but these are managed and implemented by local governments, which are authorized to receive and allocate central government funding, hire secondary school and high school teachers, build schools, purchase teaching equipment, etc. While submitting to the government's leadership, each school has a certain level of autonomy. For example, although the Ministry of Education and Culture sets the syllabus, the specific subjects covered span a wide range. Schools, therefore, have the flexibility to tailor their courses and teaching methods to fit their own circumstances. Theoretically speaking, all teachers are employees of the ministry, but the decisions to hire or fire teachers for and from specific schools lie with the school principal, thus ensuring quality and mobility of the teaching staff. In order to bring active citizen participation into play, the Israeli government also encouraged some local and civil organizations to set up private schools. For instance, the Women's International Zionist Organization ran 80 kindergartens, 30 daycare centers and 70 clubs from 1962 to 1963. Currently, various types of private schools exist throughout the country and they have become a main part of Israel's universal education system.

Second, the country has established an effective system of preschool education. Early childhood education has been regarded with importance since the early days of Hebrew education. There were no schools at the time and homeschooling was the main form of education. Jewish law dictates that parents, especially the father, should be responsible for their children's early education, and should pave the way for them to become ethical, wise, and law-abiding citizens. Some Jewish associations require children to start learning the Talmud from the age of 3. Since its founding, Israel has devoted much effort to implementing universal preschool education, with an aim to reap the advantages of an early start. In general, preschoolers start school at the age of 2 to develop their language and motor capabilities as well as to learn to recognize their surroundings. Children between the ages of 3 and 4 enter nurseries set up by local authorities, women's groups or some private organizations, where they receive more systematic knowledge training. The education and culture ministry also funds preschool education in some poorer areas. According to the country's education legislation, preschool marks the first year of free education for a child. According to the *Middle East Economic Handbook* published in the United Kingdom in 1996, 97% of Israeli children attend preschool at the age of 3. This puts it at the top of international rankings in this area. Between 1993 and 1994, as many as 320,000 Israeli children between the ages of 2 and 6 were schooled under the country's preschool system, comprising more than 90% of children of school-going age. Israel's achievements in preschool education attracted the attention of the United Nations and some international education organizations very early on. Comparative studies conducted by the International Institute for Educational Planning in the late 1970s and early 1980s found that preschool education in Israel was the most comprehensive and satisfactory in the world in terms of quantity and quality. An advanced system of preschool education not only enabled children to acquire basic knowledge from a young age, but also cultivated their creativity, judgment, analytical skills, learning abilities, social skills and aesthetic sensibilities. Children also developed a thirst for knowledge, love for the community and labor, as well as respect for law and civic-mindedness.

Third, the system integrates modern and traditional cultures. Although Israel is a modern democratic country, it has preserved its rich religious and cultural traditions. In this environment, where modernity meets tradition, East meets West, and the religious and the secular co-exist, education must adapt itself to the multi-faceted cultural environment. To this end, the Israeli government paid special attention to traditional education while incorporating the best of modern culture. In 1959, the education and culture ministry initiated a nationwide program to heighten Jewish consciousness in order to remind its citizens that Israel was the only Jewish country in the world and of their individual responsibility and mission as a member of a Jewish society. In the curriculum stipulated by the ministry, courses on Hebrew, Jewish history, Jewish law, Jewish beliefs and religious laws were mandatory for Jewish children throughout their schooling years. In order to preserve the national character and because of strong influence from religious forces, Israel set up many public and private schools, which made it a high priority to offer traditional education. For a long period of time since its founding, Israel had tried to create a new Israeli culture that blended Eastern and Western cultures, and this thinking shaped all aspects of its education policy, education system and the educational programs.

Fourth, the simultaneous development of Jewish and ethnic minority education. Israel's ethnic minorities (mainly Arabs) and Jewish people have the same rights and obligations under the *Compulsory Education Law*. The Israeli government promoted the learning of Arabic nationwide and made it compulsory in primary education. The curriculum in Arab language schools is basically the same as that in the Hebrew schools, except that in Arab schools Arabic is taught as a first language, Hebrew classes begin in the fourth year in primary school, and English in the sixth. These schools also follow the holiday traditions of the Arab people. As a result, the education attainment levels for Arabs have risen significantly. For instance, in 1948, the school enrollment rate for Arab girls was 25%, but this increased to 80% in 1964. There were 920,000 Arab school children in 1973, compared to 140,000 in 1949. Of course, if we look at current education attainment levels and literacy rates, there is still a huge gap between Arabs and Jews, and there is still a long way to go before real equality is achieved (especially in terms of attitudes). Additionally, other notable characteristics of the Israeli education system include the combination of formal education and adult education, and attention to both knowledge education and skills training.

III. Stable growth of education expenditure

Israel's leaders have long viewed education as key to the country's strong foundations and national development. Past leaders have shared a strong consensus on the importance of investment in education. David Ben-Gurion emphasized "without education there is no future" while Golda Meir pointed out that "the investment in education is a farsighted one." Former president Yizhak Navon devoted himself to his new job as the minister of education and culture after stepping down from his presidency, something rarely seen in other countries. This was because he recognized that investment in education meant investment in the economy. Since the mid-1970s, Israel's investment in education has never fallen below 8% of gross national product (GNP), surpassing the level of investment made by developed countries such as the United States (See Table 1).

Table 1   Israel's Education Expenditure as a Proportion of Gross National Product (Percentage)

Year	Percentage	Year	Percentage
1962/1963	6.0	1982/1983	8.6
1965/1966	7.6	1983/1984	8.4
1972/1973	7.5	1984/1985	8.5
1975/1976	8.0	1985/1986	8.5
1979/1980	8.8		

Israel's investment in education was as high as 9.5% of GNP in 1995. In the same year, the Peres administration announced that it would lower the share of defense expenditure from 33% to 9% of GNP, reallocating the savings toward education and technology. Education expenditure in Israel is largely funded by the government, and before 1978, the government's investment in education came from general government revenue. After 1978, the country began implementing the education tax, with the National Insurance Institute collecting taxes based on family income. Education taxes accounted for 0.4% of all payable tax. Meanwhile, the government paid close attention to the use of foreign funds for educational development. For instance, donations from overseas Jewish communities through the Jewish Agency for Israel once accounted for a large proportion of Israel's education spending, especially in 1968 when it hit 27.7%. Although local governments in Israel also contribute toward education spending, it is a small share. For instance, in

1990, the central government contributed more than 60% of the education expenditure while local governments only 8%. In 1992, the central and local governments together contributed 77% of the expenditure on national education, with the bulk coming from the former. Education expenditure in Israel increased steadily throughout the 1990s, and high levels of investment provided the material basis for the development of education.

IV. Integrating education with social production

The Jewish people are known for their pragmatism. They believe that getting educated is the responsibility and obligation of every individual, but that book learning and knowledge of the Torah cannot replace practical skills. The Talmud states: "He who does not teach his son a trade teaches him to steal." The Jewish text Pirkei Avot (Chapters of the Fathers) encapsulated the close relationship between the study of the Torah and labor with the words of Rabban Gamaliel: "The best arrangement in life is to combine the study of the Torah with a physical occupation, for the vast effort required by both of them leaves no time for sin, while the study of the Torah that is not combined with work will ultimately cease and will lead to sin." Due to the influence of this traditional notion, Hebrews have attached great importance to acquiring a skill from ancient times, and children, regardless of the background and economic conditions of their family, had to acquire some skill by adulthood, and the skills of some tribal leaders were said to rival those of artisans. Before the founding of Israel, Palestine Jews living in kibbutzim had attached great importance to labor education for young children. Teachers not only taught children the value and meaning of labor but also organized them into "children's societies" where they were engaged in daily labor. In this way, children learnt all kinds of farming and rearing techniques from a young age and they ran small vegetable and animal farms as well as gardens under the guidance of their teachers.

Israel has continued this Jewish tradition after the founding of the nation, with children engaged in systematic labor education from their first year in primary school, in which they acquire basic labor skills, learn about raw materials and production processes and are taught how to use basic tools of labor. At the upper primary and secondary levels, students are taught various labor skills in areas such as materials processing, cartography, tabulation, electrical and electronic work, sewing and tailoring, housework and housekeeping, etc. Those in Grade 8 of normal schools (equivalent to 7th grade in China) have to take a course on "The Israeli Industry and National Economy" which introduces them to the basic principles of industrial production, main operating mechanisms of the national economy, product manufacturing and marketing as well as the basic laws of finance. Labor education at the upper secondary level has an obvious vocational bent, covering agricultural and industrial skills. Students learn a specific skill of their interest, and this teaching method enables them to complete basic education and labor training by the time they finish secondary school, with a considerable number having also developed a special skill. This will help them decide what to study in university and give them better employment opportunities in the future. Israel has an advanced system of higher education. Between 1948 and 1949, there were only 1,640 university graduates, but the number increased to 99,000 between 1984 and 1985, meaning that there were 77 university graduates for every 1,000 workers (while the United States had 111, Japan 42, United Kingdom 30, and France 50). The number of undergraduates in Israel's universities increased to 200,000 in 1993, accounting for 18% of the total workforce. With the educated populace growing in size, the trend of industrialization in higher education was also becoming more obvious. While also developing research capabilities, Israel's universities have put much energy into product development with many institutions of higher learning establishing their own companies, such as the Yissum Research and Development Company of the Hebrew University of Jerusalem, Yeda Research and Development Company of the Weizmann Institute of Science, Ramot at Tel Aviv University and the research and development company of the Technion-Israel Institute of Technology. These enterprises play an important role in producing commercial applications of scientific research outcomes. With support from the government, many industrial parks geared toward high tech industrial development have established their presence around university campuses. These industrial parks enjoy credit and tax benefits, and companies seeking to operate in these industrial parks have to be vetted and appraised by the universities for their technological and production capabilities. Within these industrial parks, universities and enterprises work together closely to turn new research findings into products that can be put into production quickly. Once production reaches a certain scale, it is moved out of the industrial park for expanded production. Currently, the Kiryat Weizmann Science Park next to the Weizmann Institute, the Kiryat Atidim jointly developed by the Tel Aviv city hall and Tel Aviv University, and the Har Hotzvim Science Park of the Hebrew University have all become cradles of the country's high technology industries. In addition, the number of patents obtained by Israeli universities is a measure of the effectiveness of collaboration between universities and industries. A recent study has shown that universities are the main owners of patents filed domestically and abroad and Israeli universities have greatly surpassed their counterparts in other countries in terms of the scale of such activities. Also, in terms of research and development expenditure, the patent funding that Israeli universities receive is more than 2 times that of American universities and more than 9 times that of Canadian universities.

In short, the close integration with social production explains why education in Israel has been able to play an indispensable role in harnessing intellectual resources, raising the quality of the workforce and keeping the industrial structure updated, making it an enduring force for promoting economic modernization. Despite many problems and challenges such as how to manage the relationship between the religious and the secular and how to make the welfare model of education more suited to the trend of marketization in economic development, the Israeli education system is scientifically sound and highly effective. Israel's successful experience in developing the country through promoting education provides useful lessons to other countries.

[Originally published in *the Journal of Northwest University* (Philosophy and Social Sciences Edition) , 2000, Vol. 30, No. 1.]

A Comparative Study on Vocational Education in China and Israel[*]

LIU Yang[**]

The knowledge economy enables employees to develop in the direction of lifelong learning. In this context, China is taking vocational education seriously. There are, however, problems with vocational education in China that must be addressed. In this report, we look closely at the rapid growth of the Israeli economy and the country's miraculous achievements in science, technology, and culture from the perspective of vocational education.

I. Significant differences

We compare Chinese and Israeli vocational education in

---

*   Translated by Andrew H. Keller, polished by Liang Fan.

**   Tianjin University Institute of Vocational and Technical Education.

terms of conceptualization, curriculum design, and teaching standards.

(I) Different conceptualization

Scholars and students of education in China have long understood vocational education to mean the cultivation of professional competence. Their conception of capability is heavily weighted toward cognitive capability, and they hold the view that the possession of capabilities is a particular psychological characteristic, manifested through an understanding of the subjective and objective world, and practical skills and attitudes in the process of individual development. When trying to define its own goals for and content of vocational education, Israel has formed a perspective on knowledge and capability that is focused on knowledge application and practical capabilities. Israel's conceptualization of vocational education, different as it is from that the prevailing one in China, is why Israel lays emphasis on experience and practice.

(II) Differences in curriculum design

China's approach to curriculum design is to use the discipline or subject matter as a whole the basis Over the years, work in curriculum design has focused on the writing of teaching plans and teaching programs. Under the leadership of national educational authorities, specialized departments or agencies would be chartered to do this work. On the whole, China's curriculum for vocational education has a bias toward the teaching of theories. Although Israel has a uniform national teaching program, the country highly values regional diversity, and schools can design courses based on their own circumstances. This gives vocational schools the flexibility to design curriculums and to organize teaching according to the real needs of society. Israel's vocational education curriculum is thus quite pragmatic.

（III）Differences in the caliber of teachers

People teaching in China's vocational schools are mostly graduates of technical schools, vocational colleges that grant degrees in less than 4 years, and post-secondary vocational institutions. There is a proficiency gap between teachers who have graduated from these types of schools and the qualification requirements of the Ministry of Education. On the one hand, the level of formal training is in general quite low for teachers in senior vocational schools. On the other hand, the vast majority of teachers who have had more formal training are university graduates and often lack appropriate work experience and unfamiliar with engineering technology. Israel's development trend for vocational education teachers is much different. In Israel it is believed that part-time teachers typically possess a wealth of theoretical and practical knowledge, and vocational education teams should be a combination of professional and part-time teachers, dominated by the latter. Overall, teams of part-time teachers are an important force supporting the development of Israeli vocational education, and their importance continues to grow. Employment criteria for teachers are also more stringent in Israel, which has established a teacher qualification system with fairly exacting standards.

II. Reasons for the differences

There are significant differences between Chinese and Israeli vocational education, and these differences are the combined result of a number of factors.

(I) Traditional factors

The Jewish people have always believed that neither book learning nor studying the legal codes can replace labor skills. In the hearts of the Israeli people, vocational education is a pillar that can support their survival and livelihood. Therefore, vocational education in Israel is not considered an inferior form of education. Instead, it is believed to be an essential tool that would allow an individual to gain a footing in society and realize development. Israeli society has a tradition of respecting practical skills and vocational education.

In China, Confucianism reigned for more than a thousand years. The mentality that "an accomplished scholar is not an instrument," has seriously hampered Chinese vocational education. The notion of training laborers for the sake of labor is foreign to China, in either official or un-official education, both of which see the selection of governmental officials through examinations as the sole goal of education, and skills and technical know-how as "clever but useless knacks." The imparting of vocational skills exists only among folks of plain births, and they are passed down through the system of apprenticeship. This is why the Chinese have traditionally denigrated vocational education.

(II) Institutional factors

Training highly qualified professionals is key to Israel's success in science and technology. Specialized vocational middle schools and agricultural middle schools train a large number of skilled workers and junior engineers for factories and agricultural production. In order to ensure that the country's youth meets the basic needs of the market when they enter the labor market, the government passed the *Vocational Training Act*, which provides policy, legal, and regulatory guarantees for the development of vocational education.

By contrast, in China, the large number of legislations and the actual development of vocational education are in discordance with each other. Just a few years into the new century, the State Council and Ministry of Education introduced "Decisions on Vigorously Advancing Vocational Education Reform and Development," "State Council Decisions on Vigorously Developing Vocational Education" and other important policies for vocational education, creating an appearance of a flourishing policy landscape as far as vocational education is concerned. However, China's eagerness to achieve expeditious development of vocational education through institutional design has not produced the intended results. Data show that China's vocational education is facing serious difficulties. The stark contrast between the large number of policies and regulations on one hand and the deficiencies in the practice of vocational education on the other makes evident China's ineffectiveness in its efforts to implement vocational education–related polices. This is now proving to be the bottleneck in

China's development in this area.

(III) Economic factors

In Israel's early years, its economy was still underdeveloped, and per capita GDP was little more than 1,000 US dollars. But the Israeli government was able to make large investments in vocational education, something which promised no immediate return. This was clearly a bold move. The government did not hesitate to invest heavily in a variety of vocational education facilities. National expenditures on vocational education through labor departments were around 1.3 million US dollars annually. Today, we can say that such spending has proven nothing less than visionary.

In China, insufficient government investment in vocational education is an important factor in its deterioration and retarded development. Growth in the country's expenditures on this area, including on technical schools, is outpaced by growth in tax revenue, and is slower even than the growth in education expenditure as a whole. Due to the general unevenness in the allocation of education funding, the proportion earmarked for vocational educationhas decreased substantially.

III. Lessons to be learned

We conclude that China should learn from Israel's advanced experience in vocational training and change the status quo. Specifically, we can take away three lessons from Israel's experience:

(I) In terms of the conceptualization of vocational education, we should take a comprehensive and holistic view. Vocational education is a system with many elements, such as teachers, students, school assets, liabilities, and revenues. How to effectively manage vocational education so that it achieves optimal results and creates the most social and economic benefit is the central issue. Only such a holistic ways of understanding the essence of vocational education can promote its development.

In terms of curriculum development, we should correct the overwhelming bias toward book learning and appropriately increase the depth and breadth of practical training and studies, and increase training in independent thinking, self-learning, self-examination, and learning by doing. This will enable students to learn and distill theories, and even to develop theories by drawing on practice. This alone would help them meet the requirement of integrating theory and practice.

(II) From the teacher's point of view, for vocational teachers to seriously carry out their mission of offering a complete vocational education and producing qualified professionals useful tosociety, they must constantly strengthen and enrich the content of vocational education and accept new ideas, new cultures, and new knowledge. Only in this way can teachers complete the task of teaching for the new era.

Resource scarce as Israel is, and facing as many problems as she has on its road to development, the country's achievements in economy, technology, and culture are nothing less than astonishing. By comparing vocational education in China and Israel through identifying the differences, and analyzing the reasons for them, our goals is to try to chart a better course for the further development of vocational education in China.

(Originally published in *Work & Study Abroad,* 2011, Vol. 3.)

China-Israel Relations

Sixty Years of China-Israel Relations: An Overview

An Analysis of the Evolution and Current State of China-Israel Relations

Chronicle of Major Events in China-Israeli Relations（1949-2013）

Sixty Years of China-Israel Relations: An Overview[*]

YIN Gang[**]

The China-Israel relationship is unusual in the history of international relations. The People's Republic of China and the State of Israel were founded around the same time. There was no direct conflict of interest between the two, nor were there any historical animosities, making it ideal for developing bilateral relations on an equal footing. However, even though Israel was the first Middle East country to recognize the People's Republic of China, it was the last country in that region to establish formal diplomatic relations with the latter. As the situation in the Middle East evolved, China and Israel

---

[*] Translated by Lu Caixia, polished by Liang Fan.
[**] Researcher, Institute of West Asian and African Studies, Chinese Academy of Social Sciences.

finally normalized their relations in 1992. China currently maintains normal and friendly exchanges with all Middle East countries, and Israel is no exception.

I. Amicable historical exchanges and missing the best opportunity to establish diplomatic relations

Amicable relations between Chinese and Jews can be traced back a thousand years. In the third year of the Dading reign in the Jin Dynasty (1163 AD), Jews who had arrived in the Chinese hinterland built a synagogue in Kaifeng, [1] marking the formation of one of the earliest Jewish community within China's borders. This community had frequent contacts with Jewish communities in Ningxia and Yangzhou in terms of the flow of people, religious texts and funds [2] during the Ming and Qing dynasties while the Jewish community in Hangzhou during the Yuan Dynasty was fairly active in the economic realm, whose size exceeded that of the community in Kaifeng. [3] The Kaifeng Jews' own historical accounts, field surveys conducted by foreign missionaries in the Ming and Qing dynasties and relevant official Chinese records all

---

[1]　See the stone inscription "Record of the Reconstruction of the Temple of Purity and Truth" in front of the Kaifeng synagogue giving evidence of its reconstruction in 1489 (second year of the Hongzhi reign in the Ming Dynasty).

[2]　Ibid. See also the 1512 (seventh year of the Zhengde reign in the Ming Dynasty) stone inscription "A Record of the Synagogue Which Honors the Scriptures."

[3]　See He Gaoji and others (trans.), 1983. *The Notes on China of Father Matteo Ricci,* Zhonghua Book Company, Beijing, pp. 116-117.

point to the equal treatment accorded to members of the Jewish communities by both ordinary people and officials during the Jin, Yuan, Ming and Qing dynasties, with some Jewish people even holding important positions. The combination of the pull of the imperial examination system, the Ming Dynasty's restrictions on the use of foreign languages and scripts as a result of a policy of assimilation, the insular nature of Jewish communities and the cutting off of overseas contacts caused the Kaifeng Jewish community, once numbering thousands, to disintegrate in the mid - 19 century.

At a time when ancient Jewish communities in China were disappearing, Jewish businessmen began to arrive in China and to form modern communities. Jewish synagogues were built in Shanghai and Harbin in 1887 and 1907 respectively. With the development of the Chinese Eastern Railway, the persecution of Jews by Tsarist Russia and the influence of the October Revolution, the Harbin Jewish population ballooned in the early 20 century, and reached 1.12 million in 1920 and spread to cities such as Tianjin, Dalian and Qingdao. [1] This had a huge impact on the local society, culture and economic development. The Sassoon and Kadoorie families, who were active in Shanghai, as well as the property magnate Hardoon, had considerable influence over the development of Shanghai's modern industry and urban development. During the Second World War, 30,000 Jews who had been forced by anti-Semitism to flee Nazi Germany went to Shanghai. In 1939, at the

---

[1]   XU Xin, 1992. "Jews in Harbin: a Historical Perspective," *Latest Developments in Israel*, No. 19, p. 31.

persuasion of Jewish banker Jacob Berglas and the suggestion of Sun Ke, then president of the Legislative Yuan, the Nationalist government seriously considered a proposal to accept 10,000 Jewish refugees and resettle them in Tengchong, Yunnan. Long Yun, the governor of Yunnan province at the time, readily approved the proposal but the plan had to be abandoned later due to a combination of deteriorating war conditions, China-German relations, domestic security concerns and other factors. [1]

Because China was free of anti-Semitism, some Chinese Nationalist leaders were sympathetic toward the Zionists as a result of active lobbying and financial assistance by Jewish community leaders. Some Jewish people also came forward to participate in the anti-Japanese war in China, such as Jakob Rosenfeld, who served as a field doctor in the New Fourth Army and later became the Minister of Health in the first column of the Northeast Democratic United Army, and Hans Shippe, who was killed in operations against a Japanese mopping-up campaign in Shandong province.

The Nationalist government maintained a neutral stance over the 1947 United Nations General Assembly resolution on the partition plan for Palestine and the first Arab-Israeli War in 1948, and abstained from voting on Resolution 181. On the other hand, the main news publications of liberated areas in

---

[1] See "The Plans of the Nationalist Government at Chongqing for Resettling the Jewish Refugees in China)," *Archives of the Republican Period,* 1993, No. 3, pp. 17-21. See also "One Hundred Thousand Jews May Find Home in China" , *Israel's Messenger*, Shanghai, July 14, 1939, pp. 114-151.

China declared their support for the establishment of an Israeli state, pointing out that the war was a ploy by the British to provoke Arab reactionary governments into an anti-Semitic war, and that the Jewish people were putting up a determined and righteous resistance. [1] The Communist Party of China (CPC) held the same position as the former Soviet Union early in the Arab-Israeli conflict.

On March 1, 1949, the Nationalist government, which had withdrawn in defeat to Guangzhou, announced its recognition of Israel through its foreign ministry, but the Israelis politely kept their distance. [2]

The People's Republic of China (PRC) was formally established on October 1, 1949. On January 4, 1950, the legal adviser of the Israeli foreign ministry signed documents recognizing the new Chinese government and decided that "should there be a tussle for the Chinese seat in the UN, we should be in favor of letting the new government have it." [3] On January 9, Israel's foreign minister Moshe Sharett informed his Chinese counterpart Zhou Enlai in a cabled message of Israel's recognition of the PRC. On January 16, Liu Shaoqi sent a cable of acknowledgement on Zhou's behalf. On January 28, the Chinese foreign ministry contacted its embassy in the former

---

[1] See Xinhua News Agency report from Shanbei dated June 2, 1848, *People's Daily*, June 5, 1948.

[2] See Central News Agency report from Guangzhou dated March 1, 1949, Central Daily News, March 2, 1949.

[3] "From the International Division to the Asia Division: Issues Concerning the Position on China," Archival Records of the Ministry of Foreign Affairs 1561/9, Israel State Archives.

332 / CHINA AND ISRAEL: Through the Eyes of Scholars and Journalists

Soviet Union to enquire if Israel had officially acknowledged receipt of the document. ① However, the Israeli foreign ministry felt that the Chinese reply was merely customary and did not indicate a decision to establish formal relations with Israel; hence it decided not to rush things, opting instead to establish contact with the Chinese in Moscow. ② On June 13 the same year, the Chinese foreign ministry informed its embassy in the former Soviet Union of its decision to exchange diplomatic missions with Israel, and the Chinese representative subsequently met the Israeli consul to enquire when Israel was sending a diplomatic mission to China.

On diplomatic contact between the two countries in 1950, the Chinese also had this understanding: China and Israel "had already established diplomatic relations but had yet to exchange diplomatic missions." ③

II. China's policy adjustment and the freezing of China-Israeli relations

Between 1953 and 1955, diplomats of both countries based in Myanmar and other countries met several times, and Arab countries were also beginning to adjust their polices toward China. On June 29, 1954, Premier Zhou Enlai met Israeli

---

① See the Bureau of Archives of the Ministry of Foreign Affairs, Original document 107-D0035, Open document 107-00087-01 (1), p. 4.

② Letter from the foreign minister to the head of the East Asia department dated January 29, 1950, Israel State Archives, 130.02/2385/31.

③ "Diplomatic Victories of the People's Republic of China in the Past Four Years" in *World Fact Book*, World Affairs Press, 1954 , p. 54.

envoy to Myanmar David Hacohen and invited him to visit China. [①] On September 23 the same year, while delivering the government's work report at the National People's Congress, Premier Zhou announced that China was in contact with Israel on matters concerning the normalization of bilateral relations, but he also said that China hoped to develop economic and cultural relations with countries in the Middle East and Near East. [②]

David Hacohen led a trade delegation to China in January 1955 while China was in talks with Egypt on establishing diplomatic relations. The head of the Asia Division in Israel's foreign ministry Daniel Lewin was also part of the delegation. Both sides signed a trade agreement but did not go into specific discussions on establishing diplomatic relations. This visit was featured rather prominently in Chinese newspapers, according to which its purpose was "to give Arab countries a push from the back into establishing relations with us by inviting the Israeli delegation to China." [③]

At this time, the preparatory meeting for the first Afro-Asian conference (Bandung Conference) had already ended and the decision by Arab countries not to let Israel participate was confirmed. On China's stance toward the Arab countries' decision to exclude Israel from the conference, it is worth nothing that the *People's Daily* published an editorial saying that "the Afro-Asian conference should not become an exclusive

---

① David Hacohen, Time to Tell, Hezel Press, New York,1985, pp. 227-8.
② See *World Fact Book,* 1955 , p. 976.
③ See "Zhou Enlai's letter to Liu Shaoqi, Chen Yi, Deng Xiaoping and Xi Zhongxun," the Bureau of Archives of the Ministry of Foreign Affairs, Open document 107-00087-01, p. 19.

regional organization," and that "the door remains open for African and Asian countries that have yet to be invited." [1] Clearly, China had its reservations about the exclusion of Israel.

During the Bandung Conference, Premier Zhou Enlai had two one-to-one meetings with Egyptian President Gamal Abdel Nasser, and he listened carefully as the vice-chairman of the Syrian delegation spoke about the Palestine issue. The vice-chairman Ahmad Shukeiri would later become the first chairman of the Palestine Liberation Organization (PLO) established 9 years later. Israel officially informed the Chinese three days after the Bandung Conference ended that "Israel desires to establish full diplomatic relations with the Government of the People's Republic of China," [2] but this was too late. Three weeks later, a reply came from the director of Asian affairs in the Chinese foreign ministry that China wished to remain in private contact with Israel on matters regarding the establishment of diplomatic relations. [3] On May 30, Egypt finally severed relations with Taiwan and established diplomatic relations with the PRC. When the Israeli envoy in Moscow came to China on a private visit in July 1956, China's vice minister of foreign affairs Zhang Hanfu candidly told him that under the circumstances, the time was not right for the two countries to establish diplomatic relations. [4]

---

[1]   *People's Daily* editorial, January 5, 1955.

[2]   Letter from the head of the Asia Division in Israel's foreign ministry to his Chinese counterpart dated April 29, 1955, Archival Records of the Ministry of Foreign Affairs 3334/37, Israel State Archives.

[3]   Ibid, Chen Jiakang's reply to Daniel Lewin dated May 21, 1955.

[4]   The Bureau of Archives of the Ministry of Foreign Affairs, Open document 107-00039-01 (1), pp. 30-32.

III. Supporting the Arab Liberation Movement while not denying Israel's right to exist

In the conflicts between Arab countries and Israel that occurred after 1956, China consistently maintained that while it objected to Israel's policies, it did not object to its right to exist, and it did not approve of the actions taken by extremist factions in the PLO. Premier Zhou Enlai had on many occasions told visiting PLO delegations that while China objected to the policies of the Israeli government, it did not see the Israeli people as enemies. He also strongly condemned terrorist actions such as the hijacking of civilian aircraft and the killing of hostages, and objected to the slogan of "throwing Israelis into the sea." [①]

The Chinese may have ceased official contact with Israel, but this did not mean that all contact was severed between the two countries. The CPC had all along maintained normal exchanges with its Israeli counterpart and the latter sent delegations to the Eighth National Congress of the CPC in 1956 as well as China's 10th National Day celebrations in 1959. Documents from the Israeli communists were also translated into Chinese. Both Premier Zhou Enlai and Chairman Mao Zedong were in contact with leaders of the Israeli communists. During the international meeting of communist and workers'parties held in Moscow in November 1957, Mao Zedong had a one-to-one meeting with Shmuel

---

① See Pei Jianzhang (eds), 1989. *Zhou Enlai : Ideas and Practice in Foreign Affairs,* World Affairs Press, pp. 132-134.

Mikunis, then leader of the Maki (Communist Party of Israel) and listened carefully to the latter's complaints on the erosion of Jewish culture in the former Soviet Union and also expressed his incomprehension at the Soviet decision to ban the publication of Jewish prayer books. Subsequently, Mao Zedong personally took this matter up with Khrushchev. A year later, tens of thousands of Jewish prayer books as well as many works on Jewish literature and Hebrew dictionaries appeared on the shelves of bookstores in Moscow. In his discussion with Mikunis, Mao Zedong also spoke about the lives of Jews in ancient China, which greatly surprised the Israeli communist leader. [1]

On August 2, 1963, in view of the fact that the United States, Britain, and the former Soviet Union had concluded the Partial Nuclear Test Ban Treaty a week earlier, Premier Zhou Enlai wrote a letter to foreign heads of governments proposing the convening of an international conference of world leaders to discuss the question of the complete prohibition and total destruction of nuclear weapons. Israeli prime minister Levi Eshkol also received the letter that bore Zhou Enlai's signature. In his reply, Eshkol expressed his desire to establish formal relations with China. [2]

During this period of frozen bilateral relations, Jews who had participated in the Communist revolution and remained in China continued to be held in high regard by Chinese leaders. Of the seven Chinese delegates of foreign origin in the Seventh

---

[1] See Yedioth Ahronoth, May 6, 1973.
[2] Archival Records of the Ministry of Foreign Affairs 3436/16-17, Israel State Archives, "Correspondence between Zhou Enlai and Levi Eshkol."

Chinese People's Political Consultative Conference in 1988, five had Jewish backgrounds.

The normal activities of Jewish communities in China were similarly unaffected. Tens of thousands of Jews left China peacefully and voluntarily. The Jewish people remaining in Shanghai were treated with respect by the Chinese government and the people, while Jewish communities in Shanghai, Harbin and Tianjin gained legal status after registration, and kept in contact with international Jewish organizations and Israel. By the start of the Cultural Revolution in 1967, most Jewish people of foreign nationality had left China. The favorable circumstances of the Jewish people who had chosen to stay were evident in the concluding remarks of a 1957-1958 report to the World Jewish Congress by the Council of the Jewish Community in Shanghai: "In conclusion, it must be mentioned that the Chinese people and the Chinese People's Government have been both generous and kind to the Jewish residents and the Jewish Community Associations in China. Special consideration and respect have been consistently shown to our religious requirements by the authorities. The Council takes pleasure to place on record its sincere gratitude to this great nation." ①

Israel has also steadfastly recognized the PRC as the only legitimate government of China and did not initiate exchanges with the Taiwanese authorities, and it also supported our country in regaining our rightful seat at the UN.

---

① Report, Council of the Jewish Community, Shanghai, July 1, 1957- June 30, 1958.

IV. Developments and obstacles in China-Israel relations after the establishment of formal diplomatic relations

Since the early years of China's reform and opening up, many Jewish businessmen and entrepreneurs have been active in various parts of China, and Jewish money is once again flowing into China, with much of it coming from conglomerates controlled by former members of the Jewish community in Shanghai. In 1979, China began receiving Israeli non-governmental business representatives, and non-governmental economic and technological exchanges with Israel. These unofficial exchanges had a positive impact on China's defense capabilities and technological advancement.

In the mid 1980s, as Arab-Israeli relations were generally moving in the direction of a political solution, China promptly adjusted its policy toward Israel and formally resumed diplomatic contact with the latter in 1985. Academic, trade as well as postal and telecommunications exchanges between China and Israel gradually got on track.

In the spring of 1990, China and Israel exchanged unofficial liaison offices, with the Israelis setting up a representative office of the Israel Academy of Sciences and Humanities in Beijing while the Chinese set up a representative office of the China International Travel Service in Tel Aviv.

In November 1991, 12 years after the normalization of relations between Egypt and Israel in 1979, the Arab countries finally found themselves at the negotiating table with Israel at the Madrid Peace Conference. On January 24, 1992, the governments of China and Israel finally signed the joint communiqué to formally establish diplomatic relations. From then on, China-Israel relations have entered a new phase and flourished. Since October 1992, the two countries have signed numerous agreements in areas such as government-to-government trade, avoidance of double taxation, investment protection, trade and economic cooperation, as well as cooperation in industrial research. They also signed a memorandum of understanding on cooperation in high technology sectors. In November 2005, Israel formally recognized China's full market economy status. [1]

Bilateral cooperation in the agricultural sector is especially active. Israel set up China-Israel agricultural training centers in Beijing and demonstration farms for agricultural produce, flowers and plants as well as dairy produce in places such as Beijing, Shandong, Shaanxi, Yunnan and Xinjiang. This helped promote technological improvement for China's agriculture. In addition to the thousands of Chinese technical personnel who are trained by Israelis in China, every year about a hundred students from China go to Israel for advanced education. There are at any given time about a hundred Israeli students studying in China. [2]

Since the two countries established diplomatic relations, all Israeli leaders who have served as prime ministers or presidents of the country have visited China. Before the Middle East peace

---

[1] http://fmprc.gov.cn/chn/pds/gjhdq/gj/yz/1206-4/xgxw/t3849161htm.

[2] http://fmprc.gov.cn/chn/pds/gjhdq/gj/yz/1206-41/sbgx/.

process came to a standstill in 2000, both the Chinese premier and president made state visits to Israel. From then on, China has toned down its political relationship with Israel.

Currently, more than 260 Israeli companies involved in commercial and technological trade have established a presence in China. [1] Chinese construction companies have also undertaken many projects in Israel, including the construction of tunnels and railways. The number of Chinese workers in Israel was at one point close to 40,000. [2] According to statistics from the Chinese customs, trade between China and Israel reached 6 billion US dollars in 2008, with 4.2 billion US dollars in exports and 1.8 billion US dollars in imports. [3] Israel has set a goal to raise this to 10 billion US dollars within a few years.

It must be pointed out that former members of the Jewish community in Shanghai and their descendants have played a special and important role in promoting economic and trade cooperation between the two countries. The Kadoories and Eisenbergs have also made huge investments in China's energy, high technology and nuclear power sectors, and were praised by Deng Xiaoping and other Chinese leaders for their contributions.

(Originally published in *West Africa,* 2010, Vol. 4.)

---

[1]　http://israeltrade.org.cn/zhongwen/companiesphp#8.
[2]　http://chinanews.com.cn/news/2006/2006-04-11/8/7153461.shtml.
[3]　http://il.mofcom.gov.cn/aarticle/zxhz/tjsj/200903/20090306140350.html.

An Analysis of the Evolution and Current State of China-Israel Relations[*]

PAN Guang[**]

For more than six decades, China-Israel relations have evolved along a path less traveled, on which it reached a stage of comprehensive and stable development only after many ups and downs. A strong impetus to enhance bilateral relations notwithstanding, some obstacles remain. This article provides a review, an analysis and commentary on the history and prospects of this relationship.

---

[*] Translated by Lu Caixia, polished by Liang Fan.
[**] Professor at the Shanghai Academy of Social Sciences, Dean of Center of Jewish Studies Shanghai.

I. From the founding of the two countries to the establishment of diplomatic ties: A turbulent journey

The end of the 1940s was a period of epic change for both the Chinese and Jewish people. The People's Republic of China and the State of Israel were founded in the east and west of Asia in 1949 and 1948, respectively. At the time, there was no direct conflict of interests between the two countries and the establishment of diplomatic relations, which would have provided an excellent opportunity for further development of a long-standing friendship, should have been a matter of course. However, due to complex factors, it was not until 43 years later when the two countries normalized relations. During these four decades, their relationship went through roughly four stages.

The first stage: Friendly contact. When the State of Israel was established on May 14, 1948, the Chinese press, including papers published by the Communist Party of China, all applauded the development. On May 27, the *Central Hebei Guide*, a newspaper published by the Communist Party of China in the liberated areas of North China, commented: The new Jewish nation, which is called the State of Israel, has declared its establishment on the 14th. To the Jewish people, who have lived for two millennia without a homeland, drifting from place to place and suffering humiliation and bloodshed, their wish for a Jewish nation is beginning to materialize." ①

On October 1, 1949, the People's Republic of China (PRC)

---

① *Central Hebei Guide,* May 27, 1948.

was formally established, and this development was welcomed by the Israeli government and people. The Israeli government formally recognized the PRC on January 9, 1950, making Israel the first Middle East country to do so. This made it to the front page of the *People's Daily* on January 17, 1950 and the headline read: "Israel, Afghanistan and Finland Decide to Establish Diplomatic Relations with Our Country, Foreign Minister Zhou Replies to the Countries Respectively to Express Welcome." [1]

In the months that followed, China and Israel seemed to be heading toward the establishment of normal diplomatic relations. Unlike most other countries, Israel had no official ties with the former Nationalist regime; hence there were no direct obstacles in building relations with the PRC. Chinese and Israeli representatives met for the first time in Moscow in June 1950 to discuss specific arrangements for formalizing diplomatic relations. However, the Korean War broke out at this time, vastly increasing the odds of a direct confrontation between China and the United States in Korea. Under such circumstances, American pressure led to subtle changes in the Israeli government's attitude toward the issue of establishing diplomatic relations with China. At the end of June, Israel's foreign ministry informed its representative in Moscow: "The Government has decided in principle to establish diplomatic relations with People's Republic of China. However, nothing will be done in this direction until the situation in the Far East clears up. This is for you only, and you are to do nothing until

---

[1]　*People's Daily,* January 17, 1950.

you hear further from here." ① As such, the escalating Cold War caused the two countries to miss their first opportunity to develop normal relations.

Between 1953 and 1954, representatives from the two countries met in Moscow, Yangon, Helsinki and London, with Yangon being the main point of contact for the two sides.

On September 23, 1954, while delivering the government's work report to the National People's Congress, Premier Zhou Enlai pointed out that: "China is in contact with Afghanistan and Israel with regards to the establishment of normal diplomatic relations." ② From then on, in the lead up to the Bandung Conference, relations between China and Arab countries developed rapidly.

Between May and September of 1956, China established diplomatic ties with Egypt, Syria and Yemen. This halted contact between the two countries regarding the formalization of relations, and a two-decade long "deep freeze" of bilateral relationship followed.

The second stage: "Frozen" relationship.

Although China-Israel relations remained in "deep freeze" during this period, this did not imply that the Chinese people were not on friendly terms with Jewish people worldwide. Both the Chinese and Jewish people supported each other in their opposition to wars of invasion and the protection of world peace. Economic and cultural exchanges continued. American

---

① Michael Curtis and Susan Aurelia Gitelson (eds), 1976. *Israel in the Third World,* New Jersey : Transaction Publishers, p. 225.

② Xinhua News Agency Beijing, September 23, 1954.

Jewish politicians such as Henry Kissinger played an important role in the rapprochement between China and the United States as well as other Western countries. They also tried to establish links between China and Israel.

Unlike the former Soviet Union or Eastern European countries, the PRC has never known anti-Semitism. This was consistent throughout the history of China, and remained unchanged as regimes rose and fell.

In the 17 years before the start of the Cultural Revolution, many Jewish people lived in New China and the organizations they formed locally (such as the Council of the Jewish Community in Shanghai) were able to operate smoothly with the support of the Chinese government. Meanwhile, those who had left China settled in various parts of the world and formed communities of "Chinese Jews," reflecting their strong emotional ties to the country.

In 1956, in a conversation with visiting Singaporean Jewish politician David Marshall (former Singapore Chief Minister and Ambassador to France), Premier Zhou Enlai came to know about the policy obstacles that some Jewish people in China faced when trying to relocate to other countries. He then instructed the relevant departments to expedite the exit process for these people. [1] After some efforts by the Chinese, the former Soviet government also changed its policy and allowed some Jewish people living in China to

---

[1] Chan Heng Chee, 2001. *A Sensation of Independence: David Marshal, A Political Biography,* Singapore:Times Books International, pp. 220-223. See Joan Bieder, 2007. *The Jews of Singapore*, Singapore: Suntree Media, p. 131.

move to the Soviet Union. [1] At the same time, as the PRC had no formal ties with most Western countries, Hong Kong became the main intermediary for trade between China and the West. Jewish communities in Hong Kong with traditional ties to the Chinese mainland, especially the Sephardi merchants, played an important role in promoting such trade.

The third stage: Relationship thawing. Since the Cultural Revolution ended in 1976, China has entered a period of reform and opening up and established diplomatic ties with more and more countries. Its relations with many, including major Western countries such as the United States, also improved and grew. Against this backdrop, China-Israel relations also began to ease. In October 1977, Egyptian President Anwar El-Sadat visited Israel to negotiate the peaceful resolution of the Egyptian-Israeli conflict with Israeli leaders. News publications in China enthusiastically welcomed this move and gave prominent publicity on the prospects for a political solution to the Middle East issue. In July 1980, China's vice minister of foreign affairs He Ying enumerated three principles governing China's attitude toward the Palestine issue, of which the third was that "Every country in the Middle East should enjoy the right to be independent and to exist," and this of course included Israel. Chinese leaders reaffirmed China's support for the Egyptian-Israeli peace process during a visit to Egypt in 1982, and reiterated the view that all countries in the

① Chan Heng Chee, 2001. *A Sensation of Independence: David Marshal, A Political Biography,* Singapore:Times Books International, pp. 220-223. See Joan Bieder, 2008. *The Jews of Singapore*, Singapore: Suntree Media, p. 131.

Middle East had the right to exist. In September 1988, Chinese foreign minister Qian Qichen outlined a five-point proposal from China to resolve the Middle East issue: (1) The Middle East issue should be resolved through political means; (2) Support for peace talks hosted by the UN and attended by the five permanent members of the Security Council and parties involved; (3) Support for all appropriate forms of dialogue among parties involved; (4) Israeli withdrawal from occupied Arab territories and guarantee of Israel's security; (5) Mutual recognition by Palestine and Israel and peaceful co-existence of the Arab and Jewish peoples. The series of constructive suggestions by China on the Middle East issue created propitious conditions for improving its relations with Israel.

Meanwhile, Israel was also taking further steps to develop its relationship with China. In 1985, the Israeli cabinet held a meeting to discuss its China policy, and Minister without Portfolio Ezer Weizman was appointed to manage this. The Israeli foreign ministry subsequently allocated funds to reopen its consulate in Hong Kong, which had been closed for 10 years, appointing Reuven Merhav to be the Consul General. [1] The objective of the Israeli government was to utilize all means to establish contact with the Chinese and break the deadlock in China-Israel relations, so as to be able to formalize diplomatic ties as soon as possible. This proposal received the unanimous approval of both the Likud and the

---

[1] Jonathan Goldstein (eds) , 2006. *China, the Jewish National Movement and Israel*, Beijing, China Social Sciences Press, p. 121.

Labor parties, two major political parties in Israel, and was also supported by the public.

The Jewish community in Hong Kong also played a special role in facilitating the establishment of China-Israel diplomatic ties. Hong Kong had been an important intermediary of trade between the two, whose volume would reach tens of millions of dollars in some years. Shaul Eisenberg, who had sought refuge in Shanghai during the Second World War, was the key mover of such trade. He had a special fondness for China, the country that had saved him in his hour of need, and he helped promote indirect trade between the two countries long before formal ties were established.

In 1978, Eisenberg saw the huge business potential in China's reform and opening up and was determined to take China-Israel trade to a higher level. With the blessing and support of Israeli leaders, Eisenberg began exporting high technology and related products to China. [1] Meanwhile, Eisenberg's work also laid the foundation for closer relations between the two countries, prompting comment from former Israeli Prime Minister Rabin that "Mr. Eisenberg opened the doors to China for Israel." [2]

The fourth stage: Establishing formal diplomatic relations. After the mid-1980s, non-governmental exchanges between China and Israel developed quickly, in areas ranging from economy and trade to culture and tourism, and in interactions

---

[1]   *Time Magazine,* October 25, 1993.

[2]   *Time Magazine,* October 25, 1993.

between political parties and organizations. Owing to the efforts of the two governments, conditions were now right for both parties to reestablish official contact.

From March 1986 to January 1987, Chinese and Israeli officials met several times in Paris to discuss the possibility of taking official exchanges further and to make preparations for higher-level contact. In March and September 1987, China's permanent representative to the United Nations Li Luye twice met Abraham Tamir, director general of the Israeli Foreign Ministry in New York and the two held specific discussions on bringing official contact to a higher level. On September 30, Chinese State Councilor and foreign minister Wu Xueqian met Israeli acting prime minister and foreign minister Shimon Peres in New York. This was the first time in the history of bilateral relations that such a high level of official contact took place. The next Chinese foreign minister Qian Qichen also met his Israeli counterpart Moshe Arens in Paris in January 1989, where the two sides agreed to maintain regular contact through their respective permanent representatives to the UN. Soon after, by mutual agreement, China set up a representative office of the China International Travel Service in Tel Aviv while Israel set up the representative office of the Israel Academy of Sciences and Humanities in Beijing. This signaled not only the renewal of China-Israel ties, but also a new level of friendly contact that exceeded that in the 1949-1950 and 1954-1956 periods in certain respects. In 1991, these two organizations were given diplomatic rights, which signified that China and Israel had established de facto consular relations.

Meanwhile, sweeping changes in the international and Middle East situations also provided the opening for China and Israel to transform their relationship.

First, the Gulf War and the dissolution of the Soviet Union greatly weakened the influence of hardliners who were advocating war in the Middle East, and enhanced the strength of those who called for a peaceful resolution to the conflict. Under this circumstance, peace supporters within and beyond the Middle East worked together to make the Madrid Conference a reality. As such, China, a permanent member of the UN Security Council, faced the issue of how to get involved in the Middle East peace process. The problem for the China was that there is no basis for its legitimately participating in it if it had formal diplomatic relations with only one of the two parties to the conflict, and not the other.

Second, many countries in Central and Eastern Europe, as well as in the former Soviet Union and even Mongolia had established diplomatic ties with Israel. This made it even stranger that China, a major player on the world stage, had not. And as Arab countries saw that it was inevitable that more and more countries would try to establish diplomatic relations with Israel, they know they had to come to terms with that fact.

Sensing that conditions were finally ripe for formalizing relations, China's vice minister of foreign affairs Yang Fuchang and Israeli deputy prime minister and foreign minister David Levy visited Tel Aviv and Beijing in December 1991 and then again in January 1992 to complete the formalization process. On January 24, 1992, the Chinese and Israeli foreign ministers officially signed the joint communiqué to establish diplomatic relations at the ambassadorial level, marking a new chapter in relations between the two countries and the Chinese and Jewish peoples.

Looking back at the tortuous journey over these 43 years, we can see that obstacles to formalizing relations mainly came from changes in the external environment and external interference, and not from problems intrinsic to the bilateral relationship or domestic resistance. Hence, as external conditions improved and the international atmosphere began to turn around, these obstacles became easy to overcome.

II. Post-formalization: steady and comprehensive development in bilateral relations

In the 17 years since the two countries formalized diplomatic ties, there has been steady and comprehensive development in bilateral relationship. This is manifested in three ways.

First, there have been frequent mutual visits by the leaders of both countries, who have engaged in beneficial discussions on bilateral relations and international issues. In September 1992, the Chinese State Councilor and foreign minister Qian Qichen visited Israel. In December of the same year, Israeli president Chaim Herzog visited China. Israel's foreign minister Shimon Peres and prime minister Yitzhak Rabin visited China in May and October 1993, respectively. Rabin, who had just concluded the Israel-Palestine peace deal with Yasser Arafat in September, received an exceptionally warm welcome in China. In October 1994, Chinese vice premier Zou Jiahua visited Israel, and in October the following year, Chinese president Jiang Zemin and Israeli prime minister Yitzhak Rabin met in New York, where they exchanged views on advancing bilateral relations. In 1997, Chinese leaders Li Lanqing, Qian Qichen and Wen Jiabao visited Israel in succession. In May the following year, Israeli prime minister Benjamin Netanyahu visited China. This was followed by a visit from Israeli president Ezer Weizman in April 1999. In November the same year, Li Peng, Chairman of the Standing Committee of the Chinese National People's Congress, visited Israel. This was followed by a visit by Chinese president Jiang Zemin in April 2000, making it the first time in history that a Chinese head of state visited a Jewish nation.

Table 1　Important Bilateral Exchanges from 2000 to 2008

China	Year	Israel	Year
Jiang Zemin, President	2000	Shimon Peres, Minister of Regional Cooperation	2000
Vice Minister of Foreign Affairs Yang Wenchang	2002	Shimon Peres, Deputy Prime Minister and Minister of Foreign Affairs	2002
State Councilor Tang Jiaxuan	2004	Moshe Katsav, President	2003
		Ehud Olmert, Acting Prime Minister and Minister of Industry, Trade and Labor	2004
		Silvan Shalom, Deputy Prime Minister and Minister of Foreign Affairs	

China	Year	Israel	Year
Minister of Foreign Affairs Li Zhaoxing	2005	Ron Prosor, Director General of the Ministry of Foreign Affairs	
Wang Jiarui, Minister of the International Department of CPC Central Committee			
L Xinhua, Special Envoy of the Chinese government and Vice Minister of Foreign Affairs			
Sun Bigan, Special Envoy of the Chinese government on the Middle East issue. (Twice in June and August)	2006	Tzahi Hanegbi, Chairman of the Knesset's Foreign Affairs and Defense Committee	
Li Yuanchao, Secretary, CPC Jiangsu Provincial Committee			
Liu Qi, member of the Political Bureau of the CPC Central Committee, Secretary of the CPC Beijing Municipal Committee		Yakov Litzman, Chairman of the Knesset's Finance Committee, Party Chairman, United Torah Judaism	
Zhai Jun, Assistant Minister of Foreign Affairs			
Sun Bigan, Special Envoy of the Chinese government on the Middle East issue.(Thrice in April, July and December)	2007	Ehud Olmert, Prime Minister	2007
Chang Keren, Vice Minister of Culture		Shaul Mofatz, Deputy Prime Minister, Minister of Transportation and Road Safety	
Sun Zhengcai, Minister of Agriculture		Majallie Whbee Deputy Speaker of the Knesset	
Hu Siyi, Vice Minister of Water Resources			

China	Year	Israel	Year
Liu Yunshan, member of Politburo, member of the Secretariat and head of the Publicity Department of the of the CPC Central Committee.	2008	Tzipi Livni, Acting Prime Minister, Minister of Foreign Affairs	2008
		Eliyahu Yishai, Deputy Prime Minister and Minister of Industry, Trade and Labor	
		Shimon Peres, President (for the opening ceremony of the Beijing Olympics)	
		Colette Avital, Deputy Speaker of the Knesset	

Source: Website of the Ministry of Foreign Affairs, the People's Republic of China.

Second, bilateral economic and technological cooperation was progressing swiftly and trade between the two countries soared. In October 1992, the governments of both countries signed a trade pact granting each other the status of most-favored nation. Since then, the two countries have signed agreements on avoiding double taxation, investment protection, economic and trade cooperation, cooperation in industrial research, customs cooperation, financial cooperation and cooperation in maritime shipping. A bilateral committee on economic and trade cooperation meets once every year to promote such cooperation. In November 2005, Israel formally recognized China's full market economy status. When Israeli deputy prime minister and Minister of Industry, Trade and Labor Eliyahu Yishai visited China in January 2008, both countries signed a memorandum of understanding for increased cooperation in high technology sectors and an agreement to invest in the Infinity I-China Fund.

With the above-mentioned agreements as the cornerstone, China-Israel cooperation in the economic and technological spheres grew by leaps and bounds and achieved significant results, particularly for sectors including agricultural, telecommunications, medical, mining, construction, energy, diamond-processing and aviation. In 1993, the two countries signed a memorandum of understanding on agriculture and set up the Chinese-Israeli International Center for Training in Agriculture at the Beijing University for Agricultural Engineering and a demonstration farm in the Beijing suburbs. In 1997, both countries formally established a joint committee on agriculture. The two countries have achieved steady progress in agricultural cooperation in recent years and the China-Israel demonstration farm in Yongledian, which the Israelis helped set up, has become a symbol of friendship between the two. Israel has also built demonstration farms for agricultural produce, plants and flowers, as well as dairy produce in places such as Shandong, Shaanxi, Yunnan and Xinjiang. Smooth development in the MASHAV project for agricultural cooperation between the two countries enabled skilled workers in China's agricultural industry to receive training by working on Israeli-run farms. In November 2008, the "Chinese-Israel Agricultural Cooperation Week" was held in Yangling, Shaanxi. The two countries also jointly funded and established a 5 million US dollars scientific research fund in 1995. For the past decade or so, the fund has played an important role in promoting collaboration in scientific research. In 2000, the Shanghai Diamond Exchange was established in Pudong with cooperation between the two countries, and it has since become the most important diamond distribution center in the Far East region.

Prior to the establishment of diplomatic relations, the total value of annual bilateral trade stood at tens of millions of dollars. That figure had since soared to 5.3 billion US dollars in 2007.[1] At the time of this writing, bilateral trade in the first 10 months of 2008 had reached approximately 5 billion US dollars, a 17% increase over the same period in the previous year. The value of Chinese exports came approximately to 3.5 billion US dollars, a 19% increase over the same period the year before, while imports accounted for about 1.5 billion US dollars, an 11% year-on-year increase.[2]

Third, there has been rapid development in people-to-people interactions and cultural exchanges. The two countries have signed numerous cooperation agreements and memoranda of intent in areas such as culture, sports, tourism and education and cultural, arts and sports groups from both countries have conducted mutual visits. All these have strengthened the traditional ties of friendship between the people of both countries. In May 1993, the two countries signed an agreement on cultural exchange. In November 1994,

---

[1]   Website of the Ministry of Foreign Affairs, People's Republic of China http://www.mfa.gov.cn

[2]   Website of the Ministry of Foreign Affairs, People's Republic of China http://www.mfa.gov.cn

performances by the legendary Israel Philharmonic Orchestra created a sensation in Beijing and Shanghai. Meanwhile, Beijing opera and acrobatic troupes also received a resounding welcome in Israel.

In March 1992, the civil administrations of the two countries signed a memorandum of understanding allowing the Israeli national airline to offer direct flights to Beijing. In September the same year, El Al commenced flight service between Tel Aviv and Beijing. In October 1993, the two sides signed another civil aviation agreement that would turn the Israeli direct service to Beijing into a regular weekly flight.

In June 1994, the two countries signed an agreement on tourism cooperation. Soon after, China became hugely popular as a travel destination for Israelis, and more and more Chinese tourists were also visiting Israel. Many Israeli and Chinese cities became sister cities, including Beijing and Tel Aviv as well as Shanghai and Haifa. In June 2005, the Chinese authority officially declared Israel a tourist destination for Chinese tourists. In October 2007, the two countries signed a memorandum of understanding to allow Chinese tourists to sign up for tours to Israel. The first Chinese tour group arrived in Israel in September 2008.

Bilateral exchanges in education also produced great results. Many professors and experts from both countries made mutual visits, participated in joint research projects and organized joint conferences. The universities and research institutes of the two countries also signed various agreements for further exchanges and cooperation. Thousands of Chinese nationals have studied and are studying in Israel, and the number of Israeli students in China is also increasing yearly. In May 2007, a Chinese cultural festival was organized in Israel and a Confucius Institute was established at Tel Aviv University. [1]

For 17 years, communities of "Chinese Jews" from all over the world have played an important role in promoting bilateral relations, who have in turn benefited from and been encouraged by its rapid development. In the meantime, as China becomes more developed and prosperous, the number of Jewish people coming to China is surging again. New Jewish communities and organizations have sprung up in cities such as Shanghai, Beijing, Guangzhou and Shenzhen. In particular, Jewish organizations in Hong Kong are witnessing a golden age in their development. Jewish organizations in Taiwan, though smaller in scale, are also very active and developing steadily. They too have benefited from warming Cross-Strait relations.

III. Routine factors: driving forces and obstacles in China-Israel relations

Looking at the evolution of China-Israel relations over the past six decades or so, we can identity some routine factors that have shaped China-Israel relations.

---

[1] Website of the Ministry of Foreign Affairs, People's Republic of China http://www.mfa.gov.cn.

(I) Forces sustaining the momentum of bilateral relations

Much progress has been made in China-Israel relations despite numerous impediments. This is because there are strong forces that have helped to sustain its momentum. These forces come from the following sources:

First, there are commonalities between Chinese and Jewish cultures and friendship between the two peoples goes back a long time. Chinese and Jewish civilizations have much in common, including the high regard for education and familial ties, keen business sense and an aptitude for wealth management, and the resolve to unite and fight against enemies in difficult times. The combination of these shared foundational values and the absence of anti-Semitism made it possible for many Jewish people to live and work happily in China throughout history. Shanghai was the only big city in the world to open its doors to Jewish refugees when they faced the threat of Nazism in Europe. The common experience of the devastating loss of human life during the Second World War united the two peoples in the fight against Fascism. Some Jewish people living in China also participated in the Chinese revolution and nation-building. Some of them are making active contributions today to China's reform and development. The forces that have sustained the momentum of China-Israel relations are forged of precisely these historical, cultural and emotional ingredients.

Second, there have been no mutual tension or conflicts that may have obstructed the development of bilateral relations directly. As mentioned earlier, unlike most other countries in the word, Israel has had no official links to China's old Nationalist regime, and even during the two decades of "frozen" relations, Israel consistently maintained its "One China" policy. Meanwhile the two countries have virtually no direct or fundamental conflicts of interests as far as bilateral issues are concerned. It is indeed quite rare, as was already noted, for two sovereign countries free of any direct conflict to take so long to establish formal diplomatic ties. In some ways, however, this peculiarity would prove to become something of a favorable factor in the normalization of bilateral relations.

Third, the two countries have complemented and learnt from each other in the era of economic globalization. Unlike the previous two factors, this is something that did not become apparent until rapid development began in China. In 2004, a report published by the Jewish People Policy Institute in Jerusalem opined that China's development could profoundly affect the future of the Jewish people and that the Jewish people, with their international connections, should take seriously the huge opportunities brought by China's peaceful development. It also urged policymakers to incorporate Jewish policies on China into a grand strategic frame and predicted that cooperation between the two great civilizations would have a profoundly positive impact on the world. [1] This grand theory of "Chinese opportunity" reflected the views of many Israeli elites and Jewish elites around the world, and provided the

---

[1]   Salomon Wald, 2004. *China and the Jewish People,* Jewish People Policy Institute, Jerusalem.

theoretical underpinning for Israelis and Jewish involvement in China's reform and development. At the same time, China can learn lessons from successful Israeli and Jewish experiences in various areas. It is evident, therefore, that the willingness and commitment to learn from each other in the process of economic globalization are becoming a new impetus to advancing China-Israel relations.

Fourth, China and Israel have developed close cooperation in security and counterterrorism. There have been growing instances of national and religious conflict in the post-Cold War world. The international situation has further deteriorated since the September 11 attacks and the Iraq War, and extremism and terrorism have again reared their ugly heads globally. These are common threats that both Israel and China must face, and the two countries have had fruitful cooperation in counterterrorism and national security. For instance, when China organized the Beijing Olympics and the Shanghai World Expo, it drew a great deal from Israel's counterterrorism experiences in security planning. Such cooperation is gradually becoming a new area of growth in China-Israel relations.

Fifth, China-Israel relations have benefited from the overall trend of peaceful development in the world and progress in the Middle East peace process. From a long-term perspective, peaceful development will be the dominant trend in world development, events such as the September 11 attacks and the Iraq War notwithstanding. At the same time, more and more people are realizing that dialogue and negotiation are the only means to resolving various kinds of conflict and the only correct means to reaching fair resolution to various problems in the Middle East, including the Palestine-Israel conflict. Despite setbacks, the Middle East peace process is irreversible. Such developments help reduce the differences between China and Israel on issues such as the Palestine-Israel conflict and other disputes in the Middle East, thereby deepening of China-Israel relations.

（Ⅱ）Sources of setbacks

China-Israel relations had its share of obstructions in its past development, and these will likely resurface in the future. The following factors account for the difficulties and problems in the relationship.

First, there are undeniable differences in social systems and values between the two countries. In addition, their development processes are also dissimilar. This inevitably causes the two countries to have different views on many issues, which can sometimes result in disputes. This basically explains why China and Israel have often experienced tension such as can be given rise to by differences in principle, value or ideology.

Second, China and Israel have not been in agreement with each other on Arab-Israeli and Palestinian-Israeli conflicts. Indeed, even though the two countries hold different views on many international issues, it is their disagreements over the Arab-Israeli conflict, and in particular the Palestine-Israel conflict that has had the most adverse impact on their relations.

Third, American interference and its exercise of "veto

power." American interference once caused China and Israel to miss the first opportunity to establish diplomatic relations. However, as Sino-US relations improved, the United States also began to see normal relations between China and Israel in a positive light. Some Jewish politicians and entrepreneurs in the US have been active in forging links between the other two countries. When China-Israel diplomatic ties were finally formally established in 1992, American public opinion appeared to welcome the move and the country apparently made no further attempts to thwart the development of that relationship. Unfortunately, the failed Phalcon deal in 2000 showed that when it was likely that progress in China-Israel relations would affect her core interests, the US would try to exert influence by exercising its "veto power" over Israel's decisions.

Three conclusions can be drawn in light of the above:

First, the history of China-Israel bilateral relations has been variably shaped by both positive and negative forces. This is why it has not been more smooth and there have been as many twists and turns throughout the process. This situation will likely continue in the future.

Second, we should no more assume that everything is fine and that all problems have been resolved when bilateral relations are in good shape thanks to the powerful forces of positive factors than we should be too alarmed and pessimistic when the relationship encounters a setback.

Third, ensuring sustained development of China-Israel relations in the long-term requires us to know not only how to bring all positive factors into play, but also how to be forward-looking and more efficacious in adjudicating conflicts and settling disputes.

(Originally published in *Social Science Journal*, 2009, No. 12.)

Chronicle of Major Events in China-Israel Relations (1949–2013)[*]

CHENG Hong[**]

1949

October 11: Chairman Mao Zedong sends a cable to Israeli Communist Party leader Micoud Nice to report that because of difficulties in transportation, China will not be able to send a representative to the 11th Israeli Communist Party Congress, but he congratulates the Israeli party and wishes success for the congress.

October 21: The 11th Congress of the Communist Party of Israel convenes. Previously, a cable had been sent to the Communist Party of China (CPC) to send a representative to

---

[*]   Translated by Andrew H. Keller, polished by Liang Fan.

[**]   Researcher, Institute of West Asian and African Studies, Chinese Academy of Social Sciences.

participate.

December 10: The Asian Women's Conference formally convenes in Beijing. Israel sends an official representative, who speaks at the conference.

1950

January 9: Israeli Minister of Foreign Affairs Moshe Sharrett sends a cable on behalf of the Israeli government to Chinese Minister of Foreign Affairs Zhou Enlai indicating that Israel has decided to establish diplomatic relations with China.

October 2: The Israeli Communist Party secretary sends a cable to Chairman Mao congratulating him on the first anniversary of the founding of the People's Republic of China.

1951

July 3: Israeli Communist Party General Secretary Micoud Nice sends a congratulatory cable for the CPC's 30th anniversary.

1952

May 29: The Israeli Communist Party convenes its 12th Party Congress. On May 28, the CPC Central Committee sends a congratulatory cable.

August 1: Israel publishes the second collection of Chairman Mao's writings in Hebrew.

1953

October 2: Israeli Communist Party Central Committee sends a congratulatory cable to the CPC for the 4th anniversary of the founding of the People's Republic of China.

1954

September 27: Israeli Communist Party Central Committee

sends a congratulatory cable to the Central Committee of the CPC for the 5th anniversary of the founding of the People's Republic of China. Israeli Prime Minister and Foreign Minster Sharett sends a cable to Chinese Premier Zhou Enlai to congratulate China on its 5th anniversary.

1955

January 31: A six-member Israeli trade delegation led by the Israeli ambassador to Burma arrives in Beijing.

October: The Israeli Communist Party Central Committee sends a cable to the CPC Central committee congratulating it on the 6th anniversary of the establishment of the People's Republic of China. Israeli Prime Minister and Foreign Minister Sharett calls Prime Minister and Foreign Minster Zhou Enlai to congratulate China on the 6th anniversary of its founding.

1956

September: Israeli Communist Party delegation is invited to Beijing to participate in the 8th National Congress of the CPC. The leader of the Israeli delegation gives a speech at the congress. Israeli Communist Party Central Committee sends a cable to congratulate the Central Committee of the CPC on the 7th anniversary of the founding of the People's Republic of China.

September 30: Israeli Foreign Minister Golda Meir sends a cable to Chinese Premier and Foreign Minister Zhou Enlai to congratulate China on the 7th anniversary of its founding.

1957

September 30: Israeli Prime Minister and Acting Foreign Minister David Ben-Gurion sends a cable to Chinese Premier and Foreign Minister Zhou Enlai congratulating China on the 8th anniversary of its founding. Israeli Communist Party Central Committee sends a cable to the CPC Central Committee congratulating China on the 8th anniversary of its founding.

1959

September 27: At the invitation of the CPC Central Committee, the Israeli Communist Party representative and chairman of the Israeli Communist Party Control Commission arrives in Beijing to visit China and participate in the ceremony to celebrate the 10th anniversary of the founding of the People's Republic of China.

1960

September 27: The Israeli Communist Party Central Committee sends a congratulatory cable to the CPC Central Committee for the 11th anniversary of the founding of the People's Republic of China.

1961

May 27: The CPC Central Committee sends a cable to the Israeli Communist Party Congress to congratulate the Israeli Communist Party on the satisfactory and successful completion of its 14th Party Congress.

September 29: The Israeli Communist Party Central Committee sends a congratulatory cable to the CPC Central Committee for the 12th anniversary of the founding of the People's Republic of China.

1962

October 1: The Israeli Communist Party Central Committee sends a congratulatory cable to the CPC Central Committee for the 13th anniversary of the founding of the People's Republic of China.

1963

September 30: Israeli Communist Party Central Committee sends a congratulatory cable to the CPC Central Committee for the 14th anniversary of the founding of the People's Republic of China.

1964

September 30: Israeli Communist Party Central Committee sends a congratulatory cable to the CPC Central Committee for the 15th anniversary of the founding of the People's Republic of China.

1965

September 30: Israeli Communist Party Central Committee Political Bureau Secretary Mel Werner sends a congratulatory cable to the CPC Central Committee for the 16th anniversary of the People's Republic of China.

1987

March 27: Responding to Israel's with to meet with the permanent members of the U.N. Security Council, Chinese Permanent Representative to the U.N. Li Luye meets with Israeli Foreign Ministry Chief of Staff Tamir in New York.

June 29-July 9: In response to the invitation of the CPC Central Committee, an Israeli Communist Party delegation led by the Israeli Communist Party secretary general visits China.

September 30: In response to the Israeli side's request to meet with the foreign ministers of the permanent members of the U.N. Security Council, Chinese State

Councilor and Minister of Foreign Affairs Wu Xueqian meets with Israeli Deputy Prime Minister and Foreign Minister Shimon Peres.

1989

January 9: Chinese Foreign Minister Qian Qichen meets with Israeli Foreign Minister Arens in Paris. The two sides exchange views on the situation in Middle Easts.

September 28: Chinese Foreign Minister Qian holds a meeting with Israeli Foreign Minister Arens on the situation in the Middle East.

1990

October 2: Chinese Foreign Minister Qian holds talks with Israeli Foreign Minister David Levy on Middle East issues.

1991

September 10: At the invitation of the International Liaison Department of the CPC Central Committee, a Israeli United Workers Party delegation completes a goodwill visit to China.

September 30: Israeli Communist Party Central Committee sends a cable to the CPC Central Committee and Secretary General Jiang Zemin to congratulate China on the 42nd anniversary of its founding.

December 6: An Israeli Communist Party delegation led by the secretary general arrives in Beijing and begins a goodwill visit to China. During the visit, CPC Central Committee Politburo Standing Committee Member Li Ruihuan meets with the Israeli Communist Party secretary general, and the two sides exchange views on the international communist movement.

1992

January 22 to 26: At the invitation of Chinese Foreign Minister Qian Qichen, Israeli Deputy Prime Minister and Foreign Minister of State David Levy visits China. Levy is the first Israeli government official to make an official visit to China. On January 24, the two foreign ministers hold talks in Beijing. After the talks, the two foreign ministers sign a joint communiqué establishing diplomatic relations. In Chinese, Hebrew, and English, the communiqué reads, "The government of the People's Republic of China and the government of the State of Israel decided to establish diplomatic relations on the ambassadorial level beginning January 24, 1992." The same day, Chinese Premier Li Peng meets with Levy in Beijing, and the two sides exchange views on bilateral relations, international issues, and Middle East issues.

January 26: The two sides issue the joint communiqué establishing diplomatic relations, and the Chinese Embassy in Tel Aviv officially opens.

February 9: In accordance with the joint communiqué, the Chinese Embassy in Israel holds a reception to celebrate the establishment of diplomatic relations and the opening of the embassy.

March 22: At the invitation of the Israeli Communist Party and the United Workers party, a delegation from the CPC International Liaison Department arrives in Tel Aviv to begin a nine-day visit to Israel. During this visit, the delegation holds talks with the leaders of both parties separately and meets with well-known Palestinian Faisal Husseini and Hanan Ashrawi,

Palestinian spokesperson to the Middle East Peace Talks.

April 5: At the invitation of the Israeli Chamber of Commerce and Manufacturers Association, a private Chinese trade delegation arrives in Jerusalem and begins a six-day visit to Israel. This is the largest private Chinese trade delegation to Israel since the two countries established diplomatic relations. During the visit, Israeli Prime Minister Yitzhak Shamir meets with the Chinese delegation.

September 15-17: At the invitation of Israeli Foreign Minister Shimon Peres, Chinese State Councilor and Foreign Minister Qian Qichen makes an official visit to Israel. During the visit, he meets separately with Israeli President Chaim Herzog and Prime Minister Yitzhak Rabin.

October 30: China and Israel sign an intergovernmental trade agreement in Jerusalem. Under the agreement, the two countries open reciprocal trade, and products enjoy preferential tariffs in each other's markets. The two sides decide to set up a mixed committee.

December 6: A China National Tourism Administration delegation finishes a five-day visit to Israel. During the visit, the two nations sign a memorandum of understanding to cooperate further on tourism.

December 24-30: Israeli President Chaim Herzog and his delegation make an official visit to China. This is the first time a president of Israel has visited China. Herzog also visits Shanghai and Xi'an.

1993

January 6: At the invitation of the Israeli film industry, the

China Film Company holds a Chinese film festival in Jerusalem. This is the first time Chinese films are shown in Israel.

February 14: China and Israel sign a technology cooperation agreement in Jerusalem in order to strengthen cooperation between the two countries in research and development.

May 7: At the invitation of the CPC, an Israeli Labor Party delegation led by Chaim Chaddock visits Beijing. During the visit, CPC Central Committee Politburo Standing Committee Member Hu Jintao meets with Chaddoc and his party.

May 19-24: At the invitation of Chinese Vice Premier and Foreign Minister Qian Qichen, Israeli Foreign Minister Shimon Peres makes an official visit to China. During the visit, the two foreign ministers hold talks. Qiao Shi, chairman of the Chinese National People's Congress, meets with Peres in Beijing.

August 3: Israeli Labor Party leader and Prime Minister Yitzhak Rabin receives a CPC delegation led by Gansu Provincial Secretary Gu Jinchi.

October 10: At the invitation of Chinese Premier Li Peng, Israeli Prime Minister Yitzhak Rabin arrives in Beijing for a five-day official goodwill visit to China. This is the first time an Israeli Prime Minister has visited China and the first time Rabin has visited a country outside of the Middle East since signing a peace agreement between Israel and the Palestinian Liberation Organization. During the visit, Premier Li Peng holds talks with Prime Minister Rabin. Chinese President Jiang Zemin also meets with Rabin.

October 27: A Chinese agricultural delegation visits Israel.

During the visit, the two countries sign a "Memorandum of Understanding Between the Chinese Ministry of Agriculture and the Israeli Ministry of Agriculture."

1994

March 11: Israeli Minister of Industry and Trade's Mitchell Harish and his party arrive in Beijing. During the visit, the two countries sign the "Minutes of the First Meeting of the China-Israel Mixed Committee" and "Cooperation Agreement Between the China National Import and Export Committee Inspection Bureau and the Israeli Standards Bureau."

March 14: The China-Israel Trade Fair is held in Beijing. Nearly 200 businessmen from the two countries hold negotiations on communications, electronics, machinery, chemicals, biotechnology and investment, and light industry.

June 18: At the invitation of the CPC, an Israeli Communist Party delegation led by the general secretary arrives in Beijing for a visit to China.

July 1: At the invitation of the People's Liberation Army Chief of General Staff Zhang Wannian, Israeli Defense Force Chief of Staff Ehud Barak arrives in Beijing to begin a ten-day visit to China.

October 3: Chinese Vice Premier Zou Jiahua and his party arrive in Tel Aviv to begin an official visit. During the visit, Israeli Prime Minister Yitzhak Rabin holds talks with Vice Premier Zou. Israeli President Ezer Weizman also meets with Zou.

November 23: Chinese Vice Premier Zou Jiahua meets with the Israeli Minister of Communications, Science, and Art in

Beijing.

1995

March 24: Israeli Minister of Education, Culture, and Sports Amnon Rubinstein and his party arrive in Beijing for an official visit to China.

April 12: Chinese Premier Li Peng meets with Israeli Finance Minister Avraham Shochat.

April 18: At the invitation of the CPC, an Israeli Labor Party delegation led by General Secretary Nissim Zvili arrives in Beijing for a visit to China. During the visit, CPC General Secretary and Chinese President Jiang Zemin meets with Zvili in Beijing.

May 27: At the invitation of the Knesset Foreign Affairs and Defense Committee, a China National People's Congress delegation led by Zhu Liang arrives in Jerusalem for a week-long goodwill visit.

September 26: At the invitation of Israeli Minister of Industry and Trade Mitchell Harish, the Chinese Minister of Foreign Trade and Economic Cooperation Wu Yi and her party arrive in Jerusalem to begin an official visit to Israel. During the visit, Israeli Prime Minister Yitzhak Rabin meets with Wu and her party. The two countries sign four cooperation agreements, including the minutes of the second meeting of the Economics and Trade Mixed Committee and technology transfer for electronic communications, medical equipment, food processing, and high technology.

October 23: Chinese President Jiang Zemin meets with Israeli Prime Minister Yitzhak Rabin.

November 5: Chinese President Jiang Zemin sends a cable to Israeli President Ezer Weizman expressing condolences for the unfortunate death of Israeli Prime Minster Rabin. On the same day, Chinese Premier Li Peng sends a cable to Israeli Prime Minister Shimon Peres to express his condolences as well.

November 6: Chinese Vice Premier and Foreign Minister Qian Qichen goes to the Israeli Embassy in China to express condolences for the death of Prime Minister Rabin. On the same day, China appoints Deputy Director of the National Planning Commission Gan Ziyu, who is visiting Israel, as a special envoy of the Chinese government to attend the state funeral of Prime Minister Rabin.

1996

March 5: Chinese Premier Li Peng sends a message of sympathy to Israeli Prime Minister Shimon Peres regarding several recent terrorist bombings in Israel.

May 4: Chinese Vice Premier and Foreign Minister Qian Qichen meets with the visiting delegation led by Israeli Justice Minister David Libai.

September 11: Council for Promoting Israel-China relations is founded in Tel Aviv.

November 1: At the invitation of Chinese National People's Congress Foreign Affairs Committee, a delegation of the Knesset Foreign Affairs and Defense Committee arrives in Beijing for a goodwill visit to China.

1997

January 2: Chinese People's Association for Friendship with Foreign Countries President Qi Huaiyuan and his party arrive in Jerusalem for a goodwill visit to Israel. During the visit, Qi and his party meet with Israeli President Ezer Weizman, Foreign Minister David Levy, and Finance Minister Dan Meridor.

January 4: Council for Promoting Israel-China relations holds a rally in Tel Aviv to celebrate the 5th anniversary of the establishment of Sino-Israeli diplomatic relations.

February 17: At the invitation of the Israeli government, a Chinese government delegation led by Vice Premier Li Lanqing arrives in Jerusalem for a visit to Israel. During the visit, Israeli President Ezer Weizman meets with Vice Premier Li. The two sides sign an agreement on mutual administrative assistance and cooperation.

February 24-26: At the invitation of Chinese Vice Premier and Foreign Minister Qian Qichen, Israeli Deputy Prime Minister and Foreign Minister David Levy makes an official visit to China. During the visit, Chinese President Jiang Zemin and Premier Li Peng meet separately with Levy.

March 30: Israeli First Deputy Prime Minister and Foreign Minister Levy meets with Chinese Minister of Communications Huang Zhendong who is visiting Jerusalem. After the meeting, the two sides sign the "Maritime Agreement Between the Government of the People's Republic of China and the Government of the State of Israel."

April 1: Israeli Labor Party Chairman and former Prime Minister Shimon Peres meets with Chinese Foreign Liaison Department Head Li Shuzheng and her CPC delegation in Tel Aviv.

November 2: At the invitation of the Israeli government, CPC Central Committee Member and Secretary of the Secretariat Wen Jiabao and his party arrive in Jerusalem for a four-day goodwill visit to Israel. During the visit, Israeli President Ezer Weizman meets with Wen and his party.

November 12: The first meeting of the China-Israel joint Committee on Agriculture is held in Jerusalem on November 12. The two countries sign a memorandum of understanding on the implementation of a number of agricultural cooperation projects. The two sides agree to further strengthen cooperation in the field of agriculture.

December 18: Chinese Vice Premier and Foreign Minister Qian Qichen leaves Beijing for visits to Lebanon, Syria, Israel, Palestine, Egypt, and South Africa.

December 22: Israeli Prime Minister Benjamin Netanyahu meets with Qian in Jerusalem.

1998

April 6: Chinese Vice Premier Qian Qichen meets with Israeli Prime Minister and Honorary President of the China-Israel Relations Promotion Conference Shimon Peres and his party in Beijing.

May 25-28: At the invitation of Chinese Premier Zhu Rongji, Israeli Prime Minister Benjamin Netanyahu makes an official visit to China. During the visit, Zhu and Netanyahu hold talks. President Jiang Zemin also meets with Netanyahu.

September 2: Chinese President and Central Military Commission Chairman Jiang Zemin meets with Israeli Defense Minister Yitzhak Mordechai in Beijing.

October 19: National People's Congress Chairman Li Peng meets with an Israeli Supreme Court delegation led by Supreme Court President Aharon Barak in Beijing.

1999

April 25-May 1: At the invitation of Chinese President Jiang Zemin, Israeli President Ezer Weizman makes a state visit to China. During the visit, Jiang, Premier Zhu Rongji, and NPC Chairman Li Peng meet with Weizman.

October 6: Israeli President Ezer Weizman holds a grand reception to celebrate the 50th anniversary of the founding of PRC at the Presidential Palace in Jerusalem.

November 15-December 4: NPC Chairman Li Peng makes official goodwill visits to Mauritius, South Africa, Kenya, Israel, Palestine, and Oman.

November 25: At the invitation of the Israeli government and Knesset, NPC Chairman Li Peng arrives in Jerusalem for an official visit to Israel. During the visit, Li meets separately with Israeli President Ezer Weizman and former Israeli Prime Minister Shimon Peres.

2000

March 1: Chinese Minister of Industry and Trade Shi Guangsheng and Israeli Trade Minister Larne Cohen initial the "China-Israel Industrial Technology Research and Development Cooperation Framework Agreement" and sign the minutes of the 3rd meeting of the China-Israel Economic and Trade Mixed Committee.

April 12-27: Chinese President Jiang Zemin makes official state visits to Israel, Palestine, Turkey, Greece, and South

Africa . While visiting Israel, President Jiang meets with Israeli President Weizman and Prime Minister Barak. The governments of the two countries sign the "Framework Agreement in the Field of Industrial Technology Research and Development Between the Government of the People's Republic of China and the Government of the State of Israel" and the "Cooperation Agreement Between the People's Republic of China Ministry of Education and State of Israel Ministry of Education."

August 16: Chinese Foreign Minister Tang Jiaxuan meets with Israeli Minister of Regional Cooperation Shimon Peres in Beijing to exchange views on Middle East peace talks, especially Palestinian-Israeli peace talks.

2001

February 21: At the request of Israeli Foreign Minister Shlomo Ben-Ami, Chinese Foreign Minister Tang Jiaxuan speaks with Ben-Ami over the phone on the situation in the Middle East and the Middle East peace process.

September 10: At the invitation of the Israel-China Relations Promotion Association, Chinese People's Association for Friendship with Foreign Countries President Chen Haosu and his party arrive in Israel for a three-day visit. During the visit, Israeli President Moshe Katsav meets with Chen and his entourage.

2002

February 27: Israeli President Moshe Katsav holds a reception at the presidential palace in Jerusalem to celebrate the 10th anniversary of the establishment of diplomatic relations between China and Israel.

March 24-26: Israeli Prime Minister and Foreign Minister Shimon Peres is invited to China for an official visit. During the visit, Chinese Premier Zhu Rongji and Foreign Minister Qian Qichen meet with Peres separately.

June 4: Chinese Vice Premier Qian Qichen meets with Natan Sharansky, a member of the Israeli delegation to the leaders conference of the "Asian Conference on Interaction and Confidence-Building Measures" and Vice Premier and Minister of Housing and Construction in Almaty and the two exchange views on the situation in the Middle East.

August 12: A memorandum of understanding signing ceremony is held in Beijing for the Sino-Israeli Dry Farming Agriculture Demonstration Project.

September 15: Chinese Foreign Minister Tang Jiaxuan meets with Israeli Deputy Prime Minister and Foreign Minister Shimon Peres while attending the 57th General Assembly of the United Nations. The two discuss bilateral relations and exchange views on Middle East issues.

2003

January 5: Three Chinese workers are killed in a suicide bombing in Tel Aviv.

January 14: The Israeli Foreign Ministry and Interior Ministry hold a funeral for the three Chinese workers.

May 18-22: Chinese middle East Envoy Wang Shijie visits Israel and Palestine. During the visit, Wang meets separately with Israeli Foreign Minister Silvan Shalom, Former Prime Minister Shimon Peres, and Palestinian President Yasser Arafat, Prime Minister Mahmoud Abbas, and Foreign Mister Nabil

Shaath. In bilateral talks, Wang puts forward China's five-point proposal for the Middle East peace process and a "Roadmap" plan.

October 18: Chinese Middle East Envoy Ambassador Wang Shijie begins visits to Syria, Egypt, Saudi Arabia, Israel, and Palestine.

December 14-20: At the invitation of Chinese President Hu Jintao, Israeli President Moshe Katsav makes a state visit to China. During the visit, Chinese President Hu Jintao, NPC Standing Committee chairman Wu Bangguo, and Premier Wen Jiabao meet separately with Katsav in Beijing.

2004

November 25: China and Israel hold a signing ceremony in Beijing for the financial cooperation agreement between the two countries.

December 28: Israeli President Moshe Katsav and Prime Minister Ariel Sharon meet separately with Chinese State Councilor Tang Jiaxuan in Jerusalem.

2005

March 30: Chinese Special Envoy for Middle East issues Ambassador Wang Shijie begins visiting Palestine, Israel, and Egypt and exchanges views with the relevant parties on the situation in the Middle East and the progress of the Middle East peace process.

June 20: Israeli Prime Minister Ariel Sharon meets with Chinese Foreign Minister Li Zhaoxing in Jerusalem.

August 31: Israeli Deputy Prime Minister and Labor Party Chairman Shimon Peres meets with a CPC delegation led by

Minister Wang Jiarui in Tel Aviv.

September 14: Chinese Middle East Envoy Ambassador Wang Shijie begins visits to Palestine, Israel, Jordan, Egypt, and Morocco and exchanges views with the relevant parties on the situation in the Middle East and advancing the Middle East peace process.

November 1: The Israeli government officially recognizes China's full market economy status. On the same day, Chinese Vice Minister of Commerce Wei Jianguo signs the "Memorandum on Strengthening Economic and Trade Cooperation" with the director general of the Israeli Ministry of Labor.

2006

August 6: Chinese Special Envoy to the Middle East Sun Bigan leaves to visit Syria, Lebanon, Israel, Egypt, and Saudi Arabia and exchanges views with the relevant parties on the regional situation and the conflict between Lebanon and Israel in particular.

December 16: Chinese Foreign Minister Li Zhaoxing meets with former Israeli Justice Minister Yossi Beilin, who is in Beijing to attend the "Israeli-Palestinian Peacemaker Seminar."

2007

January 9-11: At the invitation of Chinese Premier Wen Jiabao, Israeli Prime Minister Ehud Olmert makes an official visit to China. This is the first time Olmert has visited China since his election as prime minister. During the visit, Chinese President Hu Jintao and Premier Wen Jiabao meet with Olmert separately, and the two sides exchange views on international and regional issues of common interest.

May 25: To celebrate the 15th anniversary of the establishment of diplomatic relations between China and Israel, a "Chinese Cultural Festival" is held in the International Convention Center in Jerusalem.

July 19: Israeli President Shimon Peres meets with visiting Chinese Special Envoy on the Middle East in Jerusalem.

October 28-30: At the invitation of Chinese Foreign Minister Yang Jiechi, First Israeli Deputy Prime Minister and Foreign Minister Tzipi Livni makes an official visit to China.

October 29: Chinese State Administration of Foreign Experts Affairs and the Israeli Embassy in Beijing hold a ceremony to celebrate the 15th anniversary of cooperation between the Chinese State Administration of Foreign Experts Affairs China Association for International Exchange and the Israeli Ministry of Foreign Affairs Center for International Cooperation.

2008

July 10: The Israeli president's office issues a statement officially announcing that Israeli President Shimon Peres will accept the invitation to attend the Beijing Olympics opening ceremony on August 8.

October 17: CPC Central Committee Secretariat and Minister of Propaganda Liu Yunshan meets with an Israeli Labor Party delegation led by Colette Avital, deputy speaker of the Knesset and International Secretary of Israeli Labor Party.

November 19: Responding to an invitation CPC Central

Committee Member, Secretariat, and Propaganda Minister Liu Yunshan leads a delegation from Beijing to Iran, Bahrain, Egypt, Israel, and Palestine for goodwill visits.

2009

January 14: Chinese Special Envoy on the Middle East Sun Bigan meets with Israeli President Shimon Peres in Jerusalem. The two sides exchange views on the current situation in Gaza.

April 23: Israeli President Shimon Peres meets with Chinese Foreign Minister Yang Jiechi in Jerusalem.

March 20-July4: Chinese Special Envoy on the Middle East Wu Sike visits Egypt, Palestine, Israel, Jordan, Syria, Lebanon, and Russia to exchange views on the current situation in the Middle East with the relevant parties.

October 28: Israeli President Shimon Peres meets with a CPC delegation to Jerusalem led by CPC Central Committee Member and Ningxia Hui Autonomous Region Party Secretary Chen Jianguo.

2010

March 24: Chinese Vice Premier Hui Liangyu meets with Israeli President Shimon Peres in Jerusalem.

April 26: Chinese Vice Premier Hui Liangyu meets with Chaim Herzog, the Israeli Minister of Social Affairs, in Beijing.

May 10: Chinese Vice Premier Li Keqiang meets with Yuval Steinitz, Israeli Minister of Finance, in Beijing. The two sides exchange views on bilateral relations, trade, and scientific and technological cooperation.

June 6: Chinese Special Envoy to the Middle East Wu Sike meets with Israeli Foreign Minister Avigdor Lieberman in

Jerusalem. The two exchange views on bilateral relations and Middle East peace talks.

June 11-23: Chinese Special Envoy on the Middle East Wu Sike visits Jordan, Israel, Palestine, Turkey, and Egypt to exchange views on the latest developments in the Middle East with the relevant parties.

November 7: Israeli President Shimon Peres meets with a delegation led by CPC Central Committee Member and Tianjin Party Secretary Zhang Gaoli in Jerusalem.

December 13: Chinese State Councilor and Defense Minister Liang Guanglie meets with Israeli Navy Commander Eliezer Marom in Beijing.

2011

February 28: Israeli Prime Minister Benjamin Netanyahu meets with a Chinese economic and trade delegation led by Minister of Commerce Chen Deming. On March 2, Israeli President Shimon Peres meets with Minister Chen and his party in Jerusalem.

March 23-April 2: Chinese Special Envoy on the Middle East Wu Sike leaves to visit Israel, Palestine, Syria, Lebanon, and Qatar. During his visits, he exchanges views on the peace process and the current situation in the Middle East with the relevant parties.

June 14: Chinese Vice Premier Li Keqiang meets with Israeli Deputy Prime Minister and Defense Minister Ehud Barak and his party in Beijing.

June 21: Israeli President Shimon Peres meets with a Chinese government cultural delegation led by Chinese Minister of Culture Cai Wu in Jerusalem. On June 22, Israeli Prime Minister Benjamin Netanyahu meets with Wu and his party in Jerusalem.

2012

January 24: Chinese President Hu Jintao and Israeli President Shimon Peres exchange congratulatory messages to celebrate the 20th anniversary of the establishment of diplomatic relations between the two countries. The same day, Chinese Premier Wen Jiabao and Israeli Prime Minister Benjamin Netanyahu also exchange congratulatory messages.

February 19: Chinese Special Envoy on the Middle East Wu Sike meets with Israeli Deputy Prime Minister and Foreign Minister Avigdor Lieberman and Yitzhak Molcho, Prime Minister Netanyahu's Special Envoy and the two sides exchange views on major issues of common concern.

March 15-22: Israeli Deputy Prime Minister and Foreign Minister Avigdor Lieberman responds to an invitation and makes an official visit to China. During the visit, Chinese Vice president Xi Jinping meets with Lieberman.

April 4: Vice Chairman of the NPC Standing Committee and President of the Chinese Association for International Understanding Zhou Tienong visits Israel. During the visit, he meets separately with Israeli Knesset Deputy Speaker Raleb Majadele, Deputy Prime Minister and Minister of Foreign Affairs Avigdor Lieberman, and Sino-Israeli Friendship Group Chairman David Rotem.

May 22: Chinese Vice President and Central Military Commission Vice Chairman Xi Jinping meets with Israeli

Defense Forces Chief of Staff Benny Gantz in Beijing.

2013

April 29: Chinese Special Envoy on the Middle East Wu Sike meets separately with Israeli Deputy Foreign Minister Ze'er Elkin and Justice Minister Tzipi Livni and exchanges views on the Middle East peace process and other regional issues.

May 6-10: Israeli Prime Minister Benjamin Netanyahu is invited to China for an official visit. During the visit, he meets with Chinese President Xi Jinping.

May 26-28: A Chinese Tibetology delegation visits Israel. During the visit, the delegation engages in in-depth exchanges with Israeli government officials and academics and explains the peaceful liberation of Tibet, especially the achievements since reform and opening-up.

June 17-19: Chinese People's Political Consultative Conference Vice President and Chinese People for Peace and Disarmament Association President Han Qide leads a delegation to visit Israel. During the visit, Han attends the 5th meeting of the Presidents of Israel and meets separately with Israeli President Shimon Peres and Israeli Knesset Speaker Yuli Edelstein.

October 21-23: CPC Central Committee Publicity Department Head Liu Qibao leads a CPC delegation to Israel. During the visit, Liu meets with Israeli President Shimon Peres.

图书在版编目（CIP）数据

眼睛里的你：中国与以色列 / 杨光主编 . —北京：社会科学文献
出版社，2014.4
ISBN 978-7-5097-5795-6

Ⅰ . ①眼… Ⅱ . ①杨… Ⅲ . ①以色列—概况 ②中外
关系—研究—以色列 Ⅳ . ① K938.2 ② D822.338.2

中国版本图书馆 CIP 数据核字（2014）第 049960 号

眼睛里的你
——中国与以色列

主　编 / 杨　光

出 版 人 / 谢寿光
出 版 者 / 社会科学文献出版社
地　　址 / 北京市西城区北三环中路甲 29 号院 3 号楼华龙大厦
邮政编码 / 100029

责任部门 / 国际出版分社（010）59367197　　责任编辑 / 王玉敏　梁　帆
电子信箱 / guoji@cass. cn　　　　　　　　　责任校对 / 杜若佳
项目统筹 / 王玉敏　李延玲　　　　　　　　　责任印制 / 岳　阳
经　　销 / 社会科学文献出版社市场营销中心（010）59367081　59367089
读者服务 / 读者服务中心（010）59367028

印　　装 / 三河市东方印刷有限公司
开　　本 / 787mm×1092mm　1/32　　　　　印　张 / 14
版　　次 / 2014 年 4 月第 1 版　　　　　　　彩色印张 / 0.5
印　　次 / 2014 年 4 月第 1 次印刷　　　　　字　数 / 211 千字
书　　号 / ISBN 978-7-5097-5795-6
定　　价 / 149.00 元